Pasta

BLOOMSBURY KITCHEN LIBRARY

Pasta

Bloomsbury Books
London

This edition published 1994 by Bloomsbury Books,
an imprint of The Godfrey Cave Group,
42 Bloomsbury Street, London, WC1B 3QJ.

ISBN 1 85471 552 6

Printed and bound in Great Britain.

Contents

Basic Pasta Dough

Serves
4

Calories
205

Protein
7g

Cholesterol
60mg

Total fat
7g

Saturated fat
1g

Sodium
30mg

| 175 to 200 g | strong plain flour | 6 to 7 oz | 1 | egg white | 1 |
| 1 | egg | 1 | 1 tbsp | safflower oil | 1 tbsp |

To prepare the dough in a food processor, put 175 g (6 oz) of the flour, the egg, egg white and oil in the bowl of the machine and process the mixture for about 30 seconds. If the mixture forms a ball immediately and is wet to the touch, mix in flour by the tablespoon until the dough feels soft but not sticky. If the mixture does not form a ball, try pinching it together with your fingers. If it is still too dry to work with, blend in water by the teaspoon until the dough just forms a ball. If you have a pasta machine, the dough may be immediately kneaded and rolled out.

To prepare the dough by hand, put 175 g (6 oz) of the flour into a mixing bowl and make a well in the centre. Add the egg, egg white and oil to the well and stir them with a fork or wooden spoon, gradually mixing in the flour. Transfer the dough to a lightly floured surface and knead it for

a few minutes. The dough should come cleanly away from the surface; if it is too wet, add flour by the tablespoon until the dough is no longer sticky. If the dough is too dry and crumbly to work with, add water by the teaspoon until it is pliable. Continue kneading the dough until it is smooth and elastic – about 10 minutes; alternatively, knead the dough in a pasta machine.

If you are not using a pasta machine, wrap the dough in greaseproof paper or plastic film and let it rest for 15 minutes before rolling it out.

Editor's Note: In a traditional pasta dough, two eggs are used with 175 g (6 oz) of flour. Here, to reduce the amount of cholesterol in the dough, an egg white has been substituted for one of the whole eggs.

Semolina Pasta Dough

| 125 g | strong plain flour | 4 oz | 150 g | fine semolina | 5 oz |

To prepare the dough in a food processor, first blend the flour and semolina together, then gradually mix in up to 15 cl (¼ pint) of water until the mixture just forms a ball. If the mixture is wet to the touch, blend in flour by the tablespoon until the dough feels soft but not sticky. If the mixture does not form a ball, try pinching it together with your fingers. If it is still too dry to work with, blend in water by the teaspoon until the dough just forms a ball. If you have a pasta machine, the dough may be immediately kneaded and rolled out.

To prepare the dough by hand, blend the flour and semolina in a bowl and make a well in the centre. With a fork or wooden spoon, gradually mix in up to 15 cl (¼ pint) of water until the dough can be pressed together into a solid ball. Transfer the dough to a lightly floured surface and knead it for a few minutes. The dough should come cleanly away from the surface; if it is too wet, incorporate flour a tablespoon at a time until the dough is no longer sticky. If the dough feels dry and crumbly, incorporate water by the teaspoon until it is pliable. Continue kneading until the dough is smooth and elastic – about 10 minutes; alternatively, knead the dough in a pasta machine.

If you are not using a pasta machine, wrap the dough in greaseproof paper or plastic film and let it rest for 15 minutes before rolling it out.

Spinach Pasta Dough

Serves
4

Calories
225

Protein
10g

Cholesterol
60mg

Total fat
7g

Saturated fat
1g

Sodium
120mg

175 to 200 g	strong plain flour	**6 to 7 oz**	**1**	egg	**1**
3 tbsp	finely chopped spinach (about 150 g/5 oz frozen spinach, thawed, or 250 g/8 oz fresh spinach, washed, stemmed and blanched in boiling water for 1 minute)	**3 tbsp**	**1**	egg white	**1**
			1 tbsp	safflower oil	**1 tbsp**

To prepare the dough in a food processor, purée the spinach with the egg, egg white and oil for 5 seconds. Add 175 g (6 oz) of the flour and process the mixture for about 30 seconds. If the mixture forms a ball right away and is wet to the touch, mix in flour by the tablespoon until the dough feels soft but not sticky. If the mixture does not form a ball, try pinching it together with your fingers. If it is still too dry to work with, blend in water by the teaspoon until it can be formed into a ball. If you have a pasta machine, the dough may be immediately kneaded and rolled out.

To prepare the dough by hand, put 175 g (6 oz) of the flour in a mixing bowl and make a well in the centre. Add the spinach, egg, egg white and oil to the well and mix them, gradually incorporating the flour. Transfer the dough to a lightly floured surface and knead it for a few minutes. The dough should come cleanly away from the surface; if it is too wet, add flour by the tablespoon until the dough is no longer sticky. If the dough is too dry and crumbly to work with, add water by the teaspoon until it is pliable. Continue kneading the dough until it is smooth and elastic – about 10 minutes; alternatively, knead the dough in a pasta machine.

If you are not using a pasta machine, wrap the dough in greaseproof paper or plastic film and let it rest for 15 minutes before rolling it out.

Fettuccine with Swordfish and Roasted Red Pepper

Serves 4

Working (and total) time: about 1 hour

Calories 375
Protein 24g
Cholesterol 100mg
Total fat 15g
Saturated fat 2g
Sodium 215mg

	basic pasta dough		1 tbsp	fresh lemon juice	1 tbsp
350 g	swordfish or fresh tuna steak, trimmed and cut into 1 cm (½ inch) strips	12 oz	2 tbsp	virgin olive oil	2 tbsp
			1	sweet red pepper	1
2	garlic cloves, finely chopped	2	2 tbsp	chopped parsley	2 tbsp

In an ovenproof baking dish, combine the swordfish cubes, garlic, lemon juice and 1 tablespoon of the oil. Toss well, cover, and let the mixture marinate in the refrigerator for at least 30 minutes.

Roll out the dough and cut it into fettuccine. Set the pasta aside while you prepare the fish and red pepper.

Grill the red pepper under a preheated grill, about 5 cm (2 inches) below the heat source, turning the pepper from time to time until it is charred on all sides. Transfer the pepper to a bowl and cover the bowl with plastic film, or put the pepper in a paper bag and fold it shut; the trapped steam will loosen the skin. Peel, seed

and derib the pepper, holding it over the bowl to catch any juice. Cut it into thin strips and strain the juice to remove any seeds. Set the strips and juice aside.

Preheat the oven to 200°C (400°F or Mark 6). Bake the swordfish cubes in their marinade until they are cooked through – 6 to 8 minutes.

Meanwhile, add the fettuccine to 3 litres (5 pints) of boiling water with 1½ teaspoons of salt. Start testing the pasta after 1 minute and cook it until *al dente*. Drain the pasta and transfer it to a large bowl. Add the remaining tablespoon of oil, the red pepper juice, and the parsley; toss well. Add the swordfish and its cooking liquid, toss gently, and serve at once.

Tagliarini with Prawns and Scallops

Serves 8

Working (and total) time: about 45 minutes

Calories
380

Protein
23g

Cholesterol
155mg

Total fat
12g

Saturated fat
3g

Sodium
480mg

	basic pasta dough	
	spinach pasta dough	
500 g	shelled scallops	1 lb
30 g	unsalted butter	1 oz
3 tbsp	finely chopped shallot	3 tbsp
500 g	Mediterranean prawns, shelled and deveined, the shells reserved	1 lb

¼ litre	dry vermouth	8 fl oz
1	small bay leaf	1
2 tbsp	safflower oil	2 tbsp
2 tbsp	cut fresh chives	2 tbsp
¼ tsp	salt	¼ tsp
	white pepper	

Roll out pasta doughs and cut them into tagliarini – very thin noodles. Set the tagliarini aside.

Pull off and reserve the firm, small muscle, if there is one, from the side of each scallop. Rinse scallops, pat dry, and set aside. Melt the butter in a saucepan over medium heat. Stir in shallots and cook them until they are translucent – about 2 minutes. Add the reserved prawn shells and any reserved side muscles from the scallops; cook, stirring, for 1 minute. Pour in the vermouth and simmer the mixture for 1 minute more.

Add bay leaf and 35 cl (12 fl oz) of water. Bring to the boil. Reduce heat and simmer until reduced by half – 10 to 12 mins. Set aside.

To prepare the seafood, heat the oil in a large, deep, heavy frying pan over medium-high heat.

Add the prawns and scallops, and sauté them for 1½ to 2 minutes, turning the pieces frequently with a spoon. Push the seafood to one side of the pan and strain the liquid from the saucepan into the frying pan. Set the frying pan aside.

Add the tagliarini to 6 litres (10 pints) of boiling water with 3 teaspoons of salt. Start testing the tagliarini after 1 minute and cook it until it is *al dente*. Drain the pasta and add it to the frying pan with the seafood. Season with the chives, salt and some pepper, and toss gently to distribute the prawns and scallops through the pasta. Cover the pan and place it over medium heat to warm the mixture thoroughly – about 1 minute. Serve the tagliarini at once.

Parsley-Stuffed Mini-Ravioli

Serves 6

Working
(and total)
time: about
1 hour

Calories
215

Protein
12g

Cholesterol
10mg

Total fat
4g

Saturated fat
2g

Sodium
330mg

	semolina pasta dough	
125 g	low-fat ricotta cheese	4 oz
125 g	low-fat cottage cheese	4 oz
125 g	parsley leaves, finely chopped	4 oz
30 g	Parmesan cheese, freshly grated	1 oz

¼ tsp	grated nutmeg	¼ tsp
⅛ tsp	salt	⅛ tsp
	freshly ground black pepper	
12.5 cl	skimmed milk	4 fl oz

To prepare the filling, work the ricotta and cottage cheese through a sieve into a bowl. Stir in the parsley, Parmesan cheese, nutmeg, salt and some pepper. Set the mixture aside.

Roll out the dough. and form it into ravioli that are each about 4 cm (1½ inches) square with ½ teaspoon of filling inside. Use only about half of the filling to stuff the squares.

To make the sauce, put the remaining filling in a pan over medium-high heat and stir in the milk. Cook the sauce until it is hot but not boiling – about 5 minutes. Keep the sauce warm while you cook the ravioli in 3 litres (5 pints) of boiling water with 1½ teaspoons of salt. Start testing the ravioli after 1 minute and cook them until they are *al dente*, then drain them. Pour sauce over ravioli and serve the dish immediately.

Making ravioli

1 Adding the filling. Spread the rolled dough sheet on a lightly floured surface. Place dollops of the filling on half of the sheet, taking care to space them evenly, about 2.5 cm (1 inch) apart.

2 Covering the filling. Brush the other half of the sheet lightly with water. Then fold it gently over the mounds of filling, matching the edges as closely as possible.

3 Cutting the ravioli. Starting from the folded edge, use your fingers or the side of your hand to force out the air between the mounds of filling and to seal the dough. Then cut out the ravioli with a fluted pastry wheel.

Pressed-Leaf Ravioli in Shallot Butter

Serves 6
as a
side dish or
first course

Working
(and total)
time: about
45 minutes

Calories
175

Protein
5g

Cholesterol
55mg

Total fat
8g

Saturated fat
3g

Sodium
110mg

	basic pasta dough or basic semolina dough	
30 g	combined flat-leaf parsley, dill and celery leaves, stems removed	1 oz
1 tbsp	finely chopped shallot	1 tbsp
¼ tsp	salt	¼ tsp
	freshly ground black pepper	

Divide dough into three pieces. Cover two of the pieces with plastic film or an inverted bowl to keep them from drying out, and roll out the third piece into a sheet about 1 mm (¹/₁₆ inch) thick.

Place the pasta sheet on a lightly floured surface. Distribute one third of the leaves over half of the sheet so that they are about 1 cm (½ inch) apart. Carefully flatten each leaf in place. Lightly brush the uncovered half of the sheet with water and fold it over the leaves. Press the dough down firmly to seal the leaves in, forcing out any air bubbles.

Pass the folded sheet through the pasta machine to obtain a thickness of about 1 mm (¹/₁₆ inch). With a large, sharp, chef's knife, cut the sheet into 5 cm (2 inch) squares. Set the squares aside and repeat the process with the remaining dough and leaves.

Melt the butter in a large, heavy frying pan over medium-high heat. Add the shallot and salt, and sauté the shallot until it turns translucent – about 2 minutes. Remove the pan from the heat.

Add the ravioli to 3 litres (5 pints) of boiling water with 1½ teaspoons of salt. Start testing the ravioli after 2 minutes and cook them until they are *al dente*. Drain the ravioli and add them to the frying pan with the shallot butter. Shake the pan gently to coat the pasta with the butter. Sprinkle on some pepper and serve hot.

Editor' Note: These ravioli make an excellent accompaniment to grilled lamb or veal chops. They may also be served without the shallot butter in a clear consommé.

Bow Ties with Buckwheat and Onions

Serves 4

Working
(and total)
time: about
45 minutes

Calories
210
Protein
6g
Cholesterol
15mg
Total fat
7g
Saturated fat
4g
Sodium
260mg

	semolina pasta dough (half quantity)	
30 g	unsalted butter	1 oz
90 g	onion, chopped	3 oz
	freshly ground black pepper	

100 g	toasted cracked buckwheat	3½ oz
	groats (kasha)	
1	egg white	1
¼ tsp	salt	¼ tsp
17.5 cl	unsalted chicken stock	6 fl oz

Cut the dough in half; cover one of the halves with plastic film or an inverted bowl to keep it moist. Roll out the other half into a long rectangle about 1 mm (¹/₁₆ inch) thick. Cut the rectangle into strips and form the strips into bow ties. Repeat the process to fashion bow ties from the other piece of dough.

Melt the butter in a saucepan over medium heat. Add the onion and some pepper; cook for 5 minutes, stirring occasionally. Meanwhile, put the buckwheat groats in a bowl with the egg white and blend well, then add the mixture to the saucepan. Increase the heat to high and cook, stirring constantly with a fork, until the mixture is light and fluffy – 3 to 4 minutes. Add the salt and stock, then reduce the heat to low. Cover the pan tightly; simmer the mixture, stirring once after 4 minutes, until all of the liquid is absorbed and the buckwheat groats are tender – about 6 minutes.

Meanwhile, drop the bow ties into 2 litres (3½ pints) of boiling water with 1 teaspoon of salt. Start testing the bow ties after 1 minute and cook them until they are *al dente*. Drain the bow ties and add them to the buckwheat mixture. Stir gently and serve hot.

Shaping Bow Ties

1 Cutting out the ties. With a fluted pastry wheel or a knife, trim the edges of the rolled dough sheet on a flour-dusted surface. Divide the sheet down the middle. Then cut the strips into 2.5 cm (1 inch) widths.

2 Tying The 'Knot'. Separate the pieces. Pinch the centre of each between your thumb and forefinger to form bows, holding down the 'knot' with the index finger of your other hand.

Butternut Agnolotti

Serves 6
as a
side dish
or appetizer

Working
time: about
30 minutes

Total time:
about
1 hour and
15 minutes

Calories
335
Protein
9g
Cholesterol
55mg
Total fat
12g
Saturated fat
3g
Sodium
325mg

	basic pasta dough				
1	butternut squash (about 500 g/1 lb) halved lengthwise and seeded	1	½ tsp	salt	½ tsp
			¼ tsp	white pepper	¼ tsp
35 cl	unsalted chicken stock	12 fl oz	30 g	unsalted butter	1 oz
2 tbsp	finely cut chives	2 tbsp	2 tbsp	finely chopped shallots	2 tbsp
45 g	walnuts, finely chopped	1½ oz	2 tbsp	flour	2 tbsp
1 tbsp	finely chopped fresh sage, or 1 tsp dried sage	1 tbsp	4 tbsp	sweet sherry	4 tbsp
			45 g	raisins	1½ oz
			45 g	sultanas	1½ oz

Preheat oven to 200°C (400°F or mark 6). Place squash halves, cut sides up, on an oiled baking sheet; bake until soft – 1 hour. Cool, scoop out pulp and put it in a processor with 1 tbsp of stock. Purée and transfer to a bowl. Stir in chives, walnuts, sage, half salt and half pepper.

Divide the dough into three pieces and set two aside, covered with an inverted bowl or plastic film. Roll out the third piece to thickness of about 1 mm (¹/₁₆ inch). Using a 7.5 cm (3 inch) cutter, cut it into about 12 circles. Roll out and cut the other two pieces. Place 1 teaspoon of filling near the centre of each circle. Dampen the edges, then fold in half, to seal in the filling.

Melt the butter in a heavy-bottomed saucepan over medium heat. Add the shallots and cook until translucent – about 2 minutes. Stir in the flour and cook, stirring, for 1 minute. Whisk in the remaining stock and the sherry, and continue cooking, whisking constantly, until the sauce thickens and turns smooth – about 1 minute more. Add the raisins and sultanas, reduce the heat to low and simmer for 3 minutes. Season with the remaining salt and pepper.

Cook agnolotti in 3 litres (5 pints) of gently boiling water with 1½ teaspoons of salt. Start testing agnolotti after 2 minutes and cook until *al dente*. Transfer to a warmed, lightly buttered platter. Spoon the sauce over and serve warm.

Tortellini Stuffed with Veal

Serves 6

Working
(and total)
time: about
1 hour

Calories
310

Protein
16g

Cholesterol
70mg

Total fat
13g

Saturated fat
4g

Sodium
360mg

	basic pasta dough	
2 tbsp	virgin olive oil	**2 tbsp**
1	onion, finely chopped	**1**
1	carrot, peeled and finely chopped	**1**
1	stick celery, finely chopped	**1**
4	garlic cloves, very finely chopped	**4**
250 g	veal, minced	**8 oz**
¼ tsp	salt	**¼ tsp**

	freshly ground black pepper	
1 litre	unsalted chicken stock	**1¾ pints**
4 tbsp	Marsala	**4 tbsp**
2 tbsp	tomato paste	**2 tbsp**
¼ tsp	grated nutmeg	**¼ tsp**
4 tbsp	freshly grated Parmesan cheese	**4 tbsp**
2 tbsp	chopped parsley	**2 tbsp**

Heat the oil in a large frying pan over medium-high heat. Add the onion, carrot, celery and garlic, and cook them, stirring often, until the onion is translucent – about 4 minutes. Add the veal and continue cooking, turning the mixture frequently with a spatula or wooden spoon, until the veal is no longer pink – about 5 minutes. Add the salt and some pepper, ¼ litre (8 fl oz) of the stock, the Marsala and the tomato paste. Cover the pan, reduce the heat to medium, and cook for 30 minutes. Remove the pan from the heat and stir in the nutmeg and half of the cheese.

To prepare the pasta, roll out the dough and form it into tortellini, using 1 teaspoon of the veal mixture to fill each circle. Set the tortellini aside.

To make the sauce, reduce the remaining ¾ litre (1¼ pints) of stock by one third over high heat – about 5 minutes. Stir in the parsley and keep the sauce warm.

Add the tortellini to 3 litres (5 pints) of boiling water with 1½ teaspoons of salt. Start testing the tortellini 2 to 3 minutes after the water returns to the boil and cook them until they are *al dente*. Drain the pasta and transfer it to a bowl. Pour the sauce over the tortellini and pass the remaining 2 tablespoons of Parmesan cheese seperately.

Tortellini Stuffed with Escargots

Serves 2
(about 24
tortellini)

Working
(and total)
time: about
45 minutes

Calories
370

Protein
16g

Cholesterol
120mg

Total fat
13g

Saturated fat
8g

Sodium
350mg

	basic semolina pasta dough (half quantity)	
15 g	unsalted butter	½ oz
1 tbsp	very finely chopped onion	1 tbsp
1	garlic clove, very finely chopped	1
12	giant canned snails (escargots), drained and cut in half (about 125 g/4 oz)	12

2 tsp	fresh lemon juice	2 tsp
½ tsp	chopped fresh thyme, or ¼ tsp dried thyme	½ tsp
⅛ tsp	salt	⅛ tsp
	freshly ground black pepper	
3 tbsp	finely chopped parsley	3 tbsp
4 tbsp	single cream	4 tbsp

Melt the butter in a heavy frying pan over medium heat. Add the onion and garlic and cook them, stirring often, for 3 minutes. Add the snails, lemon juice, thyme, salt and some pepper; cook for 3 minutes more, stirring frequently. Stir in the parsley and remove the pan from the heat. Transfer the snalis to a small dish and refrigerate them. Stir the cream into the pan juices and set aside.

Cut the dough into two pieces. Cover one with plastic film or an inverted bowl to keep it moist. Roll out the other into a sheet about 1 mm ($^1/_{16}$ inch) thick. With a 7.5 cm (3 inch) pastry cutter, cut the sheet into 12 circles. Place a snail half slightly off centre on one of the circles. Form the round of dough into the shape of a tortellini. Repeat the process with the remaining dough rounds and then with the piece of dough.

Cook the tortellini in 3 litres (5 pints) of boiling water with 1½ teaspoons of salt until they float to the top and are *al dente* – 4 to 5 minutes. Meanwhile, heat the sauce in the frying pan. Drain the tortellini, toss them with the sauce, and serve immediately.

Fettuccine with Oysters, Spinach and Fennel

Serves 4

Working (and total) time: about 1 hour

Calories 420

Protein 22g

Cholesterol 140mg

Total fat 14g

Saturated fat 5g

Sodium 275mg

	basic pasta dough	
30 g	unsalted butter	1 oz
1	fennel bulb, trimmed, cored and thinly sliced	1
4	spring onions, trimmed and thinly sliced	4
500 g	fresh spinach, washed and stemmed	1 lb
1	shallot, finely chopped	1
12.5 cl	dry white wine	4 fl oz
1 tbsp	chopped fresh tarragon, or 1 tsp dried tarragon	1 tbsp
16	oysters, shucked and drained, the liquid reserved (about 15 cl/¼ pint)	16

Roll out the dough and cut it into narrow fettuccine. Set aside while you prepare sauce.

In a frying pan over medium-low heat, melt half the butter. Add fennel and spring onions, cover, and cook until tender – about 10 minutes.

Meanwhile, blanch the spinach in boiling water for 40 seconds. Drain and refresh under cold water. Squeeze dry and separate the leaves. When the fennel and spring onions finish cooking, add the spinach leaves and remove from the heat.

In a small saucepan, combine the shallot, wine and half of the tarragon. Cook over medium-high heat until reduced by half – about 5 minutes. Add the reserved oyster liquid and bring it to a simmer

– about 3 minutes. Add the oysters and cook them just until their edges begin to curl – about 2 minutes. Reduce the heat to low to keep the oysters warm.

Cook the fettuccine in 3 litres (5 pints) of boiling water with 1½ teaspoons of salt. Start testing the pasta after 1 minute and cook it until it is *al dente*. Drain the pasta and transfer it to a large bowl. Swirl the remaining butter into the oyster sauce and combine the sauce with the pasta. Reheat the vegetables in the frying pan and stir in the remaining tarragon, then add the vegetables to the pasta and oyster sauce. Toss well and serve immediately.

Crab Pillows

Serves 4

Working
(and total)
time: about
1 hour and
15 minutes

Calories
350

Protein
24g

Cholesterol
145mg

Total fat
10g

Saturated fat
3g

Sodium
325mg

	spinach pasta dough	
350 g	crab meat, all bits of shell removed	12 oz
6	spring onions, green and white parts separated and thinly sliced	6
1½ tsp	finely chopped fresh ginger root	1½ tsp
10	drops Tabasco sauce	10

750 g	ripe tomatoes, skinned and seeded, or 400 g (14 oz) canned whole tomatoes, drained	1½ lb
1 tbsp	white wine vinegar	1 tbsp
1	garlic clove, finely chopped	1
⅛ tsp	cayenne pepper	⅛ tsp
2 tbsp	double cream	2 tbsp

Combine the crab meat, the green spring onion parts, the ginger and the Tabasco. Refrigerate.

Purée the tomatoes. Put purée in a saucepan. Add vinegar, garlic, cayenne pepper and the white spring onion parts, and bring to the boil. Reduce the heat and simmer the sauce for 10 minutes. Set aside.

Divide the dough into two. Roll out each piece into a strip 1 mm (¹/₁₆ inch) thick and 10 cm (4 inches) wide and place on a lightly floured surface. Cut into 12.5 cm (5 inch) lengths to form 10 by 12.5 cm (4 by 5 inch) rectangles. Spread about 2 tbsps of crab filling on one half of each rectangle, leaving a border about 1 cm (½ inch)

wide. Moisten edges lightly, fold dough over the filling to form smaller rectangles about 6 by 10 cm (2½ by 4 inches). Seal in filling. Trim the edges. Use the dull side of a knife to press down along each of the three sealed edges; this leaves a decorative indentation and reinforces the seal.

Cook pillows in 4 litres (7 pints) of boiling water with 2 teaspoons of salt for 5 minutes, turning over half way through cooking. While cooking, warm sauce over low heat, then whisk in cream. Spoon half sauce on to heated platter.

Remove pillows from the boiling water, allowing most of the water to drain off. Arrange on the platter. Serve remaining sauce separately.

Spinach Fettuccine with Chicory and Bacon

Serves 6
as an
appetizer

Working
(and total)
time: about
30 minutes

Calories
215
Protein
8g
Cholesterol
50mg
Total fat
10g
Saturated fat
2g
Sodium
265mg

	spinach pasta dough	**1½ tbsp**	virgin olive oil	**1½ tbsp**
5	rashers lean bacon, cut into 1 cm (½ inch) pieces	**5**	**⅛ tsp** salt	**⅛ tsp**
2	large heads chicory (about 325 g 11 oz), ends trimmed, leaves cut diagonally into 2.5 cm (1 inch) strips and tossed with 1 tbsp fresh lemon juice	**2**	freshly ground black pepper	

Roll out the spinach pasta dough and cut it into fettuccine. Set the fettuccine aside on a lightly floured surface.

Meanwhile, cook the bacon pieces in a large, heavy frying pan over medium heat, stirring occasionaly, until they are crisp – about 8 minutes. Remove the pan from the heat; with a slotted spoon, transfer the bacon pieces to a paper towel to drain. Pour off all but about 2 tablespoons of the bacon fat from the pan, and

return the pan to the heat. Add the olive oil and the chicory. Sauté the chicory, stirring frequently, for 2 minutes, then sprinkle it with the salt and some pepper.

While the chicory cooks, add the fettuccine to 3 litres (5 pints) of boiling water with 1½ teaspoons of salt and cook until it is *al dente* – about 2 minutes. Drain the pasta and add it to the chicory in the pan. Add the bacon pieces, toss well, and serve at once.

American Cornmeal Pasta with Chilies and Tomato

Serves 4

Working (and total) time: about 1 hour

Calories 295
Protein 8g
Cholesterol 75mg
Total fat 12g
Saturated fat 3g
Sodium 265mg

	Cornmeal Pasta Dough	
90 g	finely ground cornmeal	3 oz
90 g	strong plain flour	3 oz
1	egg	1
1	egg white	1
1 tbsp	virgin olive oil	1 tbsp
	Hot Chili and Tomato Sauce	
1 tbsp	safflower oil	1 tbsp
5	garlic cloves, thinly sliced	5

2	small dried red chili peppers, finely chopped, or ½ tsp crushed red pepper flakes	2
1	sweet green pepper, seeded, deribbed and chopped	1
¼ tsp	salt	¼ tsp
1	large ripe tomato, skinned, seeded and finely chopped	1
1 tbsp	red wine vinegar	1 tbsp
15 g	unsalted butter	½ oz

Mix cornmeal and flour in a large bowl. In a small bowl, whisk the egg, egg white and 3 tbsps water. Make a well in the centre of the cornmeal and pour in the eggs. Stir, gradually incorporating cornmeal mixture. When almost all has been incorporated, add the olive oil and work it into the dough by hand.

Transfer dough to a flour-dusted surface and begin kneading it. If dough is stiff and crumbly, add water, a teaspoon at a time; if too wet and sticky, gradually add flour, a tablespoon at a time, until dough no longer sticks to your hands. Knead dough until it is soft and pliable – 10 to 15 mins. Wrap dough in plastic film; let it rest for 15 mins.

Dust surface with cornmeal. Remove film and roll into a 60 by 23 cm (29 by 9 inch) rectangle; cut crosswise into 1 cm (½ inch) wide strips.

Heat safflower oil in a frying pan over medium heat. Add garlic and chili peppers, cook, stirring, until garlic turns golden – 4 mins. Add green pepper and salt, cook for 5 mins more. Stir in tomato, vinegar and butter, cook for 2 mins more.

Add dough strips to 3 litres (5 pints) of boiling water with 1½ tsps salt; cover pan. Return to the boil and cook for 6 mins. Drain, add to sauce, toss and serve.

Pasta in a Sauce of Green Peppercorns and Mustard

Serves 4

Working (and total) time: about 30 minutes

Calories 375

Protein 13g

Cholesterol 75mg

Total fat 11g

Saturated fat 2g

Sodium 385mg

	Buckwheat Pasta Dough	
175 g	strong plain flour	6 oz
50 g	buckwheat flour	1¾ oz
1	egg	1
1	egg white	1
1 tbsp	safflower oil	1 tbsp
	Mustard-Peppercorn Sauce	
1 tbsp	safflower oil	1 tbsp
1 tbsp	finely chopped shallots	1 tbsp
12.5 cl	dry white wine	4 fl oz
2 tsp	Dijon mustard	2 tsp
1 tbsp	green peppercorns, crushed	1 tbsp
35 cl	semi-skimmed milk	12 fl oz
1	tomato, skinned, seeded and coarsely chopped	1
½ tsp	salt	½ tsp
	parsley sprigs for garnish	

Put flours, egg, egg white and oil into a processor and process for 30 seconds. If mixture forms a ball immediately and is wet to touch, mix in flour by the tablespoon until dough feels soft but not sticky. If it does not form a ball, and it is too dry to work with, blend in water by the teaspoon until it just forms a ball. Transfer to a floured surface and knead for a few minutes.

Alternatively, by hand, put flours into a bowl and make a well in the centre. Add egg, egg white and oil; stir, gradually mixing in the flour. Transfer dough to a floured surface and knead for a few mins. Dough should come cleanly away from surface; if too wet, add flour by the tablespoon until no longer sticky. If too dry and crumbly, add water by the teaspoon until pliable. Continue kneading dough until smooth and elastic – about 10 mins.

Wrap dough in plastic film; rest it for 15 mins. Roll out on floured surface; cut into fettuccine.

Heat oil over medium-high heat. Add shallots and sauté until they are translucent – 1 min. Add white wine, mustard and peppercorns. Cook, stirring, until almost all the wine has evaporated. Add milk, return to a simmer, and reduce heat to low. Add noodles and simmer until *al dente* – 3 mins. Stir in chopped tomatoes and salt, garnish with parsley and serve.

Grated Pasta with Green Beans and Cheddar

Serves 6

Working time: about 20 minutes

Total time: about 1 hour and 20 minutes

Calories 230
Protein 12g
Cholesterol 60mg
Total fat 6g
Saturated fat 4g
Sodium 340mg

200 g	strong plain flour	7 oz
1	egg	1
1	egg white	1
¼ tsp	salt	¼ tsp
125 g	green beans, stemmed, thinly sliced on the diagonal	4 oz
¼ litre	skimmed milk	16 fl oz
¼ tsp	white pepper	¼ tsp
⅛ tsp	cayenne pepper	⅛ tsp
90 g	grated Cheddar cheese	3 oz
4 tbsp	fresh breadcrumbs	4 tbsp

Put the flour in a mixing bowl and form a well in the middle of the flour. Briefly beat the egg, egg white and ¼ teaspoon of the salt in another bowl, then pour the beaten egg into the flour. Mix with a large spoon until the flour begins to form clumps. Add enough cold water (1 to 2 tablespoons) to allow you to form the mixture into a ball with your hands. Work the last of the flour into the dough by hand, then turn the dough out on to a flour-dusted surface and knead it until it is firm and smooth – about 5 minutes. Wrap the dough in plastic film and place it in the freezer for at least 1½ hours to harden it.

Remove the dough, unwrap it and grate it on the coarse side of a hand grater. Blanch the beans in boiling water for 2 minutes, then refresh them under cold running water. Preheat the oven to 180°C (350°F or mark 4).

Bring the milk to a simmer over low heat in a large saucepan. Add the grated noodles, white pepper, cayenne pepper and the remaining ¼ teaspoon of salt. Simmer the mixture, stirring occasionally, until the noodles have absorbed almost all of the liquid – 4 to 5 minutes. Add the green beans and half of the grated cheese, and stir thoroughly.

Transfer the contents of the saucepan to an ovenproof casserole. Combine the remaining cheese with the breadcrumbs and sprinkle the mixture over the top. Bake until the crust is crisp and golden – about 20 minutes – and serve hot.

Penne Rigati with Mushrooms and Tarragon

Serves 4

Working (and total) time: about 45 minutes

Calories
385

Protein
11g

Cholesterol
0mg

Total fat
8g

Saturated fat
1g

Sodium
385mg

250 g	penne rigati (or other short, tubular pasta)	**8 oz**
15 g	dried ceps, or porcini mushrooms	**½ oz**
2 tbsp	virgin olive oil	**2 tbsp**
1	small onion, finely chopped	**1**
250 g	button mushrooms, cut into 5 mm (¼ inch) dice	**8 oz**
½ tsp	salt	**½ tsp**

	freshly ground black pepper	
3	garlic cloves, finely chopped	**3**
¼ litre	dry white wine	**8 fl oz**
750 g	tomatoes, skinned, seeded and chopped	**1½ lb**
6 tbsp	chopped parsley	**6 tbsp**
2 tbsp	chopped fresh tarragon	**2 tbsp**

Pour ¼ litre (8 fl oz) of hot water over the dried mushrooms and soak them until soft – about 20 minutes. Drain, reserving soaking liquid. Cut into 5 mm (¼ inch) pieces.

Heat the oil in a large, heavy frying pan over medium heat. Add the onion and sauté it until it turns translucent – about 4 minutes. Add the ceps and button mushrooms, salt and pepper. Cook until the mushrooms begin to brown – about 5 minutes. Add the garlic and the wine, and cook the mixture until the liquid is reduced to approximately 2 tablespoons – about 5 minutes more.

Add the penne rigati to 3 litres (5 pints) of boiling water with 1½ teaspoons of salt. Start testing the pasta after 10 minutes and continue to cook it until it is *al dente*.

While the penne rigati is cooking, pour the reserved cep-soaking liquid into the pan containing the mushrooms and cook until the liquid is reduced to approximately 4 tablespoons – about 5 minutes. Stir in the tomatoes and cook the mixture until it is heated through – about 3 minutes more. Drain the pasta and add it to the pan along with the chopped parsley and tarragon. Toss well and serve

Bucatini with Carrot and Courgette Serpents

Serves 6
as an
appetizer

Working
time: about
20 minutes

Total time:
about
30 minutes

Calories
210

Protein
6g

Cholesterol
5mg

Total fat
5g

Saturated fat
1g

Sodium
70mg

250 g	bucatini (or linguine)	**8 oz**	6	large garlic cloves, peeled, each	6
2	carrots	2		sliced into 4 or 5 pieces	
3	medium courgettes, washed, ends	3	2	anchovy fillets, finely chopped	2
	removed		**90 g**	red onion, thinly sliced	**3 oz**
2 tbsp	virgin olive oil	**2 tbsp**		freshly ground black pepper	

Fashion the carrot and courgette serpents: pressing down hard on a sharp vegetable peeler, grate along the length of a carrot to detach a wide strip until you reach the woody core, then turn the carrot over and repeat the process on the other side. Peel strips from the other carrot in the same manner, then cut each strip lengthwise into 5 mm (¼ inch) wide serpents. With a small, sharp knife, cut a long strip about 2.5 cm (1 inch) wide and 5 mm (¼ inch) thick from the outside of a courgette. Continue cutting strips to remove the green outer portion of all the courgettes. Discard any seedy inner cores. Cut each strip lengthwise into serpents 3 mm (⅛ inch) wide.

Put 3 litres (5 pints) of water on to boil with 1½ teaspoons of salt. Heat the oil in a large,

heavy frying pan over low heat. Add the garlic slices and cook them, stirring occasionally, until they are golden-brown on both sides – 10 to 15 minutes. About 5 minutes after adding the garlic to the pan, drop the pasta into the boiling water. Start testing the pasta after 12 minutes and continue to cook until it is *al dente*.

When the garlic slices have turned golden-brown, add the anchovy fillets, onion, carrots and courgettes to the pan; cover the pan, and cook for 3 minutes. Remove the cover and cook the mixture, stirring frequently, for 3 minutes more.

Drain the pasta and immediately add it to the pan. Add some pepper, toss well, and serve at once.

Fettuccine with Artichokes and Tomatoes

Serves 4

Working time: about 25 minutes

Total time: about 50 minutes

Calories 290

Protein 12g

Cholesterol 5mg

Total fat 3g

Saturated fat 1g

Sodium 345mg

250 g	fettuccine (or other narrow ribbon pasta)	8 oz
750 g	ripe tomatoes, skinned and chopped, seeds and juice reserved, or 800 g (28 oz) canned whole tomatoes, drained and chopped	1½ lb
1	onion, chopped	1
1	carrot, peeled, quartered lengthwise and cut into 5 mm (¼ inch) pieces	1
1 tsp	fresh thyme, or ¼ tsp dried thyme	1 tsp
1 tsp	chopped fresh rosemary, or ¼ tsp dried rosemary	1 tsp
¼ tsp	salt	¼ tsp
	freshly ground black pepper	
3	fresh artichoke bottoms, rubbed with the juice of 1 lemon	3
1 tbsp	red wine vinegar or cider vinegar	1 tbsp
4 tbsp	freshly grated Parmesan cheese	4 tbsp

Put the chopped tomatoes, onion, carrot, the thyme and rosemary if you are using fresh herbs, and the salt and pepper in a saucepan over medium-high heat. Bring the mixture to the boil, reduce the heat to low, and simmer the mixture for 5 minutes.

Slice the artichoke bottoms into strips 3 mm (⅛ inch) wide and add them to the pan. If you are using dried herbs, add them now. Pour in the vinegar and simmer the mixture, uncovered, for 15 minutes. Add the reserved tomato seeds and

juice, if you are using fresh tomatoes, and continue cooking until most of the liquid has evaporated and the artichoke bottoms are tender but not mushy – about 15 minutes more.

Approximately 15 minutes before the vegetables finish cooking, add the fettuccine to 3 litres (5 pints) boiling water with 1½ teaspoons of salt. Start testing the pasta after 10 minutes and cook it until it is *al dente.* Drain it and add it immediately to the sauce. Sprinkle the cheese over the top, toss lightly and serve.

Sweet-and-Sour Cabbage Cannelloni

Serves 6

Working time: about 45 minutes

Total time: about 1 hour and 30 minutes

Calories 295
Protein 9g
Cholesterol 10mg
Total fat 6g
Saturated fat 3g
Sodium 190mg

12	cannelloni (about 250 g/8 oz)	12
30 g	unsalted butter	1 oz
1	small onion, finely chopped	1
500 g	green cabbage, shredded	1 lb
1	carrot, peeled and grated	1
1	apple, peeled, cored and grated	1

¼ tsp	salt	¼ tsp
1.25 kg	ripe tomatoes, quartered	2½ lb
1 tbsp	dark brown sugar	1 tbsp
2 tbsp	white wine vinegar	2 tbsp
4 tbsp	raisins	4 tbsp
¼ litre	unsalted chicken stock	8 fl oz

To prepare cabbage stuffing, melt butter in a frying pan over medium heat. Add the onion and sauté until translucent – about 4 minutes. Pour water into the pan 5 mm (¼ inch). Stir in the cabbage, carrot, apple and ⅛ teaspoon of the salt. Cover the pan and steam the vegetables and apple, adding more water as necessary, until they are soft – about 30 minutes. Set the pan aside.

Meanwhile, pour 4 tablespoons of water into a pan over medium-high heat. Add tomatoes and cook, stirring frequently, until they are quite soft – about 20 minutes. Transfer the tomatoes to a sieve and allow their clear liquid to drain off. Discard the liquid and purée the tomatoes into a bowl. Stir in the brown sugar, vinegar, raisins, and the remaining ⅛ teaspoon of salt.

To prepare cannelloni, add tubes to 4 litres (7 pints) of boiling water with 2 teaspoons of salt. Start testing cannelloni after 15 minutes and cook until *al dente*. With a slotted spoon, transfer the tubes to a large bowl of cold water.

Preheat the oven to 200°C (400°F or mark 6). Drain the cannelloni and fill each one carefully with about one twelfth of the cabbage stuffing.

Arrange the tubes in a single layer in a large baking dish. Pour the stock over the tubes and cover the dish tightly with aluminium foil. Bake for 30 minutes. Ten minutes before serving time, transfer the sauce from the bowl to a saucepan and bring it to the boil. Reduce the heat to low and let the sauce simmer gently while the cannelloni finish cooking. Serve the cannelloni immediately; pass the sauce separately.

Penne with Squid in Tomato-Fennel Sauce

Serves 4

Working time: about 35 minutes

Total time: about 1 hour

Calories 360

Protein 20g

Cholesterol 120mg

Total fat 5g

Saturated fat 1g

Sodium 315mg

250 g	penne (or other short, tubular pasta)	**8 oz**
350 g	squid	**12 oz**
1 tbsp	safflower oil	**1 tbsp**
4 tbsp	anise-flavoured liqueur, or 1 tsp fennel seeds	**4 tbsp**
6	spring onions, trimmed and finely chopped	**6**

750 g	tomatoes, skinned, seeded and chopped, or 400 g (14 oz) canned tomatoes, drained and chopped	**1½ lb**
1	fennel bulb, stalks discarded, bulb grated	**1**
¼ tsp	salt	**¼ tsp**
	freshly ground black pepper	

To clean a squid, first gently pull the quill-shaped pen out of its body pouch. Then, holding the body pouch in one hand and the head in the other, pull the two sections apart; the viscera will come away with the head. Rinse the pouch thoroughly and rub off the thin, purplish skin. Remove the triangular fins and skin them, then slice into strips. Cut the tentacles from the head, slicing just below the eyes. Cut out the hard beak from the centre and discard it. Slice the pouch into thin rings.

Heat the oil in a large, heavy frying pan over medium-high heat. Sauté the squid for 1 to 2 mins. Pour in the liqueur, and cook for 30 secs more. With a slotted spoon, transfer the squid to a plate. Add the tomatoes, fennel, fennel seeds and spring onions to the pan. Reduce the heat to low and simmer, stirring occasionally, until the fennel is soft – 20 to 25 mins.

When fennel has been simmering for about 10 mins, add the penne to 3 litres (5 pints) of boiling water with 1½ tsps of salt. Start testing after 10 mins and cook until *al dente*.

When the pasta is almost done, return the squid to the sauce and gently heat it through. Season the sauce. Drain the pasta, transfer it to a bowl, toss it with the sauce and serve.

Gorgonzola Lasagne

Serves 8		Calories 205
Working time: about 45 minutes		Protein 9g
		Cholesterol 15mg
Total time: about 1 hour and 30 minutes		Total fat 8g
		Saturated fat 3g
		Sodium 245mg

250 g	lasagne ('no pre-cooking' variety)	8 oz	500 g	Batavian endive, washed,	1 lb
4	sweet red peppers	4		trimmed and sliced crosswise	
350 g	red onions, sliced into 1 cm	12 oz		into 2.5 cm (1 inch) strips	
	(½ inch) rounds		½ tsp	salt	½ tsp
1 tbsp	fresh thyme, or ¾ tsp dried	1 tbsp		freshly ground black pepper	
	thyme		4 tbsp	freshly grated Parmesan cheese	4 tbsp
2 tbsp	virgin olive oil	2 tbsp	125 g	Gorgonzola cheese, broken	4 oz
				into small pieces	

Preheat grill. Arrange peppers on baking sheet with the onion surrounding them. Grill until peppers are blistered all over and onions are lightly browned – 10 to 15 minutes. (Turn peppers a few times, onions once.) Put peppers in a bowl, cover with plastic film, set aside. Separate the onion slices into rings and reserve.

Peel peppers when cool, working over a bowl to catch the juices. Remove the stem, seeds and ribs. Set one pepper aside and slice the remaining three into lengthwise strips about 2 cm (¾ inch) wide. Strain the juices and reserve.

Quarter reserved pepper; purée with pepper juices and 2 tsps thyme. Preheat oven to 180°C (350°F or Mark 4).

Heat oil in a frying pan over medium-high heat. Add endive, ⅛ tsp salt, remaining fresh thyme, and plenty of pepper. Sauté endive until wilted and almost all liquid has evaporated – 5 minutes. Remove from the heat.

Line the bottom of a baking sheet with a layer of lasagne. Cover with half of the endive and sprinkle with 1 tbsp Parmesan cheese. Spread half of the pepper strips over the top, then cover them with half of the onion rings. Repeat this procedure, covering the whole with ½ of the pepper purée. Add a last layer of lasagne; top this with remaining purée and Parmesan, and Gorgonzola. Bake for 30 mins. Leave for 10 mins before serving.

Pasta Salad with Lobster and Mange-Tout

Serves 4

Working time: about 40 minutes

Total time: about 1 hour

Calories 375

Protein 17g

Cholesterol 40mg

Total fat 12g

Saturated fat 1g

Sodium 270mg

250 g	radiatori (or other fancy pasta)	8 oz
4 tbsp	very thinly sliced shallots	4 tbsp
1 tbsp	red wine vinegar	1 tbsp
3 tbsp	virgin olive oil	3 tbsp
2	garlic cloves, lightly crushed	2
¼ tsp	salt	¼ tsp
	freshly ground black pepper	
1	live lobster (about 750 g/1½ lb)	1
2 tbsp	lemon juice	2 tbsp
250 g	mange-tout, trimmed and strings removed, sliced in half with a diagonal cut	8 oz
1 tbsp	chopped fresh basil or flat-leaf parsley	1 tbsp

Pour 2.5 cm (1 inch) water into a large pot. Bring to the boil and add lobster. Cover tightly and steam lobster until it turns a bright orange – about 12 mins.

In meantime, put half of the shallots in a bowl with the vinegar and let them stand for 5 mins. Whisk in 2 tbsps oil, then the garlic, ⅛ tsp salt, and some pepper. Set the vinaigrette aside.

Remove lobster from pot and set it on a dish to catch the juices. Pour 2 litres (3½ pints) of water into the pot along with 1 tablespoon of the lemon juice, and bring the liquid to the boil.

When lobster has cooled enough to handle, twist off tail and claws from the body. Crack the shell and remove meat from the tail and claws. Add the shells and the body to the boiling liquid

and cook for 10 minutes. Cut the meat into 1 cm (½ inch) pieces and set it aside in a bowl.

Remove shells from the boiling liquid; add the pasta. Start testing after 13 mins and cook until *al dente*.

While pasta is cooking, pour remaining oil into a frying pan over medium-high heat. Add mange-tout together with remaining shallots and ⅛ teaspoon of salt. Cook, stirring, until the mange-tout turn bright green – about 1½ minutes. Add the contents of the pan to the lobster.

When pasta is cooked, drain and rinse briefly under cold water. Discard the garlic from the vinaigrette, then combine vinaigrette with pasta. Add lobster mixture, basil, remaining lemon juice and some more pepper, and toss well.

30

Pinto Beans and Wagon Wheels

250 g	wagon wheels (or other fancy-shaped or short, tubular pasta)	8 oz
190 g	dried pinto or red kidney beans, soaked for 8 hours in water to cover and drained	6½ oz
2 tbsp	safflower oil	2 tbsp
175 g	boneless topside of beef, cut into 1 cm (½ inch) cubes	6 oz
1	sweet green pepper, seeded, deribbed and cut into 1 cm (½ inch) squares	1

1	small onion, finely chopped	1
1	garlic clove, very finely chopped	1
1.25 kg	ripe tomatoes, skinned, and chopped, or 800 g (28 oz) canned whole tomatoes, drained and chopped	2½ lb
5	drops Tabasco sauce	5
1 tbsp	coarsely chopped fresh coriander	1 tbsp
	freshly ground black pepper	
½ tsp	salt	½ tsp
4 tbsp	grated Cheddar cheese	4 tbsp

Cook beans at a rapid boil in ¾ litre (1¼ pints) of water for 10 minutes to destroy toxins, then drain and set them aside.

While beans are boiling, heat safflower oil in a frying pan over medium-high heat. Brown the beef in oil, stirring frequently, for 3 minutes. Remove meat from the pan and set it aside.

Add onion and green pepper to pan and cook until onion turns translucent – about 3 mins. Add garlic and cook 30 secs more; return beef to the pan. Stir in tomatoes, beans and ¼ litre (8 fl oz) of warm water, and bring to a simmer.

Cover, reduce heat and simmer until beans are tender – about 1¼ hours.

Approximately 10 minutes before the pinto beans finish cooking, add the wagon wheels to 3 litres (5 pints) of boiling water with 1½ teaspoons of salt. Start testing the pasta after 8 minutes and continue to cook until it is *al dente*.

Drain wagon wheels and add to the bean mixture; stir in Tabasco sauce, coriander, black pepper and salt. Simmer for 3 minutes more, transfer contents of the pan to a serving dish; sprinkle cheese over the top and serve at once.

Fluted Shells with Spicy Carrot Sauce

Serves 6
as an
appetizer or
side dish

Working
time: about
15 minutes

Total time:
about
1 hour

Calories
185
Protein
7g
Cholesterol
40mg
Total fat
4g
Saturated fat
2g
Sodium
200mg

250 g	fluted shells (or other shell-shaped pasta)	8 oz
250 g	carrots, peeled and finely chopped	8 oz
1	stick celery, finely chopped	1
4	garlic cloves, finely chopped	4
¼ tsp	crushed red pepper flakes	¼ tsp
1 tbsp	fresh thyme, or 1 tsp dried thyme	1 tbsp
½ litre	unsalted chicken or vegetable stock	16 fl oz
4 tbsp	red wine vinegar	4 tbsp
15 g	unsalted butter	½ oz
¼ tsp	salt	¼ tsp
	freshly ground black pepper	

Put the carrots, celery, garlic, red pepper flakes, thyme and enough water to cover them in a saucepan. Bring the mixture to the boil, then cover the pan and reduce the heat to medium. Simmer the vegetables until they are tender – about 20 minutes.

Pour ¼ litre (8 fl oz) of the stock into the carrot mixture and cook until the liquid is reduced to approximately 4 tablespoons – about 10 minutes. Add the remaining stock and the vinegar, and

cook until only 4 tablespoons of liquid remain – about 10 minutes more.

While you are reducing the second portion of stock, cook the pasta in 3 litres (5 pints) of boiling water with 1½ teaspoons of salt. Start testing the pasta after 5 minutes and cook it until it is *al dente*.

Stir the butter, salt and pepper into the sauce. Drain the pasta, put it in a bowl, and toss it with the sauce.

Chilled Spirals with Rocket Pesto

Serves 4

Working time: about 25 minutes

Total time: about 2 hours

Calories 535

Protein 17g

Cholesterol 10mg

Total fat 22g

Saturated fat 4g

Sodium 395mg

350 g	spirals	12 oz	60 g	Parmesan cheese, freshly grated	2 oz
125 g	rocket, washed, cleaned and stemmed	4 oz	¼ tsp	salt	¼ tsp
1	small garlic clove, coarsely chopped	1		freshly ground black pepper	
30 g	pine-nuts	1 oz	1	sweet red pepper, seeded, deribbed and finely diced	1
3 tbsp	virgin olive oil	3 tbsp	2 tbsp	balsamic vinegar, or 1 tbsp red wine vinegar	2 tbsp
1 tbsp	safflower oil	1 tbsp			

Add the spirals to 4 litres (7 pints) of boiling water with 2 teaspoons of salt. Start testing the pasta after 8 minutes and cook it until it is *al dente*.

. Meanwhile, prepare the pesto: put the rocket, garlic, pine-nuts, olive oil and safflower oil into a blender or food processor. Blend for 2 minutes, stopping two or three times to scrape down the sides. Add the cheese and the salt; blend the mixture briefly to form a purée.

Drain the pasta, transfer it to a large bowl, and season it with some black pepper. Add the diced red pepper, the vinegar and pesto, and toss well. Chill the pasta salad in the refrigerator for 1 to 2 hours before serving it.

Ziti with Italian Sausage and Red Peppers

Serves 4

Working time: about 30 minutes

Total time: about 40 minutes

Calories 300

Protein 11g

Cholesterol 10mg

Total fat 7g

Saturated fat 2g

Sodium 330mg

250 g	ziti (or other tubular pasta)	**8 oz**
3	sweet red peppers	**3**
125 g	spicy Italian pork sausages	**4 oz**
2	garlic cloves, finely chopped	**2**
2 tsp	fresh thyme, or ½ tsp dried thyme	**2 tsp**
1	large tomato, skinned, seeded and puréed	**1**
1 tbsp	red wine vinegar	**1 tbsp**
⅛ tsp	salt	**⅛ tsp**

Preheat the grill. Place the peppers 5 cm (2 inches) below the heat source, turning them from time to time, until they are blackened all over – 15 to 18 minutes. Put the peppers in a bowl and cover it with plastic film. The trapped steam will loosen their skins.

Squeeze the sausages out of their casings and break the meat into small pieces; sauté the pieces over medium-high heat until they are browned – about 3 minutes. Remove the pan from the heat and stir in the garlic and the thyme.

Add the pasta to 3 litres (5 pints) of boiling water with 1½ teaspoons of salt; start testing it after 10 minutes and cook it until it is *al dente*.

While the pasta is cooking, peel the peppers,

working over a bowl to catch the juices. Remove and discard the stems, seeds and ribs; strain the juices and reserve them. Slice the peppers lengthwise into thin strips.

Set the pan containing the sausage mixture over medium heat. Add the pepper strips and their reserved juices, the puréed tomato, the vinegar and the 8 teaspoon of salt. Simmer the sauce until it thickens and is reduced by one third – 5 to 7 minutes.

Drain the pasta, return it to the pan, and combine it with the sauce. Cover the pan and let the pasta stand for 5 minutes to allow the flavours to blend.

Vermicelli, Onions and Peas

Serves 8
as a
side dish

Working
time: about
15 minutes

Total time:
about
1 hour

Calories
185
Protein
5g
Cholesterol
0mg
Total fat
4g
Saturated fat
1g
Sodium
120mg

250 g	vermicelli or spaghettini	**8 oz**	**¼ tsp**	salt	**¼ tsp**
2 tbsp	virgin olive oil	**2 tbsp**		freshly ground black pepper	
500 g	onions, chopped	**1 lb**	**¼ litre**	dry white wine	**8 fl oz**
1	leek, trimmed, cleaned and thinly sliced	**1**	**75 g**	shelled peas	**2½ oz**

Heat the oil in a large, heavy frying pan over low heat. Add the onions, leek, salt and a generous grinding of pepper. Cover the pan tightly and cook, stirring frequently to keep the onions from sticking, until the vegetables are very soft – about 45 minutes.

Cook the pasta in 3 litres (5 pints) of boiling water with 1½ teaspoons of salt. Start testing the pasta after 7 minutes and cook it until it is *al dente*.

While the pasta is cooking, finish the sauce: pour the wine into the pan and raise the heat to high. Cook the mixture until the liquid is reduced to about 4 tablespoons – approximately 5 minutes. Stir in the peas, cover the pan, and cook for another 1 to 2 minutes to heat the peas through. If you are using fresh peas, increase the cooking time to 5 minutes.

Drain the pasta and transfer it to a serving dish; pour the contents of the frying pan over the top and toss well. Serve immediately.

Penne with Smoked Pork and Mushroom Sauce

Serves 8

Working time: about 15 minutes

Total time: about 45 minutes

Calories 315
Protein 11g
Cholesterol 5mg
Total fat 6g
Saturated fat 2g
Sodium 215mg

500 g	penne (or other short, tubular pasta)	**1 lb**
1.25 kg	Italian plum tomatoes, quartered, or 800 g (28 oz) canned whole tomatoes, drained	**2½ lb**
4	whole dried red chili peppers	**4**
2 tbsp	virgin olive oil	**2 tbsp**
1	onion, finely chopped	**1**
500 g	mushrooms, wiped clean and sliced	**1 lb**
60 g	smoked pork loin or smoked back bacon, julienned	**2 oz**
4	garlic cloves, finely chopped	**4**
12.5 cl	dry white wine	**4 fl oz**
2 tbsp	chopped parsley, preferably flat-leaf	**2 tbsp**
15 g	unsalted butter	**½ oz**

In a large saucepan, combine the tomatoes, chili peppers and 4 tablespoons of water. Cook over medium heat until the tomatoes have rendered their juice and most of the liquid has evaporated – about 20 minutes. Work the mixture through a sieve and set it aside.

Add the penne to 3 litres (5 pints) of boiling water with 1½ teaspoons of salt. Begin testing the pasta after 10 minutes and cook it until it is *al dente*.

While the pasta is cooking, heat the oil in a large frying pan over medium-high heat. Add the onion and sauté it, stirring constantly, until it turns translucent – about 3 minutes. Add the mushrooms and sauté them for 2 minutes, then add the pork and garlic and sauté for 2 minutes more. Pour in the wine and cook the mixture until the liquid is reduced by half – about 3 minutes. Stir in the reserved tomato mixture and the parsley, and keep the sauce warm.

Drain the penne and transfer it to a serving dish. Toss it with the butter and the sauce and serve.

Macaroni Baked with Stilton and Port

Serves 6

Working time: about 20 minutes

Total time: about 45 minutes

Calories 300
Protein 11g
Cholesterol 15mg
Total fat 9g
Saturated fat 4g
Sodium 400mg

250 g	elbow macaroni	8 oz	¼ litre	unsalted chicken stock	8 fl oz
1 tbsp	safflower oil	1 tbsp	125 g	Stilton, crumbled	4 oz
2	shallots, finely chopped	2	2 tsp	Dijon mustard	2 tsp
2 tbsp	flour	2 tbsp	⅛ tsp	white pepper	⅛ tsp
12.5 cl	ruby port	4 fl oz	4 tbsp	dry breadcrumbs	4 tbsp
¼ litre	semi-skimmed milk	8 fl oz	1 tsp	paprika	1 tsp

Preheat the oven to 180°C (350°F or Mark 4). Pour the oil into a large, heavy-bottomed saucepan over medium heat. Add the shallots and cook them, stirring occasionally, until transparent – approximately 2 minutes. Sprinkle the flour over the shallots and cook the mixture, stirring continuously, for 2 minutes more.

Pour the port into the pan and whisk slowly; add the milk and the stock in the same manner, whisking after each addition, to form a smooth sauce. Gently simmer the sauce for 3 minutes. Stir in half of the cheese along with the mustard and pepper. Continue stirring until the cheese has melted.

Meanwhile, cook the macaroni in 3 litres (5 pints) of boiling water with 1½ teaspoons of salt. Start testing the pasta after 10 minutes and cook it until it is *al dente*.

Drain the macaroni and combine it with the sauce, then transfer the mixture to a baking dish. Combine the breadcrumbs with the remaining crumbled cheese and scatter the mixture evenly over the top. Sprinkle the paprika over all and bake the dish until the sauce is bubbling hot and the top is crisp – 20 to 25 minutes. Serve immediately.

Linguine with Mussels in Saffron Sauce

Serves 4

Working (and total) time: about 30 minutes

Calories
475

Protein
23g

Cholesterol
30mg

Total fat
8g

Saturated fat
2g

Sodium
560mg

350 g	linguine (or spaghetti)	**12 oz**
1 kg	large mussels, scrubbed and debearded	**2 lb**
1 tbsp	safflower oil	**1 tbsp**
1	shallot, finely chopped	**1**
2 tbsp	flour	**2 tbsp**
12.5 cl	dry vermouth	**4 fl oz**
⅛ tsp	saffron threads, steeped in 17.5 cl (6 fl oz) hot water	**⅛ tsp**
4 tbsp	freshly grated pecorino cheese	**4 tbsp**
¼ tsp	salt	**¼ tsp**
	freshly ground black pepper	
1 tbsp	cut chives	**1 tbsp**

Put the mussels and 12.5 cl (4 fl oz) of water in a large pan. Cover, and steam the mussels over high heat until they open – about 5 minutes. Remove the mussels from the pan and set them aside. Discard any that do not open.

When the mussels are cool enough to handle, remove the meat, working over the pan to catch any liquid; set the meat aside and discard the shells. Strain the liquid left in the pan through a very fine sieve. Set aside.

Heat the safflower oil in a heavy frying pan over medium-high heat. Add the finely chopped shallot and sauté it for 30 seconds. Remove the pan from the heat. Whisk in the 2 tablespoons of flour, then the dry vermouth and the saffron

liquid (whisking prevents lumps from forming). Return the frying pan to the heat and simmer the sauce over medium-low heat until it thickens – 2 to 3 minutes.

Meanwhile, cook the linguine in 3 litres (5 pints) of boiling water with 1½ teaspoons of salt. Start testing the pasta after 10 minutes and cook it until it is *al dente*.

To finish the sauce, stir in 4 tablespoons of the strained mussel-cooking liquid along with the cheese, salt, pepper, chives and mussels. Simmer the sauce for 3 to 4 minutes more to heat the mussels through.

Drain the linguine, transfer it to a bowl and toss it with the sauce. Serve immediately.

Orzo and Wild Mushrooms

Serves 4
as an
appetizer or
side dish

Working
time: about
30 minutes

Total time:
about
40 minutes

Calories
255
Protein
8g
Cholesterol
10mg
Total fat
4g
Saturated fat
2g
Sodium
165mg

200 g	orzo	7 oz	35 cl	unsalted chicken stock	12 fl oz
30 g	dried ceps or other wild	1 oz	1	garlic clove, finely chopped	1
	mushrooms, soaked in ¼ litre (8 fl oz)		1 tsp	fresh thyme, or ¼ tsp dried thyme	1 tsp
	hot water for 20 minutes		¼ tsp	salt	¼ tsp
15 g	unsalted butter	½ oz		freshly ground black pepper	

Remove the mushrooms from their soaking liquid and slice them into thin strips. Strain the liquid through a fine-meshed sieve and reserve 12.5 cl (4 fl oz) of it.

Melt the butter in a heavy-bottomed saucepan over medium-high heat. Add the pasta and the sliced mushrooms to the pan and cook the mixture for 5 minutes, stirring frequently. Add the reserved mushroom soaking liquid, 12.5 cl (4 fl oz) of the stock, the garlic, thyme, salt and

pepper. Cook, stirring all the while, until the orzo has absorbed most of the liquid – 7 to 8 minutes.

Reduce the heat to low and pour in another 12.5 cl (4 fl oz) of stock; cook, stirring constantly, until the liquid has been absorbed – 3 to 4 minutes. Repeat this process once more with the remaining stock, cooking the mixture until the pasta is tender but still moist. Serve the dish immediately.

Star-Stuffed Peppers

Serves 4

Working time: about 45 minutes

Total time: about 1 hour and 15 minutes

Calories 380
Protein 17g
Cholesterol 25mg
Total fat 10g
Saturated fat 1g
Sodium 350mg

250 g	stellette (stars)	**8 oz**
150 g	skinned, boneless chicken breast, meat cut into small pieces	**5 oz**
3	spring onions, trimmed and thinly sliced	**3**
1	large garlic clove, crushed	**1**
1½ tbsp	coarsely chopped fresh ginger root	**1½ tbsp**
2 tbsp	safflower oil	**2 tbsp**

90 g	canned pimientos, drained, finely chopped	**3 oz**
	freshly ground black pepper	
2 tsp	white vinegar	**2 tsp**
½ tsp	salt	**½ tsp**
4	sweet green peppers, or very mild, large green chili peppers (about 15 cm/6 inches long)	**4**
1 tsp	dark sesame oil	**1 tsp**

Mound the chicken pieces, spring onions, garlic and ginger on a cutting board and chop into fine pieces.

Heat the oil in a large, heavy frying pan over medium heat. Add the chicken mixture and sauté; breaking it up and turning it frequently with a spatula, until the meat has turned white – about 4 minutes. Stir in the pimientos, black pepper, vinegar and ¼ teaspoon of salt.

Add the stellette to 2 litres (3½ pints) of boiling water with ½ teaspoon of salt. Start testing after 2 minutes and cook until they are *al dente.* Drain them and stir them into the chicken mixture.

Preheat the oven to 180°C (350°F or Mark 4).

Slice off the peppers' tops and set them aside; with a small spoon, scoop the seeds and the ribs from inside the cavities. Dip a finger into the sesame oil and rub it over the insides of the peppers, then sprinkle the insides with the remaining ¼ teaspoon of salt. Fill the peppers with the chicken stuffing and replace their tops; reserve the stuffing that is left over.

Lightly oil a shallow baking dish and arrange the stuffed peppers in it in a single layer. Bake the peppers for 25 minutes. Remove the dish from the oven and distribute the reserved stuffing around the peppers. Return the dish to the oven for 5 minutes before serving the peppers.

Orzo and Mussels

Serves 4

Working time: about 30 minutes

Total time: about 40 minutes

Calories 400

Protein 17g

Cholesterol 20mg

Total fat 9g

Saturated fat 1g

Sodium 390mg

250 g	orzo (or other small pasta)	**8 oz**
1	orange	**1**
2 tbsp	virgin olive oil	**2 tbsp**
1	onion, finely chopped	**1**
4	garlic cloves, finely chopped	**4**
1 kg	tomatoes, skinned, seeded and finely chopped	**2 lb**
2 tsp	fennel seeds	**2 tsp**
1½ tbsp	tomato paste	**1½ tbsp**
12.5 cl	dry vermouth	**4 fl oz**
¼ tsp	salt	**¼ tsp**
3 tbsp	chopped fresh parsley, or 1 tbsp dried parsley	**3 tbsp**
1 tsp	fresh thyme, or ¼ tsp dried thyme	**1 tsp**
750 g	mussels, scrubbed and debearded	**1½ lb**

Pare the rind from the orange and cut it into tiny julienne. Put the strips in a small saucepan with ¼ litre (8 fl oz) of cold water. Bring to the boil, then remove from the heat. Rinse the rind under cold running water and set it aside. Squeeze the orange and reserve the juice.

Heat the oil in a large fireproof casserole over medium heat. Add the chopped onion and cook it for 3 minutes, stirring constantly. Add the chopped garlic and cook, stirring, until the onion is translucent – about 2 minutes more.

Push the onion-garlic mixture to one side. Add the tomatoes and the fennel seeds, and raise the heat to high. Cook the tomatoes just enough to soften them with out destroying their

texture – 1 minute. Stir the onion-garlic mixture in with the tomatoes. Add the tomato paste, orange juice, vermouth and salt, and stir well. Reduce the heat and simmer the sauce for 5 minutes. Add herbs and orange rind.

Place the mussels on top of the sauce. Cover and steam the mussels until they open – 3 to 5 minutes. If any remain closed, discard them. Remove the casserole from the heat and set it aside with its lid on to keep the contents warm.

Add the orzo to 3 litres (5 pints) of boiling water with 1½ teaspoons of salt. Start testing after 10 minutes and cook it until it is *al dente*. Drain the orzo and divide it between four deep plates. Ladle the mussels and sauce over each serving.

Vermicelli with Tomatoes and Clams

Serves 4

Working
(and total)
time: about
1 hour

Calories
455

Protein
24g

Cholesterol
55mg

Total fat
11g

Saturated fat
3g

Sodium
150mg

250 g	vermicelli or thin spaghetti	**8 oz**
15 g	unsalted butter	**½ oz**
36	small clams, the shells scrubbed	**36**
6 tbsp	red wine	**6 tbsp**
5	parsley sprigs	**5**
6	garlic cloves, finely chopped	**6**
1½ tbsp	virgin olive oil	**1½ tbsp**
1	small carrot, thinly sliced	**1**
1	onion, finely chopped	**1**

2 kg	ripe tomatoes, skinned, seeded and chopped, or 1.3 kg (48 oz) canned whole tomatoes, drained and chopped	**4 lb**
2 tsp	finely chopped fresh oregano, or 1 tsp dried oregano	**2 tsp**
1½ tsp	finely chopped fresh thyme or ½ tsp dried thyme freshly ground black pepper	**1½ tsp**

Before steaming the clams discard any that fail to close when tapped.

In a large pan, combine the clams, wine, parsley and half of the garlic. Cover and steam over medium-high heat for 5 mins. Transfer to a bowl any clams that have opened. Re-cover the pan and steam the remaining clams for about 3 mins more. Again, transfer the opened clams to the bowl; discard any remaining closed. Strain the liquid in the pan through a fine sieve and reserve 6 tbsps of it. When clams are cool, remove from their shells and reserve with any liquid in the bowl.

Pour the oil into a saucepan over medium heat. Add carrot and onion, and sauté until onion is translucent – 5 mins. Add remaining garlic, cook 3 mins more. Stir in the tomatoes and herbs. Reduce heat and cook, stirring often, until sauce is quite thick – about 15 minutes. Then add clams to sauce, with their liquid and the wine mixture. Stir in plenty of black pepper.

About 5 minutes after adding tomatoes to the sauce, put vermicelli into 3 litres (5 pints) of boiling water with 1½ teaspoons of salt. Start testing after 6 minutes and cook until *al dente*.

Drain and toss with butter. Pour the clam sauce over, and serve.

Ditalini Gratin with Chili Pepper

Serves 6
as a
side dish

Working
time: about
25 minutes

Total time:
about
30 minutes

Calories
225

Protein
10g

Cholesterol
10mg

Total fat
4g

Saturated fat
3g

Sodium
185mg

250 g	ditalini (or other small, tubular pasta)	**8 oz**
750 g	ripe tomatoes, skinned, seeded and chopped, or 400 g (14 oz) canned whole tomatoes, drained and chopped	**1½ lb**
1	onion, chopped	**1**
¼ litre	semi-skimmed milk	**8 fl oz**

1	hot green chili pepper, seeded, deribbed and finely chopped	**1**
1	garlic clove, finely chopped	**1**
¼ tsp	ground cumin	**¼ tsp**
¼ tsp	salt	**¼ tsp**
	freshly ground black pepper	
60 g	Cheddar cheese, finely diced	**2 oz**

Put the tomatoes, onion and milk in a large, heavy sauté pan and bring to the boil. Add the ditalini, chili pepper, garlic, cumin, salt and a liberal grinding of black pepper. Stir to mix thoroughly, then cover the pan and reduce the heat to medium. Simmer the mixture for 2 minutes, stirring from time to time to keep the pasta from sticking to the bottom. Preheat the grill.

Pour into the pan just enough water to cover the ditalini. Cook the pasta, removing the lid frequently to stir the mixture and keep it covered with liquid, until the pasta is just tender and a creamy sauce has formed – about 7 minutes.

Transfer the contents of the pan to a fireproof gratin dish. Sprinkle the cheese over the top and grill the pasta until the cheese is melted – 2 to 3 minutes. Serve the dish immediately.

Fettuccine with Grilled Aubergine

Serves 4

Working time: about 30 minutes

Total time: about 40 minutes

Calories 355
Protein 9g
Cholesterol 0mg
Total fat 13g
Saturated fat 1g
Sodium 235mg

250 g	fettuccine (or other narrow ribbon pasta)	8 oz
500 g	aubergines, cut lengthwise into 2.5 cm (1 inch) slices	1 lb
2½ tbsp	virgin olive oil	2½ tbsp
1	large, ripe tomato, skinned and seeded	1
50 g	oil-packed sun-dried tomatoes, drained and thinly sliced	1¾ oz
1	shallot, finely chopped	1
1	garlic clove, finely chopped	1
1 tbsp	red wine vinegar	1 tbsp
	freshly ground black pepper	
4 tbsp	chopped fresh basil	4 tbsp

Preheat the grill. Brush both sides of the aubergine slices with 1½ tablespoons of the oil. Cut each aubergine slice into cubes. Put the aubergine cubes on a baking sheet in a single layer, then grill them until they are well browned on one side. Turn the pieces over and grill once more until brown. Turn off the grill, but leave the aubergine underneath to keep it warm.

Cook the fettuccine in 3 litres (5 pints) of boiling water with 1½ teaspoons of salt; start testing the pasta after 10 minutes and cook it until it is *al dente*.

Purée the fresh tomato in a food processor or blender. Put the tomato purée in a small saucepan along with the sun-dried tomatoes, shallot,

garlic, vinegar, the remaining tablespoon of oil and a generous grinding of pepper. Place the pan over low heat, bring the mixture to a simmer, and cook it for 2 minutes. Remove the pan from the heat and stir in the basil.

When the pasta finishes cooking, drain it and transfer it to a large serving bowl. Add the warm aubergine cubes and the sauce, toss well, and serve at once.

Editor's Note: Two and a half tablespoons of the oil in which the sun-dried tomatoes are packed may be substituted for the virgin olive oil called for here.

Lasagnette with Lobster and Spring Greens

Serves 2

Working time: about 30 minutes

Total time: about 1 hour

Calories 430
Protein 25g
Cholesterol 105mg
Total fat 15g
Saturated fat 7g
Sodium 425mg

125 g	lasagnette (or other curly-edged ribbon pasta)	4 oz
1	live lobster (about 600 g/1¼ lb)	1
1	lemon or lime, cut in half	1
250 g	spring greens, washed, stemmed and cut into 1 cm (½ inch) strips	8 oz
30 g	unsalted butter	1 oz
	freshly ground black pepper	

Pour water into a large pot to a depth of 2.5 cm (1 inch). Bring to the boil and add the lobster. Cover tightly and steam the lobster until it turns bright orange – about 10 mins. Remove the lobster from the pot and set it on a dish to catch the juices; do not discard the cooking liquid. Pour 2 litres (3½ pints) of water into the pot and bring the liquid to the boil.

Holding the lobster over the dish, twist the tail away from the body. Twist the claws off the body, then crack the shell of the tail and claws. Remove the meat and slice it thinly. Add the shells and juices to the boiling liquid. Boil for 10 minutes. With a slotted spoon, remove the shells and discard them. Squeeze the juice of one of the lemon or lime halves into the liquid. Add the lasagnette and cover the pot. When the liquid

returns to the boil, remove the lid. Start testing the pasta after 11 minutes and cook it until it is *al dente*.

While the pasta is cooking, transfer 6 tablespoons of the cooking liquid to a large, heavy sauté pan and bring it to a simmer. Add spring greens and cook, stirring occasionally, until all of the liquid has evaporated and greens are completely wilted. Melt the butter in a small, heavy-bottomed saucepan over medium heat and cook it just until it turns nut brown; do not let it burn. Scatter the lobster meat over the spring greens in the pan. Squeeze the remaining lemon or lime half over the lobster.

When pasta finishes cooking, drain it and add it to the pan. Add some pepper, pour the butter over the pasta, and toss well. Serve immediately.

45

Linguine and Chilied Prawns

Serves 4

Working time: about 20 minutes

Total time: about 1 hour

Calories 495
Protein 23g
Cholesterol 135mg
Total fat 20g
Saturated fat 6g
Sodium 390mg

250 g	linguine (or spaghetti)	8 oz
45 g	unsalted butter	1½ oz
1	onion, finely chopped	1
35 cl	light beer	12 fl oz
1	bay leaf	1
500 g	large fresh prawns, peeled and deveined, the shells reserved	1 lb

2 tbsp	safflower oil	2 tbsp
1	garlic clove, finely chopped	1
1 tbsp	chili powder	1 tbsp
¼ tsp	salt	¼ tsp
	freshly ground black pepper	
¼ tsp	salt	¼ tsp
⅓	avocado, peeled and thinly sliced	⅓

To make the sauce, melt the butter in a saucepan over medium-high heat. Add the onion and cook it until it is translucent – about 2 minutes. Add the beer, bay leaf and reserved prawn shells, and bring the liquid to a simmer. Reduce the heat to low, cover the pan, and simmer the mixture for 20 minutes.

Add the linguine to 3 litres (5 pints) of boiling water with 1½ teaspoons of salt. After 8 minutes, drain the pasta and set it aside; it will be slightly underdone.

Strain the prawn-shell liquid, discarding the solids, and return the liquid to the pan; there will be a little more than ¼ litre (8 fl oz). Add the reserved linguine to the liquid and simmer it, covered, until it is *al dente* – about 4 minutes.

While the pasta finishes cooking, pour the oil into a large, heavy frying pan over medium-high heat. Add the prawns and sauté them, stirring occasionally, until they are firm and opaque – 1 to 2 minutes. Stir in the garlic and cook for 30 seconds more. Season the prawns with the chili powder, the ¼ teaspoon of salt and some pepper.

Add the avocado to the linguine and toss. Transfer the mixture to a platter, arrange the prawns on top of the pasta, and serve hot.

Farfalle in Red Pepper Sauce with Broccoli

Serves 4

Working time: about 15 minutes

Total time: about 25 minutes

Calories 285
Protein 11g
Cholesterol 5mg
Total fat 6g
Saturated fat 2g
Sodium 350mg

250 g	farfalle (or other fancy-shaped pasta)	**8 oz**
1 tbsp	virgin olive oil	**1 tbsp**
1	garlic clove, finely chopped	**1**
2	sweet red peppers, seeded, deribbed and coarsely chopped	**2**
¼ tsp	salt	**¼ tsp**
¼ litre	unsalted chicken stock	**8 fl oz**

75 g	broccoli florets, blanched, refreshed	**2½ oz**
1 tbsp	chopped fresh basil, or 1 tsp dried basil	**1 tbsp**
½ tbsp	chopped fresh oregano, or ½ tsp dried oregano	**½ tbsp**
	freshly ground black pepper	
4 tbsp	freshly grated Parmesan cheese	**4 tbsp**

Heat the oil in a large, heavy frying pan over medium heat. Add the garlic and cook it for 30 seconds, stirring constantly. Add the red peppers, salt and stock. Simmer until only 6 tablespoons of liquid remain – 7 to 8 minutes. Meanwhile, cook the farfalle in 3 litres (5 pints) of boiling water with 1½ teaspoons of salt. Start testing the

pasta after 8 minutes and cook it until it is *al dente*. Drain the pasta and transfer it to a bowl.

Purée the red pepper mixture in a blender or food processor. Strain it through a sieve back into the pan. Stir in the broccoli is heated through – 2 to 3 minutes. Toss the farfalle with the sauce and serve.

Pasta Shells and Scallops

Serves 6

Working
(and total)
time: about
25 minutes

Calories
300

Protein
18g

Cholesterol
40mg

Total fat
9g

Saturated fat
4g

Sodium
460mg

250 g	medium pasta shells	8 oz		¼ tsp	white pepper	¼ tsp
1 tbsp	safflower oil	1 tbsp		350 g	scallops, connective muscle at	12 oz
1	small onion, finely chopped	1			their sides removed, as necessary	
2 tbsp	flour	2 tbsp		4 tbsp	fresh breadcrumbs	4 tbsp
35 cl	unsalted chicken or fish stock	12 fl oz		60 g	Parmesan cheese, freshly grated	2 oz
4 tbsp	double cream	4 tbsp		¼ tsp	paprika	¼ tsp
⅛ tsp	grated nutmeg	⅛ tsp			parsley sprigs for garnish	
¼ tsp	salt	¼ tsp				

Add the pasta shells to 3 litres (5 pints) of boiling water with 1½ teaspoons of salt. Start testing the pasta after 8 minutes and cook it until it is *al dente.*

Meanwhile, to prepare the sauce, pour the oil into a shallow fireproof casserole over medium heat. Add the onion and sauté it until it turns translucent – about 3 minutes. Stir in the flour and continue to cook, stirring constantly, for 2 minutes. Remove the casserole from the heat. Slowly whisk in the stock and cream, stirring the mixture until it smooth. Add the nutmeg, salt and pepper, and stir. Preheat the grill.

Drain the pasta and add it, along with the scallops, to the sauce. Return the casserole to the heat and bring the sauce to a simmer. Cover the casserole and simmer gently until the scallops become opaque – 2 to 3 minutes.

To prepare the dish for the table, wipe any sauce from the visible inside walls of the casserole. Then top the dish with the breadcrumbs, cheese and paprika and grill it until the topping is golden – about 2 minutes. Garnish with parsley sprigs and serve hot.

Rigatoni with Red Potatoes and Radicchio

Serves 6
as an
appetizer

Working
(and total)
time: about
45 minutes

Calories
275
Protein
7g
Cholesterol
0mg
Total fat
10g
Saturated fat
1g
Sodium
100mg

250 g	rigatoni (or medium shells)	8 oz
3	unpeeled red potatoes (about 250 g/8 oz), each cut into 8 pieces	3
4 tbsp	virgin olive oil	4 tbsp
250 g	spinach, washed, stemmed, and squeezed into a ball to remove excess water	8 oz
2	garlic cloves, finely chopped	2

125 g	radicchio, torn into 4 cm (1½ inch) pieces	4 oz
2 tbsp	Dijon mustard	2 tbsp
2 tbsp	red wine vinegar	2 tbsp
4 tbsp	chopped fresh basil	4 tbsp
2	bunches spring onions, trimmed and cut into 2.5 cm (1 inch) pieces freshly ground black pepper	2

In a large, covered pan, bring 3 litres (5 pints) of water and 1½ teaspoons of salt to the boil; add the rigatoni to the boiling water. Start testing the pasta after 13 minutes and cook until *al dente*.

While pasta is cooking, pour enough water into a pan to fill it about 2.5 cm (1 inch) deep). Add ½ teaspoon of salt and set a vegetable steamer in the bottom of the pan. Bring water to the boil. Add the potatoes, cover the pan, and steam the potatoes until they are tender when pierced with the tip of a thin knife – about 8 minutes. Transfer the potatoes to a large bowl.

When pasta is cooked, drain and transfer it to the bowl with the potatoes. Pour in 1 tablespoon

of oil and toss well to coat pasta and potatoes.

Heat another tablespoon of the oil in a large, heavy frying pan over medium-high heat. When it is hot, add the spinach and garlic, and sauté them for 30 seconds, stirring constantly. Add the radicchio and cook until the spinach has wilted – about 30 seconds more. Scrape the contents of the pan into the bowl containing the pasta and the potatoes.

In a small bowl, whisk together the mustard and vinegar. Whisk in the remaining oil, then pour over the pasta. Add the basil, spring onions and some pepper to the bowl, toss well to combine, and serve.

Capelli d'Angelo with Tomatoes, Olives and Garlic

Serves 6
as an
appetizer

Working
time: about
20 minutes

Total time:
about
1 hour

Calories
190

Protein
6g

Cholesterol
0mg

Total fat
4g

Saturated fat
0g

Sodium
190mg

250 g	capelli d' angelo (or vermicelli)	8 oz
3	large, ripe tomatoes, skinned, seeded and chopped	3
4	garlic cloves, finely chopped	4
5	black olives, stoned and finely chopped	5
1	small hot chili pepper, seeded, deribbed and finely chopped	1

1 tbsp	virgin olive oil	1 tbsp
1	lime, juice only	1
1 tbsp	chopped fresh coriander	1 tbsp
⅛ tsp	salt	⅛ tsp
	freshly ground black pepper	

Put the chopped tomatoes in a strainer set over a large bowl; place the bowl in the refrigerator and let the tomatoes drain for at least 30 minutes.

Put 3 litres (5 pints) of water on to boil with 1½ teaspoons of salt. In a separate bowl, combine the garlic, olives, chili pepper, oil, lime juice, coriander, salt and pepper. Refrigerate the mixture.

Drop the capelli d'angelo into the boiling water. Begin testing them after 3 minutes and continue to cook until they are *al dente*.

While the pasta is cooking, combine the garlic mixture with the drained tomatoes; discard the juice. Drain the pasta, transfer it to a serving bowl and toss it immediately with the sauce.

Cavatappi with Spinach and Ham

Serves 4	
Working time: about 25 minutes	
Total time: about 35 minutes	

Calories 330	
Protein 13g	
Cholesterol 35mg	
Total fat 11g	
Saturated fat 5g	
Sodium 360mg	

250 g	cavatappi (or other short, tubular pasta)	8 oz	4 tbsp	double cream	4 tbsp
10 g	unsalted butter	⅓ oz	1	bay leaf	1
1	small onion, finely chopped	1		grated nutmeg	
2	garlic cloves, finely chopped	2		freshly ground black pepper	
¼ litre	unsalted chicken stock	16 fl oz	60 g	lean ham, julienned	2 oz
4 tbsp	dry vermouth	4 tbsp	500 g	fresh spinach, washed and stemmed	1 lb

Melt the butter in a large non-reactive frying pan over medium-high heat. Add the onion and garlic, and sauté them until they turn translucent – about 5 minutes. Add the stock, vermouth, cream, bay leaf, a little nutmeg and some pepper, and cook the mixture until it is reduced to about ¼ litre (8 fl oz) – 10 to 15 minutes.

While the stock mixture is reducing, add the pasta to 3 litres (5 pints) of boiling water with 1½ teaspoons of salt. Start testing the pasta after 10 minutes and cook it until it is *al dente*.

About 3 minutes before the pasta finishes cooking, remove the bay leaf from the mixture in the pan and discard it. Stir in the ham and spinach, then cover the pan and steam the spinach, then cover the pan and steam the spinach for 3 minutes. Remove the cover and stir the mixture until the spinach is completely wilted – about 30 seconds. Turn off the heat.

Drain the pasta and immediately stir it into the spinach and ham mixture. Allow the pasta mixture to stand for 1 minute. Stir it again just before serving.

Spinach Shell Salad with Chunks of Chicken

Serves 4

Working
(and total)
time: about
40 minutes

Calories
320

Protein
22g

Cholesterol
35mg

Total fat
3g

Saturated fat
1g

Sodium
270mg

250 g	medium spinach shells	8 oz	2	large shallots, thinly sliced	2
250 g	chicken breasts, skinned and boned, cut into pieces about 2.5 cm (1 inch) square	8 oz	½ tsp	ground cinnamon	½ tsp
			750 g	ripe tomatoes, skinned, seeded and chopped	1½ lb
¼ tsp	salt	¼ tsp	1	orange, rind only, cut into thin strips	1
	freshly ground black pepper				

Arrange the chicken pieces in a single layer in a deep, heatproof dish about 25 cm (10 inches) in diameter. Sprinkle the chicken with the salt and pepper. Scatter the shallot slices evenly over the chicken and top them with the cinnamon and tomatoes. Strew the orange rind over all. Cover the dish tightly with foil.

Pour enough water into a saucepan approximately 20 cm (8 inches) in diameter to fill it about one third full. Bring the water to a rolling boil. Set the covered dish on top of the saucepan like a lid and cook the chicken over the boiling water. After 5 minutes, test the chicken: if the meat is still pink at the centre,

cover the dish again and continue to steam the chicken until all trace of pink has disappeared and the meat feels firm but springy to the touch. Remove the dish from the saucepan and uncover it.

While the chicken is cooking, add the shells to 3 litres (5 pints) of boiling water with 1½ teaspoons of salt. Start testing the shells after 12 minutes and cook them until they are *al dente*.

Drain the shells and transfer them to a heated bowl. Add the chicken-and-tomato sauce and toss it with the shells. Serve hot or at room temperature.

Macaroni Salad

Serves 6

Working
(and total)
time: about
30 minutes

Calories
240

Protein
17g

Cholesterol
5mg

Total fat
8g

Saturated fat
2g

Sodium
400mg

250 g	elbow macaroni	**8 oz**
1 tbsp	safflower oil	**1 tbsp**
1	clove garlic, crushed	**1**
100 g	fresh shelled or frozen garden peas	**3½ oz**
100 g	fresh or frozen sweetcorn kernels	**3½ oz**
100 g	fine French beans, trimmed and cut into pea-size pieces	**3½ oz**
¼ tsp	salt	**¼ tsp**
	freshly ground black pepper	
1 tsp	finely chopped fresh thyme, or ½ tsp dried thyme	**1 tsp**

¼ litre	unsalted chicken stock	**8 fl oz**
1½ tbsp	white wine vinegar	**1½ tbsp**
1	small chili pepper, seeded, deribbed and finely chopped	**1**
100 g	lean ham, chopped	**3½ oz**
1	large cos lettuce, trimmed	**1**
	Garnish	
1	large tomato, skinned, seeded and neatly chopped	**1**
2	large spring onions, finely sliced	**2**
1 tbsp	finely chopped fresh basil, or ½ tbsp dried basil	**1 tbsp**

Cook macaroni in 3 litres (5 pints) of boiling water with 1½ teaspoons of salt. Start testing after 8 minutes and cook until it is *al dente*. Drain the macaroni, and rinse it briefly under cold water. Drain the pasta again, then spread it out on a clean tea towel to remove any excess moisture.

Heat the oil in a sauté pan over medium heat. Add the garlic and cook for about 30 seconds. Add the peas, sweetcorn, beans, salt, pepper, thyme and stock. Bring the mixture to a simmer and cook gently until the liquid is reduced by two thirds, about 10 minutes. Allow to cool.

Meanwhile, pour vinegar into a small bowl, add chili pepper and leave to stand for 5 minutes to allow vinegar to mellow the pepper's hotness.

Put the macaroni into a large mixing bowl, stir in the chili vinegar and the pea, sweetcorn, bean and stock mixture. Add the chopped ham and mix everything well together.

Line a large dish with lettuce leaves and spoon macaroni mixture into centre. Garnish salad with tomato, spring onions and basil.

Egg noodles with Carrots, Mange-Tout and Lamb

Serves 4

Working (and total) time: about 40 minutes

Calories 500

Protein 20g

Cholesterol 85mg

Total fat 23g

Saturated fat 10g

Sodium 295mg

250 g	fine egg noodles	8 oz
2 tsp	honey	2 tsp
2 tbsp	lime juice	2 tbsp
1½ tsp	curry powder	1½ tsp
2 tbsp	virgin olive oil	2 tbsp
250 g	lean boneless lamb, cut into strips about 2.5 cm (1 inch) long and 5 mm (¼ inch) wide	8 oz
1	garlic clove, finely chopped	1
⅛ tsp	salt	⅛ tsp
4	spring onions, trimmed and thinly sliced, white and green parts kept separate	4
12.5 cl	unsalted chicken stock	4 fl oz
1	large carrot, peeled, halved lengthwise and sliced diagonally into very thin crescents	1
125 g	mange-tout, trimmed, strings removed, each pod sliced diagonally into thirds	4 oz

In a small dish, combine the honey, lime juice and curry powder; set the mixture aside. Add the noodles to 3 litres (5 pints) of boiling water with 1½ teaspoons of salt. Start testing the noodles after 5 minutes and cook them until they are *al dente*. Drain the noodles, transfer them to a large bowl, and toss them with 1 tablespoon of the oil.

Pour the remaining tablespoon of olive oil into a large, heavy frying pan over medium-high heat. When the oil is hot, add the lamb and cook it, stirring constantly, for about 30 seconds. Stir in the garlic, ⅛ teaspoon of the salt, the white

part of the spring onions and the honey mixture. Cook for 30 seconds more, stirring constantly. Scrape the mixture into the bowl with the noodles and toss well. Do not wash the pan.

Return the pan to the stove over medium-high heat; pour in the stock, then add the carrot and the remaining ⅛ teaspoon of salt. Cook the mixture, scraping up any caramelized bits, for about 3 minutes. Add the mange-tout and cook for 1 minute more, stirring all the while. Transfer the mixture to the bowl with the noodles, add the spring onion greens, and mix thoroughly.

Wholewheat Spirals with Caviare Sauce

Serves 6

Working
(and total)
time: about
25 minutes

Calories
245
Protein
12g
Cholesterol
90mg
Total fat
11g
Saturated fat
3g
Sodium
460mg

250 g	wholewheat spirals (or other wholewheat pasta)	**8 oz**	
1 tbsp	virgin olive oil	**1 tbsp**	
1	large onion, finely chopped	**1**	
17.5 cl	plain low-fat yogurt	**6 fl oz**	

12.5 cl	soured cream	**4 fl oz**	
100 g	lumpfish roe or caviare	**3½ oz**	
2 tbsp	finely chopped parsley	**2 tbsp**	
	freshly ground black pepper		
	watercress for garnish		

Cook the wholewheat spirals in 3 litres (5 pints) of boiling water. Start testing after 10 minutes and cook them until they are *al dente*.

Five minutes before the pasta is cooked, heat the oil in a heavy-bottomed saucepan, add the chopped onion and cook it very gently until it is translucent but still firm – about 3 minutes.

Stir in the yogurt and the soured cream. Heat the mixture gently until it is hot, but do not allow the sauce to boil. Stir in the lumpfish roe or caviare – reserving some for garnish – and the parsley and pepper.

Drain the pasta, pour on the sauce, and toss the pasta and sauce gently together. Turn the spirals on to a hot serving dish and garnish with the reserved roe or caviare and watercress. Serve immediately.

Stellette with Smoked Salmon, Yogurt and Dill

Serves 6

Working (and total) time: about 25 minutes

Calories
200

Protein
12g

Cholesterol
15mg

Total fat
1g

Saturated fa
0g

Sodium
400mg

250 g	stellette (or other small pasta)	8 oz	150 g	smoked salmon, cut into long thin strips	5 oz
2 tsp	Dijon mustard	2 tsp			
2 tbsp	chopped fresh dill	2 tbsp		**Garnish**	
1 tbsp	lemon juice	1 tbsp	2	limes, cut into wedges	2
30 cl	plain low-fat yogurt	10 fl oz		fresh dill	
	freshly ground black pepper				

Bring 3 litres (5 pints) of water containing 1½ teaspoons of salt to the boil and add the stellette. Start testing after 2 minutes, then cook them until they are *al dente*. Drain them well. Rinse them briefly under cold running water and drain them once again. Then spread them out on a clean tea towel to remove any excess moisture.

In a large bowl, combine the mustard, chopped dill, lemon juice and plain yogurt. Add the stellette to the mixture and mix everything together. Season with freshly ground black pepper.

Mound the stellette on a large serving platter, and arrange the cucumber slices and the smoked salmon strips round the edge. Garnish with the lime wedges and fresh dill.

Afghan Noodles

Serves 6

Working
time: about
35 minutes

Total time:
about
45 minutes

Calories
350

Protein
24g

Cholesterol
45mg

Total fat
12g

Saturated fat
5g

Sodium
325mg

250 g	wide curly egg noodles	8 oz
¼ litre	low-fat yogurt, drained in a fine-meshed sieve or a muslin-lined sieve for 30 minutes	8 fl oz
4 tbsp	chopped fresh mint, or 2 tbsp dried mint	4 tbsp
2½ tsp	chili powder	2½ tsp
1 tbsp	fresh lemon juice	1 tbsp

1 tbsp	safflower oil	1 tbsp
1	onion, finely chopped	1
500 g	lean beef, minced	1 lb
½ tsp	salt	½ tsp
1	ripe tomato, skinned, seeded and chopped	1
15 g	unsalted butter	½ oz

To prepare the sauce, combine the drained yogurt with 3 tablespoons of the fresh mint or 1½ tablespoons of the dried mint, ½ teaspoon of the chili powder and the lemon juice.

Heat the oil in a large, heavy frying pan over medium-high heat. Add the onion and sauté it for 3 minutes. Add the beef, the remaining 2 teaspoons of chili powder and the salt, and cook the mixture for 6 minutes, stirring frequently. Stir in the tomato and cook for 2 minutes more.

Meanwhile, cook the egg noodles in 3 litres (5 pints) of boiling water with 1½ teaspoons of

salt until they are *al dente* – about 9 minutes. Drain the noodles and return them to the pan. Add the butter and stir gently until it melts and the noodles are coated.

To serve, transfer the hot noodles to a warmed serving platter. Pour the sauce over the noodles in a ring 2.5 to 5 cm (1 to 2 inches) in from the edge of the noodles, then arrange the beef mixture in the centre of the ring. Sprinkle the remaining mint over the top of the assembly and serve immediately.

Noodles with Poppy Seeds, Yogurt and Mushrooms

Serves 8
as a
side dish

Working
(and total)
time: about
25 minutes

Calories
195

Protein
6g

Cholesterol
30mg

Total fat
6g

Saturated fat
2g

Sodium
145mg

250 g	medium egg noodles	**8 oz**	**250 g**	mushrooms, wiped clean and	**8 oz**
4 tbsp	soured cream	**4 tbsp**		thinly sliced	
12.5 cl	low-fat yogurt	**4 fl oz**	**1**	onion, chopped	**1**
1 tbsp	poppy seeds	**1 tbsp**	**¼ tsp**	salt	**¼ tsp**
⅛ to ¼ tsp	cayenne pepper	**⅛ to ¼ tsp**	**12.5 cl**	dry white wine	**4 fl oz**
2 tbsp	virgin olive oil	**2 tbsp**			

In a small bowl, combine the soured cream, yogurt, poppy seeds, cayenne pepper and 1 tablespoon of the oil. In a large, covered pan, cook the egg noodles in 3 litres (5 pints) of boiling water with 1½ teaspoons of salt until they are *al dente* – about 9 minutes.

While the noodles are cooking, heat the remaining tablespoon of oil in a large, heavy frying pan over medium-high heat. Add the mushroom and onion, and sprinkle them with the ¼ teaspoon of salt. Cook, stirring frequently, until the mushrooms and onion are browned all over – 5 to 7 minutes. Add the wine to the pan and continue cooking, stirring, until almost all of the liquid has been absorbed – about 3 minutes more.

When the noodles are done, drain them and add them to the pan. Add the yogurt and poppy seed mixture, toss well and serve.

Noodles with Asparagus, Mushrooms and Prosciutto

Serves 4

Working (and total) time: about 20 minutes

Calories
445

Protein
17g

Cholesterol
65mg

Total fat
17g

Saturated fat
5g

Sodium
350mg

250 g	wide egg noodles	8 oz
250 g	asparagus, trimmed, scraped, ends peeled	8 oz
3 tbsp	virgin olive oil	3 tbsp
1	onion, finely chopped	1
60 g	shiitake mushrooms, sliced, or 125 g (4 oz) button mushrooms	2 oz
2	garlic cloves, finely chopped	2

	freshly ground black pepper	
45 g	prosciutto, cut into strips 5 mm (¼ inch) wide and 2.5 cm (1 inch) long	1½ oz
1 tsp	fresh lemon juice	1 tsp
15	fresh basil leaves	15
60 g	Parmesan cheese, freshly grated	2 oz

Cut each asparagus stalk diagonally into three pieces, then halve each piece lengthwise. Set the pieces aside.

Heat 1 tablespoon of the olive oil in a large, heavy frying pan over medium-high heat. Sauté the onion until it becomes translucent – about 5 minutes. Stir in the mushrooms, garlic and some pepper, and cook the mixture until the mushrooms are tender – about 5 minutes more. If you are using button mushrooms, cook them an additional 4 to 5 minutes to evaporate some of their moisture. Add the asparagus pieces and

cook them until they are tender – another 4 to 5 minutes. Stir in the prosciutto, lemon juice and basil leaves.

While the mushrooms are cooking, add the noodles to 3 litres (5 pints) of unsalted boiling water and cook them until they are *al dente* – approximately 9 minutes. Drain the noodles, and add them immediately to the frying pan. Add the Parmesan cheese and the remaining 2 tablespoons of olive oil, and toss thoroughly. Serve at once on warmed plates.

Eight-Treasure Noodles with Chinese Sausage

Serves 6

Working (and total) time: about 45 minutes

Calories 330

Protein 20g

Cholesterol 15mg

Total fat 13g

Saturated fat 4g

Sodium 440mg

250 g	flat wheat noodles or fettuccine	**8 oz**
1 litre	unsalted chicken stock	**1¾ pints**
1½ tbsp	safflower oil	**1½ tbsp**
1 tbsp	grated fresh ginger root	**1 tbsp**
1	small red onion, cut into 2 cm (¾ inch) squares	**1**
1	sweet red pepper, seeded, deribbed and cut into 2 cm (¾ inch) squares	**1**
3	lop cheong sausages, thinly sliced diagonally, simmered for 5 minutes in water to cover and drained, or 125 g (4 oz) barbecue pork, cut into 3 mm (⅛ inch) slices	**3**
175 g	mange-tout, halved diagonally	**6 oz**

8	dried shiitake or Chinese black mushrooms, soaked in hot water for 20 mins, drained, stemmed and quartered	**8**
450 g	canned baby sweetcorn, rinsed	**15 oz**
450 g	canned straw mushrooms, drained	**15 oz**
125 g	broccoli florets, blanched for 1 minute, rinsed and drained	**4 oz**
150 g	cauliflower florets, blanched for 1 minute, rinsed and drained	**5 oz**
2 tsp	cornflour, mixed with 2 tbsp water	**2 tsp**
1 tbsp	low-sodium soy sauce or shoyu	**1 tbsp**
1 tbsp	rice vinegar	**1 tbsp**
1 tsp	dark sesame oil	**1 tsp**

Reduce stock to about ¼ litre (8 fl oz), keep hot.

Add noodles to 4 litres (7 pints) of boiling water with 2 teaspoons of salt; start testing after 3 minutes and cook until they are *al dente*. Drain the noodles and rinse them with cold water.

In a hot wok, heat oil over medium-high heat. When oil is hot but not smoking, add ginger and onion, stir-fry for 30 seconds. Put in red pepper, sausage, mange-tout, shiitake mushrooms and

sweetcorn, continue stir-frying for 1 minute. Add straw mushrooms, broccoli and cauliflower, stir fry until very hot – about 1 minute.

Stir in cornflour mixture, soy sauce and vinegar into hot stock. Pour this into wok and stir it until it thickens, adding sesame oil at the last minute. Put noodles in wok, toss with vegetables to heat through, and then serve the dish immediately.

Chicken, Broccoli and Chilies on Egg Noodles

Serves 4

Working (and total) time: about 35 minutes

Calories 305

Protein 28g

Cholesterol 30mg

Total fat 14g

Saturated fat 2g

Sodium 455mg

350 g	fresh Chinese egg noodles, or 250 g (8 oz) dried vermicelli or thin spaghetti	**12 oz**
½ litre	unsalted chicken stock	**16 fl oz**
3½ tbsp	rice wine or dry sherry	**3½ tbsp**
1 tsp	dark sesame oil	**1 tsp**
¼ tsp	salt	**¼ tsp**
	white pepper	
2	chicken breasts	**2**

3 tbsp	safflower oil	**3 tbsp**
150 g	broccoli florets	**5 oz**
¼ tsp	sugar	**¼ tsp**
½ tsp	sesame seeds	**½ tsp**
2	hot green chili peppers, seeded and very finely chopped	**2**
1 tbsp	low-sodium soy sauce or shoyu	**1 tbsp**
4	spring onions, trimmed and finely chopped	**4**

Bring stock to the boil in a pan. Add 2 tablespoons of wine, sesame oil, salt and some pepper, and return the liquid to the boil. Reduce the heat to low and let the stock simmer very slowly.

Put the chicken in a pan and pour in enough water to cover. Bring water to the boil, then reduce the heat to low and poach breasts until tender – about 10 minutes. Remove chicken with a slotted spoon; discard cooking liquid. As soon as the chicken is cool enough to handle, separate meat from the bones. Discard the skin and bones and shred the meat by hand. Cover the chicke and set it aside in a warm place

Add the noodles to 4 litres (7 pints) of boiling water with 2 teaspoons of salt. Start testing the noodles after 3 minutes and cook them until they are *al dente*. Drain the noodles, then rinse them with cold water and set them aside in a colander.

In a wok or a heavy frying pan, heat 1 tablespoon of the safflower oil over medium-high heat. Add the broccoli florets and stir-fry them until they turn bright green. Add 1 tablespoon of the rice wine along with the sugar, and stir-fry for 30 seconds more. Transfer to a bowl, toss with the sesame seeds and cover to keep the broccoli warm.

Barbecue-Pork Noodles with Emeralds and Rubies

Serves 4

Working (and total) time: about 25 minutes

Calories 375
Protein 33g
Cholesterol 45mg
Total fat 16g
Saturated fat 4g
Sodium 555mg

350 g	fresh Chinese egg noodles, or 250 g (8 oz) dried vermicelli	**12 oz**
1 tbsp	safflower oil	**1 tbsp**
250 g	Chinese barbecue pork, trimmed of all fat, and thinly sliced into pieces about 2.5 cm (1 inch) square	**8 oz**
1 tbsp	finely chopped fresh ginger root	**1 tbsp**
125 g	mange-tout, strings removed, sliced diagonally	**4 oz**
8	dried shiitake or Chinese black mushrooms, soaked in very hot water for 20 minutes, stemmed and sliced, the soaking liquid reduced to 4 tablespoons and reserved	
150 g	fresh bean sprouts	**5 oz**
1	sweet red pepper, seeded, deribbed and sliced lengthwise	**1**
12.5 cl	unsalted chicken stock	**4 fl oz**
2 tbsp	low-sodium soy sauce or shoyu	**2 tbsp**

Add the noodles to 4 litres (7 pints) of boiling water with 2 teaspoons of salt. Start testing them after 3 minutes and cook them until they are *al dente*. Drain the noodles and keep them warm.

Heat the oil in a wok or a heavy frying pan over medium-high heat. Add the pork and ginger and stir-fry them for 2 minutes. Add the mange-tout, mushrooms, bean sprouts and red pepper slices and continue to stir-fry the mixture until the mange-tout turn bright green – about 2 minutes more.

Remove the pork and vegetables from the pan and set them aside. Add the drained noodles, the reserved mushroom-soaking liquid, the stock and soy sauce to the pan. Toss the noodles to combine them with the liquid. Return the pork and vegetables to the pan and mix gently. Divide the noodles between four large soup bowls and ladle over them any remaining liquid.

Spicy Noodles with Pork and Peanuts

Serves 4

Working time: about 30 minutes

Total time: about 1 hour

Calories 320

Protein 25g

Cholesterol 20mg

Total fat 15g

Saturated fat 4g

Sodium 525mg

350 g	fresh Chinese egg noodles, or 250 g (8 oz) dried linguine	**12 oz**
1 tbsp	safflower oil	**1 tbsp**
2	spring onions, finely chopped	**2**
2 tsp	very finely chopped fresh ginger root	**2 tsp**
1	garlic clove, finely chopped	**1**
¼ to ½ tsp	crushed red pepper flakes or sambal oelek	**¼ to ½ tsp**
175 g	boneless pork, trimmed of all fat, finely chopped	**6 oz**
2 tbsp	dry sherry	**2 tbsp**
1 tsp	soya bean paste	**1 tsp**
1 tsp	hoisin sauce	**1 tsp**
1 tbsp	low-sodium soy sauce or shoyu	**1 tbsp**
4 tbsp	unsalted chicken stock	**4 tbsp**
4 tbsp	diced water chestnuts	**4 tbsp**
4 tbsp	dry-roasted unsalted peanuts, coarsely chopped	**4 tbsp**
¼ tsp	dark sesame oil	**¼ tsp**
1 tbsp	chopped fresh coriander	**1 tbsp**
250 g	cucumber, halved, seeded and julienned	**8 oz**
50 g	fresh bean sprouts	**2 oz**
4 tbsp	shredded or julienned radishes	**4 tbsp**
1	apple, peeled, sliced and tossed with 2 tsp lemon juice	**1**

Add noodles to 3 litres (5 pints) of boiling water. Start testing them after 3 minutes and cook them until they are *al dente*. Drain the noodles, rinse them under cold water and set them aside.

Heat safflower oil in a hot wok or frying pan over high heat. Add spring onions, ginger, garlic and red pepper flakes, and stir-fry for 30 seconds. Add pork and continue stir-frying until pork is no longer pink – about 3 minutes. Pour in sherry along with soya bean paste, hoisin sauce and soy sauce, then add stock and water chestnuts. Cook for 2 minutes before stirring in peanuts and sesame oil. Add noodles and toss with sauce until they are heated through – about 1 minute.

Transfer the noodles to a serving dish. Garnish with coriander, cucumber, bean sprouts, radishes and apple. Alternatively, garnishes may be served separately so each diner may choose his own.

Shining Noodle Salad with Beef and Tomato

Serves 6

Working
time: about
30 minutes

Total time:
about
1 hour

Calories
265

Protein
16g

Cholesterol
30mg

Total fat
6g

Saturated fat
2g

Sodium
340mg

250 g	flat cellophane noodles or rice noodles	**8 oz**
Two 175 g	fillet steaks, trimmed of fat	**Two 6 oz**
60 g	red onion, thinly sliced	**2 oz**
1	lime, grated rind only	**1**
4 tbsp	fresh lime juice	**4 tbsp**
2 tsp	finely chopped fresh coriander	**2 tsp**
2 tsp	very finely chopped fresh lemon grass, or 1½ tsp grated lemon rind	**2 tsp**

2 tsp	finely chopped fresh mint	**2 tsp**
½ tsp	finely chopped hot chili pepper, or ½ tsp sambal oelek	**½ tsp**
½ tsp	finely chopped garlic	**½ tsp**
3 tbsp	low-sodium soy sauce or shoyu	**3 tbsp**
1 tbsp	safflower oil	**1 tbsp**
½ tsp	sugar	**½ tsp**
2	small round lettuces	**2**
3	ripe tomatoes, thinly sliced mint leaves for garnish	**3**

Grill steaks until rare then cool. Cut each in half lengthwise. Thinly slice into pieces 3 mm (⅛ inch) thick, and toss with onion. Set aside.

In a large bowl, combine the lime rind and juice, coriander, lemon grass or rind, mint, chili pepper or sambal oelek, garlic, soy sauce, oil and sugar. Pour half of marinade over the beef and onion, reserving the other half for the noodles. Toss well, cover, and marinate at room temperature for 30 minutes.

Pour enough boiling water over noodles to cover. Soak until *al dente* – 10 to 15 minutes, depending on their thickness. Drain noodles,

rinse in cold water, and drain again. Wrap noodles in a towel and squeeze out most of their moisture. Cut noodles into 15 cm (6 inch) lengths and toss with the reserved half of marinade.

To serve, arrange some lettuce leaves on each of six plates. At one side of each plate, just inside the edge of the leaves, arrange several tomato slices in a crescent. Mound some noodles next to the tomatoes. Arrange the beef slices on top of the noodles, then distribute the onion strips round the beef in a flower pattern. Garnish with the mint leaves and serve them at room temperature.

Nonya Rice Noodles with Prawns

Serves 6

Working
(and total)
time: about
45 minutes

Calories
350
Protein
15g
Cholesterol
60mg
Total fat
8g
Saturated fat
3g
Sodium
360mg

350 g	flat rice noodles	12 oz	12.5 cl	unsweetened coconut milk	4 fl oz
350 g	fresh prawns, shelled	12 oz	6 tbsp	fresh lemon juice	6 tbsp
2 tsp	very finely chopped fresh lemon grass, or 1½ tsp freshly grated lemon rind	2 tsp	2 tsp	low-sodium soy sauce or shoyu	2 tsp
			2 tsp	sweet chili sauce	2 tsp
1 tsp	very finely chopped fresh ginger root	1 tsp	2 tsp	ground coriander	2 tsp
			1	large onion, halved lengthwise and thinly sliced	1
½ tsp	very finely chopped garlic	½ tsp	1	sweet red pepper, seeded, deribbed and thinly sliced	1
½ tsp	salt	½ tsp			
2 tbsp	safflower oil	2 tbsp	1	lemon, cut into wedges (optional)	1
35 cl	unsalted chicken stock, reduced to ¼ litre (8 fl oz)	12 fl oz	1	bunch watercress (optional)	1

Cover noodles with boiling water; soak for 15 minutes. In a large bowl, combine the prawns with the lemon grass, (but not rind, if you are using it), ginger, garlic and salt.

Heat 1 tbsp of oil in a wok or frying pan over high heat. Add the prawn mixture and stir-fry for 3 minutes. Transfer to a plate. Reserve any juices left in the wok, then wipe the wok clean.

In a saucepan, combine coconut milk, stock, lemon juice, soy and chili sauce. Bring just to the boil. Heat remaining oil in the wok. Add the coriander and onion, and gently stir-fry until the onion is limp – about 4 minutes. Add red pepper and stir-fry the mixture for 1 minute more.

Drain the noodles and add them to the wok. Pour in the coconut milk mixture and the juices from the prawns. Cook over medium heat, stirring, until most of the liquid has evaporated. If using lemon rind in place of the lemon grass, add it now. Add the prawns and heat through. Serve garnished with lemon wedges and watercress.

Warm Sichuan Noodles with Spiced Beef

Serves 6

Working
time: about
30 minutes

Total time:
about
1 hour

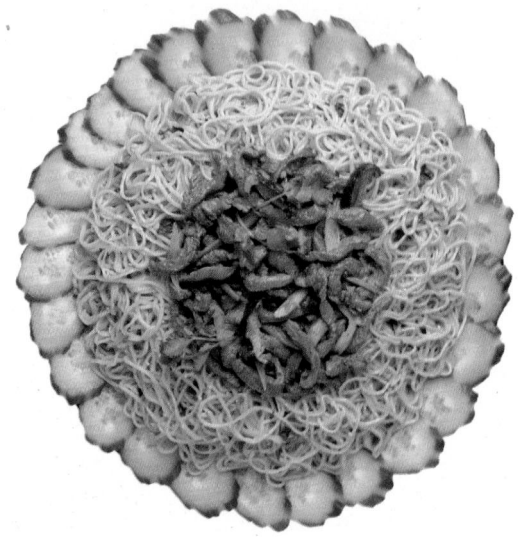

Calories
280

Protein
29g

Cholesterol
30mg

Total fat
12g

Saturated fat
2g

Sodium
340mg

500 g	fresh Chinese egg noodles, or	**1 lb**
	350 g (12 oz) dried vermicelli	
350 g	beef fillet or lean sirloin, trimmed	**12 oz**
	of all fat	
8	dried shiitake or Chinese black	**8**
	mushrooms, soaked in very hot	
	water for 20 minutes and drained	
4	spring onions, thinly sliced diagonally	**4**
1½ tbsp	safflower oil	**1½ tbsp**
	Sesame-Soy Marinade	
4 tbsp	low-sodium soy sauce or shoyu	**4 tbsp**
2 tbsp	Chinese black vinegar or	**2 tbsp**
	balsamic vinegar	
2 tbsp	rice vinegar	**2 tbsp**

1–2 tsp	chili paste with garlic	**1–2 tsp**
½ tsp	very finely chopped garlic	**½ tsp**
1½ tsp	finely chopped fresh ginger root	**1½ tsp**
1 tsp	sugar	**1 tsp**
1 tsp	dark sesame oil	**1 tsp**
2 tbsp	safflower oil	**2 tbsp**
2 tbsp	toasted sesame seeds, crushed	**2 tbsp**
5	spring onions, very finely chopped	**5**
30 g	fresh coriander, coarsely chopped	**1 oz**
	Garnish	
1	small cucumber, scored lengthwise	**1**
	with a fork and thinly sliced	
1 tbsp	toasted sesame seeds	**1 tbsp**
	coriander sprigs	

Combine the marinade ingredients and set aside.

Cut the beef across the grain into julienne. Discard the mushroom stems, and slice the caps into thin strips. In a bowl, combine the beef, mushrooms and spring onions with ⅓ of the marinade. Marinate for 30 minutes.

After this, put 4 litres (7 pints) of water on to boil. Drain and discard marinade from the beef mixture. Heat the 1½ tbsps of safflower oil in a wok; add the mushrooms, spring onions and beef strips, sauté for 1 min. Spread beef mixture out on a large plate, to cool.

Add the noodles to the boiling water. Cook until *al dente* – 3 to 5 mins. Drain and transfer to a large bowl. Toss with remaining marinade. Arrange noodles on a serving plate with cucumber slices and beef, as illustrated.

Thai Chicken in Broth, Lemon Grass and Noodles

Serves 4

Working time: about 30 minutes

Total time: about 1 hour

Calories
220

Protein
18g

Cholesterol
40mg

Total fat
4g

Saturated fat
1g

Sodium
345mg

60 g	cellophane noodles, tied together	**2 oz**
1.5 litres	unsalted chicken stock	**2½ pints**
250 g	skinned and boned chicken breasts	**8 oz**
30 g	cloud-ear mushrooms, soaked in very hot water for 20 minutes, then cut into thin strips	**1 oz**
2	citrus leaves, or 1 tbsp fresh lime juice	**2**
3	stalks fresh lemon grass, bruised with the flat of a knife and knotted, or 1½ tsp grated lemon rind	**3**
4	thin slices fresh ginger root	**4**
10	garlic cloves, peeled	**10**
2 tsp	fish sauce	**2 tsp**
2 tbsp	sweet chili sauce	**2 tbsp**
	fresh coriander for garnish	

Pour the stock into a heavy-bottomed fireproof casserole and bring it to the boil. Add the cellophane noodles, the chicken breasts, the cloud-ear strips, and the lemon grass and citrus leaves if using them. (If you are using lemon rind and lime juice, do not add them yet.) Thread the ginger slices and the garlic cloves on to skewers or wooden toothpicks, and add them to the stock with the fish sauce. Cover the casserole and remove it from the heat. Let the chicken stand undisturbed for 30 minutes.

Remove the chicken from the stock and set it aside to cool. Remove the lemon grass, ginger and garlic from the stock and discard them.

When the chicken is cool enough to handle, break it into shreds with your fingers. Remove the noodles from the stock, then untie them and cut them into 5 cm (2 inch) lengths. Reheat the stock; add the chicken, noodles and sweet chili sauce. If you are substituting lemon rind and lime juice, add them now. Ladle the mixture into individual bowls and garnish with the coriander leaves.

Beijing Wheat Noodles with Lamb and Spring Onion

Serves 4

Working time: about 40 minutes

Total time: about 2 hours

Calories 395
Protein 23g
Cholesterol 35mg
Total fat 21g
Saturated fat 8g
Sodium 405mg

250 g	fresh Chinese egg noodles, or 175 g (6 oz) dried vermicelli	**8 oz**	**12.5 cl**	red wine	**4 fl oz**
2	bunches spring onions	**2**	**1 tbsp**	low-sodium soy sauce or shoyu	**1 tbsp**
2 tbsp	safflower oil	**2 tbsp**	**1 tsp**	chili paste with garlic	**1 tsp**
250 g	boned lamb shoulder, trimmed of all fat	**8 oz**	**250 g**	fresh water chestnuts, peeled and sliced, or canned sliced water chestnuts, drained and rinsed	**8 oz**
4	large garlic cloves, sliced	**4**	**1**	star anise	**1**
¼ litre	unsalted lamb or beef stock	**8 fl oz**			

Trim and chop one bunch of the spring onions. Heat 1 tbsp of the oil in a hot frying pan over medium-high heat. Add lamb and sear it until it is browned on all sides. Transfer to a large heavy-bottomed saucepan and set aside. Add the garlic and chopped spring onions to the frying pan. Stir-fry over medium heat for 3 minutes.

Pour the stock into the frying pan, scraping loose any bits that are stuck to the sides. Add this mixture to the lamb in the saucepan. Stir in the wine, soy sauce, chili paste, water chestnuts and star anise. Bring to the boil, reduce the heat, and cover. Simmer, turning the lamb once, until the meat is tender – about 1¼ hours.

When lamb is cooked, put 4 litres (7 pints) of water on to boil with 2 teaspoons of salt.

Remove lamb, water chestnuts and star anise from the liquid; discard star anise. Reserve liquid. When meat is cooler, shred it by hand. Slice remaining spring onions into thin ovals. Heat the remaining oil in a frying pan over high heat. Add onion slices and stir-fry for 1 minute. Stir in lamb and water chestnuts; stir-fry for 1 minute.

Add noodles to boiling water. Reheat braising liquid. Start testing noodles after 3 minutes and cook until *al dente*. Drain noodles, add to the braising liquid, and toss them with the liquid; arrange in a warmed dish and top with the lamb mixture. Serve immediately.

Burmese Curried Noodles with Scallops and Broccoli

Serves 6

Working (and total) time: about 35 minutes

Calories
280
Protein
26g
Cholesterol
25mg
Total fat
9g
Saturated fat
1g
Sodium
440mg

350 g	dried rice-noodle squares or other rice noodles	**12 oz**
3 tbsp	safflower oil	**3 tbsp**
1	large onion, chopped	**1**
3 tsp	finely chopped garlic	**3 tsp**
1 tbsp	finely chopped fresh ginger root	**1 tbsp**
1 tsp	ground turmeric	**1 tsp**
½ tsp	ground cumin	**½ tsp**
1 tbsp	ground coriander	**1 tbsp**
350 g	broccoli florets	**12 oz**
1½ tsp	grated orange rind	**1½ tsp**
4 tbsp	fresh orange juice	**4 tbsp**

2 tbsp	fresh lemon juice	**2 tbsp**
½ tsp	salt	**½ tsp**
350 g	scallops, each sliced in half horizontally	**12 oz**
4	spring onions, finely chopped	**4**
250 g	fresh water chestnuts, peeled and sliced, or canned sliced water chestnuts, rinsed and drained	**8 oz**
45 g	thinly sliced shallots (optional), stir-fried in 4 tbsp safflower oil until browned and crisp, drained on paper towels	**1½ oz**

Heat 1 tbsp of the oil in a hot wok over medium heat. Add the onion, 1 tsp garlic, the ginger, tumeric, cumin and coriander. Cook, adding water as needed to prevent scorching, until the onion is soft and browned – 15 minutes.

Heat 1 tbsp of oil in a frying pan over medium heat. Add 1 tsp of garlic and cook for 30 secs, stirring. Add broccoli, cover, and cook for 3 mins. Uncover and stir, until tender – about 1 min.

Meanwhile, cook the noodles in 4 litres (7 pints) of boiling water with 2 tsps of salt. Start testing after 5 mins and cook until *al dente*. Drain, add to the onion mixture, and toss gently. Add the orange rind, orange juice, lemon juice and salt, and toss.

Heat remaining oil in a wok. Add scallops, remaining garlic, spring onions and water chestnuts. Stir-fry until they are barely done – 1 to 2 minutes.

Arrange noodles on platter, surrounded by broccoli, with scallops heaped on top. Garnish with shallots and serve.

Mushroom-Stuffed Triangles

Serves 6
as an
appetizer

Working
(and total)
time: about
50 minutes

Calories
265
Protein
10g
Cholesterol
60mg
Total fat
8g
Saturated fat
3g
Sodium
290mg

	basic or semolina pasta dough	
15 g	dried wild mushrooms, soaked for 20 mins in boiling water to cover	½ oz
250 g	mushrooms, wiped, finely chopped	8 oz
2	large shallots, finely chopped	2
3	garlic cloves, finely chopped	3
2 tbsp	balsamic vinegar, or 1 tbsp red wine vinegar	2 tbsp
4 tbsp	red wine	4 tbsp

¼ tsp	salt	¼ tsp
	freshly ground black pepper	
2 tbsp	fresh breadcrumbs	2 tbsp
1.25 kg	ripe tomatoes, skinned, seeded and chopped	2½ lb
1	large onion, chopped	1
3	carrots (about 250 g/8 oz), chopped	3
3 tbsp	double cream	3 tbsp
40 g	fresh mushrooms, wiped clean	1½ oz

Drain wild mushrooms, reserving liquid. Finely chop and transfer to a frying pan. Add fresh mushrooms, shallots, ⅔ garlic, mushroom-soaking liquid. Bring to the boil. Cook until nearly all liquid has evaporated – 5 mins. Add vinegar, wine, ½ salt and some pepper. Continue, stirring, until all liquid has boiled away – 3 mins. Stir in breadcrumbs; set aside.

Mix tomatoes, onion, carrots, some pepper, remaining garlic and salt in a pan. Add 4 tbsps water and boil. Cook until vegetables are soft and very little of liquid remains – 20 mins. Purée sauce and return it to the pan. Add cream and set aside.

Meanwhile, prepare triangles. Divide dough into 4 portions. Cover 3 with film. Roll out the fourth to form a long strip about 12.5 cm (5 inch) wide and about 1 mm (¹/₁₆ inch) thick. Cut across dough at 12.5 cm (5 inch) intervals to form squares, cut each into 4 smaller squares.

Mound about 1 tsp of filling in centre of square. Moisten edges of two adjacent sides of square. Fold moistened edges over filling to form a triangle, and press edges closed. Put triangles in a large pan of boiling water and cook until *al dente* (1-2 mins). Reheat sauce, pour over cooked, drained pasta, and serve with Parmesan.

Japanese Summer Noodles with Prawns

Serves 6

Working
(and total)
time: about
45 minutes

Calories
200
Protein
11g
Cholesterol
40mg
Total fat
1g
Saturated fat
0g
Sodium
225mg

250 g	somen, or capelli d' angelo	8 oz
18	large prawns, peeled, the tails left on and the shells reserved	18
1	slice fresh ginger root, about 3 mm ($\frac{1}{8}$ inch) thick	1
1 tbsp	low-sodium soy sauce or shoyu	1 tbsp
3 tbsp	mirin	3 tbsp
6	dried shiitake mushrooms, rinsed	6

Garnish

	watercress sprigs	
2	spring onions, thinly sliced, rinsed and drained	2
2 tbsp	grated fresh ginger root	2 tbsp
2 tbsp	wasabi, made by mixing enough water with $1\frac{1}{2}$ tbsp wasabi powder to form a stiff paste	2 tbsp

Bring $\frac{1}{2}$ litre (16 fl oz) of water to the boil. Add the prawns and the slice of ginger. Cover, remove from heat and let it stand for 5 mins. Strain the resulting stock into a second saucepan, reserving the prawns and discarding the ginger. Add the prawn shells to the stock and bring to the boil. Simmer for 15 mins, then strain through muslin into the first pan. Discard the shells. Reduce stock to about 12.5 cl (4 fl oz) and cool. Add soy sauce and 1 tbsp of the mirin, and divide this dipping sauce between six small bowls.

In a saucepan, pour 35 cl (12 fl oz) of boiling water over the mushrooms and soak for 10 mins. Add remaining mirin and simmer until almost all of liquid has evaporated – 20 mins. When mushrooms are cool enough, remove stems; cut mushrooms in half.

Add the somen to 1.5 litres ($2\frac{1}{2}$ pints) of boiling water; start testing after 2 mins and cook until *al dente*. Drain, rinse. Divide noodles between six bowls. Put three ice cubes in each bowl, and enough water to float the noodles. Arrange prawns, mushrooms and garnish as illustrated. Serve each with a dab of wasabi, 1 tsp of grated ginger and dipping sauce alongside.

Useful weights and measures

Weight Equivalents

Avoirdupois		Metric
1 ounce	=	28.35 grams
1 pound	=	254.6 grams
2.3 pounds	=	1 kilogram

Liquid Measurements

$^1/_4$ pint	=	$1^1/_2$ decilitres
$^1/_2$ pint	=	$^1/_4$ litre
scant 1 pint	=	$^1/_2$ litre
$1^3/_4$ pints	=	1 litre
1 gallon	=	4.5 litres

Liquid Measures

1 pint	=	20 fl oz	=	32 tablespoons
$^1/_2$ pint	=	10 fl oz	=	16 tablespoons
$^1/_4$ pint	=	5 fl oz	=	8 tablespoons
$^1/_8$ pint	=	$2^1/_2$ fl oz	=	4 tablespoons
$^1/_{16}$ pint	=	$1^1/_4$ fl oz	=	2 tablespoons

Solid Measures

1 oz almonds, ground = $3^3/_4$ level tablespoons
1 oz breadcrumbs fresh = 7 level tablespoons
1 oz butter, lard = 2 level tablespoons
1 oz cheese, grated = $3^1/_2$ level tablespoons
1 oz cocoa = $2^3/_4$ level tablespoons
1 oz desiccated coconut = $4^1/_2$ tablespoons
1 oz cornflour = $2^1/_2$ tablespoons
1 oz custard powder = $2^1/_2$ tablespoons
1 oz curry powder and spices = 5 tablespoons
1 oz flour = 2 level tablespoons
1 oz rice, uncooked = $1^1/_2$ tablespoons
1 oz sugar, caster and granulated = 2 tablespoons
1 oz icing sugar = $2^1/_2$ tablespoons
1 oz yeast, granulated = 1 level tablespoon

American Measures

16 fl oz	=1 American pint
8 fl oz	=1 American standard cup
0.50 fl oz	=1 American tablespoon

(slightly smaller than British Standards Institute tablespoon)

0.16 fl oz	=1 American teaspoon

Australian Cup Measures

(Using the 8-liquid-ounce cup measure)

1 cup flour	4 oz
1 cup sugar (crystal or caster)	8 oz
1 cup icing sugar (free from lumps)	5 oz
1 cup shortening (butter, margarine)	8 oz
1 cup brown sugar (lightly packed)	4 oz
1 cup soft breadcrumbs	2 oz
1 cup dry breadcrumbs	3 oz
1 cup rice (uncooked)	6 oz
1 cup rice (cooked)	5 oz
1 cup mixed fruit	4 oz
1 cup grated cheese	4 oz
1 cup nuts (chopped)	4 oz
1 cup coconut	$2^1/_2$ oz

Australian Spoon Measures

	level tablespoon
1 oz flour	2
1 oz sugar	$1^1/_2$
1 oz icing sugar	2
1 oz shortening	1
1 oz honey	1
1 oz gelatine	2
1 oz cocoa	3
1 oz cornflour	$2^1/_2$
1 oz custard powder	$2^1/_2$

Australian Liquid Measures

(Using 8-liquid-ounce cup)

1 cup liquid	8 oz
$2^1/_2$ cups liquid	20 oz (1 pint)
2 tablespoons liquid	1 oz
1 gill liquid	5 oz ($^1/_4$ pint)

'I loved this book. It made my heart sing. Written by a woman in the law with compassion, wit and legal know-how, these true life courtroom stories tell it like it is. All life is there, showing the importance to justice of lawyers who understand the human condition. Brava, Sarah Langford.' Helena Kennedy QC

'A great insight into the human side of law.' Miriam Gonzalez Durántez

'A riveting account of cases she's fought over nearly ten years in the family courts. These are harrowing stories: of newborns taken by social services, of bitter divorces, of children trapped in the turbulence of addiction, gangs, or both, an unprecedented collection, moving, enraging and desperate, all told in Langford's cool, compelling prose.' Charlotte Edwards, *Evening Standard*

'A wonderful book from a vivid new talent. Revealing, moving, funny, sad, uplifting and beautifully written, with the observational skills of Alan Bennett and the heart of Charles Dickens. Every chapter is an elegantly constructed short story complete with plot twists that alternately deliver a knife to the guts or a glimmer of hope that makes you think humanity has a chance.' Tim Shipman, political editor, *Sunday Times*

'A vivid picture of the courts at work . . . Each chapter unfolds a set of messy facts where the outcome is unclear, the justice of the case opaque. Is Langford's client guilty? Should he go to prison? Will, or should, the mother keep her children out of the reach of the father? The resolution is often as thrilling as a detective novel. And sometimes it is moving: the last chapter had this reviewer in tears. In its quiet way Langford's book is also a portrait of a particular version of Britain . . . I hope the Lord Chancellor reads it, and learns from it.' Thomas Grant QC, *The Times*

'By turns heartbreaking and hopeful, and succeeds in giving an articulate, compassionate voice to those who would otherwise struggle to be heard. The prose is engrossing, and the book is only too easy to devour in great gulps . . . Langford tackles the frustration and fears of the profession with honesty and energy.'
Olivia Potts, *Spectator*

'There are many who question the usefulness of lawyers . . . Those cynics would do well to spend time with *In Your Defence*, a collection of eleven stories of life in Britain's courtrooms by Sarah Langford. The author is a barrister who completed an English Literature degree before going into the law. Her facility with language makes this, her first book, breezy and congenial, but it is also passionate and, in places, personal. Above all, it gives the lie to the notion that lawyers are parasites.'
Alex Wade, *Times Literary Supplement*

Praise for IN YOUR DEFENCE

Best Books of 2018: *The Times*, *The Spectator*
and *New Statesman*

'I decided to dip into *In Your Defence: Stories of Life and Law* by Sarah Langford, and ended up reading it from cover to cover. Langford is a criminal barrister, but this is neither a lawyer's book for lawyers nor a "courtroom drama" exercise for non-lawyers, though courtroom drama there is. Instead she takes real case studies from her career – neither famous nor infamous trials, just the sad daily fare that is the bread-and-butter of a jobbing defence barrister – and tells her clients' stories. She describes her own feelings too, at the tangled mess her clients make of their lives. These pictures are infinitely touching.'
Matthew Parris, 'Critics' Books of 2018', *The Times*

'The law is endlessly fascinating, in its history, rituals, manners, language and, above all, the people whose lives revolve, temporarily or in the long term, around its practise. *In Your Defence: Stories of Life and Law* by the barrister Sarah Langford tells the stories of some of those caught up in its complex workings. It is riveting – and quite alarming.'
Susan Hill, author of *The Woman in Black,*
'Books of the Year', *The Spectator*

'I greatly enjoyed Sarah Langford's *In Your Defence*, an insider's account of life as a barrister. Justice and the law provide the lens: the subject is really human nature.'
Ed Smith, 'Books of the Year', *New Statesman*

'It is hard to imagine a better-written or more insightful account of life at the bar than this.'
Caroline Sanderson, *Sunday Express*

'This is an absolutely fascinating insider account of life at the bar by defence barrister Sarah Langford, told, with a novelist's eye, through the stories of eleven ordinary people she's defended. As Langford journeys through and challenges her own unconscious bias, she'll make you take a long, hard – and not entirely comfortable – look at your own.'
Sam Baker, The Pool

'This compelling book tracks eleven cases through the criminal and family courts . . . tales of despair and hope that could be about you or me. Sarah Langford's stated objective is to bring "to life ideas which otherwise so often appear in abstract: fairness, justice, truth". The result is a resounding and thought-provoking success . . . Insightful and often haunting.'
William Brodrick, *Literary Review*

'*In Your Defence* is an anthology of beautifully rendered stories of legal practice, each striking at the beating heart of our justice system. The storytelling is compelling, reading like page-turning fiction, but speaking in every chapter to fundamental truths about the meaning of justice for those trapped in the wheels of our criminal and family courts. Sarah Langford breathes vibrancy and compassion into the dusty tomes of the law, capturing and exposing the raw humanity lying beneath the system, and offering a necessary reminder of the impact of the law on those whose lives are chartered by its whims.' Secret Barrister

'A compelling read for anyone who cares about fairness, justice and humanity and should be on the reading list of all politicians and policy-makers.'
Catherine Baksi, *Observer*

IN YOUR DEFENCE
Stories of Life and Law

Sarah Langford

BLACK SWAN

TRANSWORLD PUBLISHERS
61–63 Uxbridge Road, London W5 5SA
www.penguin.co.uk

Transworld is part of the Penguin Random House group of companies
whose addresses can be found at global.penguinrandomhouse.com

First published in Great Britain in 2018 by Doubleday
an imprint of Transworld Publishers
Black Swan edition published 2019

A CIP catalogue record for this book
is available from the British Library.

ISBN 9781784163082

Typeset in 10.8/13.92pt Minion Pro by Jouve (UK), Milton Keynes.
Printed and bound in Great Britain by Clays Ltd, Elcograf S.p.A.

Penguin Random House is committed to a sustainable future
for our business, our readers and our planet. This book is made
from Forest Stewardship Council® certified paper.

To my two small sons, Wilfred and Aubrey.
You brought me back to earth.

Contents

1

Dominic

Oxford Magistrates' Court
and Oxford Crown Court

Children and Young Persons Act 1933
Section 50 – Age of criminal responsibility
*It shall be conclusively presumed that no child under
the age of ten years can be guilty of any offence.*

1

DOMINIC FELT the metal tang of blood in his mouth as he ran, fast, through the tunnel. His breath came out in rasps, echoing against the brick. He could hear the footsteps of the five police officers as they entered the mouth of the underpass behind him. The muscles in his legs burned as he tore out of the gloom and into the summer dusk, and he felt his knees weaken. He stumbled, slowed, and came to a stop. Panting hard, he bent and rested his hands on his thighs. Lifting his head, he looked at the hill path ahead of him. He was never going to make it. Almost with relief, he stood and staggered back to the exit of the tunnel, waiting for the officers to reach him. He leaned back against the raw brick and realized that he was still very drunk. As the officers got closer, Dom held up his left hand towards them, palm outwards, and looked down to spit out a shining gobbet of saliva. A moment later, he felt himself taken forward with a force so great it sent him face downwards on to the dirt path. He recognized the wrench in his shoulders as his arms were pulled back, and the rub of metal to his wrist bones as handcuffs closed around them. He felt the deeper pain of a thick-soled boot in his ribs, on his spine; the full weight of a grown man kneeling on the back of his legs. He managed to turn his head just in time to see the tread of a large black boot closing down upon his face. In the background he could hear his friend, Caz, who had now caught up with them, screaming. As his body buckled, Dom remembered, almost in abstract, that it was his nineteenth birthday.

*

When I was at law school I was taught to memorize things I would rarely use again. The difference between various types of Will. How to distinguish a joint tenancy and a tenancy-in-common. Why an 'invitation to treat' was not as exciting as it sounded. What I was not taught was how to represent a child.

In my first few years as a barrister I realized that this was a skill so vital I must master it for myself. I began to understand that representing those charged with a criminal offence meant that I was more than just a source of advice, or a mouthpiece for my client's case. I needed to be a psychiatrist, a counsellor, a social worker, a mother, and many other things besides, none of which had appeared on the pages of my law books. I had to learn how to identify mental health problems, victims of domestic abuse, alcohol and drug addictions. I grew to know who might, after court had finished, go home and try to end their life.

But the cases that first asked the most of me were those in the youth court. I would sit with my teenage clients in the hall-way of the courthouse, trying to take their instructions on the trial they were about to face as they stared at their phones, or the floor, or the sky through the window, or anywhere but at me. I became familiar with courtrooms made up of desks rather than benches. Our hearings had breaks to maintain their short attention spans, and reminders to use language my child offender could understand. I learned to play paper-scissors-stone with my younger clients under the desk, to keep them occupied while we waited for the magistrates to return with their inevitable guilty verdicts. I worked out how to talk to twelve-year-olds in a Ritalin stupor; how to ask them about the summer when they robbed, threatened and stabbed their way through the nights. I also discovered, crucially, that my clients did not want me to try to be their friend. Too often they would treat the social worker – who came in lieu of an absent parent, with a sing-song voice and attempts at camaraderie – with withering contempt. I tried to convince my young clients that deference was not the same as weakness. In doing so I gained their trust and, occasionally, respect. This respect would enable me to hush the gang of twenty waiting in the corridor for their missing member; or to chase my teenage client down the court stairwell, persuading them to come back to the courtroom and face their custodial sentence.

When I first met Dominic he had turned eighteen, and so, now technically an adult, his criminal career had moved from the youth court up to the magistrates' and crown courts. But it was the youth court that marked his first conviction for burglary, not long after his eleventh birthday. In that same year, still not into adolescence, Dominic was sentenced twice more, just three months apart. If he had lived anywhere else in Europe he would, at eleven years old, still have been considered a child. But Dominic lived in England and so, from the age of ten, he was old enough to be a criminal. Over the three years following his first conviction, another four burglary offences were added to his record. Then, at fourteen, a period of forced respite came with his first incarceration. He entered adulthood, therefore, as someone already marked – the landscape of his future shrunk to a single pathway, leading in only one direction.

Over the years Dominic had developed – or been taught – an old-fashioned kind of criminal code. Never grass anyone up. Treat the police, sex offenders and men who hit women with contempt and violence, but your lawyers with respect. Burglaries should only ever be commercial, not domestic – it is not right to break into people's homes. Bigger shops were worth less guilt, as they all had insurance and the staff turnover was high, and *no one really cared about working there anyway*. But post offices and independent retailers deserved letters of apology which said he knew he would be sent down but, when he got out, could he come and work there for free, to make it up to them? And if you were stupid enough to get caught, then you pleaded guilty – but only if the evidence was there to get you. Whenever I walked down into the bowels of court and to our conference room in the cells, Dom would stand up to greet me – *Morning, Miss!* – as though I were his headmistress and he was in detention.

But when I was first given one of Dominic's cases, I did not know any of this about him. I only knew that he had been charged with assaulting three police officers, and that his solicitor would pay me £125 to set off to Oxford Magistrates' Court for the next two days to represent him at his trial.

The case papers arrived in my pigeonhole in chambers – as was always the way before they were sent digitally – and I read through them with a sinking heart. Now nineteen, Dom had as many pages of previous convictions as years of life. He would surely have to plead guilty, I thought, scanning through the police officers' statements. They were almost identical, although I knew from experience that the officers would deny, with expressions of horror, any suggestion of collusion.

I wondered who was likely to be prosecuting the trial. The magistrates' court – unlike the crown court – rarely has independent barristers representing the state. Instead, the Crown Prosecution Service will often send the same in-house lawyer to court. There they will prosecute each and every case which comes into their courtroom that day. This, inevitably, means they are as much a part of the place as the legal advisor, who runs the court and advises the magistrates on the law; or the court ushers, who rush in and out of court with flapping black gowns, ensuring everyone is where they need to be; or the magistrates, the panel of three citizens who volunteer to sit in judgment on those who appear before them. Walking into this as a defence barrister can be a lonely business. In those early years, when I would walk into a magistrates' courtroom to find the prosecutor sharing a joke with the legal advisor and the court usher, the chances of an acquittal seemed to melt in my hands. So I worked hard to push myself in; to make sure they liked me, trusted me, had confidence that I knew what I was doing. In part, that trust was formed by an understanding that I had carefully read and understood the evidence against my client and, if the case was hopeless, that I had told my client so. And, I conceded, zipping Dominic's case papers into my wheelie bag, there was no trial so hopeless as five police officers giving evidence against a nineteen-year-old with whom they were so familiar that all were on first-name terms.

Two days later, I walked across the forecourt of Oxford train station. I decided to take the back route to court and, as I bumped my case down the steps and walked alongside the river, I noticed it was lined with spring wildflowers. At the end of the path I turned the corner and rattled my bag over the cobbles and through the quiet, winding lanes. Eventually I came to the rectangular brick building, ingloriously overlooking a car park, that is the magistrates' court. Opposite the court, almost hidden, is an alleyway. Standing there in the sunshine, I longed to cross towards it and wind my way down its narrow path. I knew that, were I to do so, I would come out opposite the crested gates of Christ Church, its meadow heavy with life about to burst into bloom. Instead I turned away, and walked towards the court, preparing myself to do what I could, in the hour we had before his case began, to persuade my client not to have a trial.

I moved past the people dragging on the end of a last cigarette, before hauling my bag past the security guards and up the long flight of stairs into court. Oxford Magistrates' Court is set along one floor. One wall is lined with a row of tiny brick conference rooms, the other punctuated by double swing doors leading to four courtrooms, and a small thin door leading to the windowless advocates' room. The main part of the floor is taken up by a waiting area filled with rows of bolted-down seats and the noisy chaos of those waiting their turn on the wheel of justice. Once you have pushed open the heavy oak doors to the courtroom, however, all inside is quiet grandeur. The doors are stained dark brown and covered with the same studded green leather that pads the three magistrates' chairs, elevated at one end. These look down on two rows of advocates' benches and – at the back of court – a glass-slatted dock.

That morning, I walked into the courtroom to find the prosecutor in Dominic's trial alone, going through her papers. I knew this was probably the first time she had ever seen them. I greeted her cheerfully and checked to see which of the police officers had arrived, ready to give evidence. She asked, half-joking, whether we were 'really going to waste the day on such a hopeless trial'. I smiled in response, and said I had to go and find my client. As I pushed open the courtroom doors I longed to be able to turn and promise her that I would be back within the hour, ready to watch my client plead guilty to all three charges.

But then I met Dominic.

I stood in the waiting room and called his name. A tall, slim boy with dark curly hair and hard blue eyes rose in answer, picked up his bag and came towards me with a languid confidence. He had been waiting with a gang of friends who had come to watch his trial from the court's public gallery. Among this cluster of boys sat two girls. One was Caz, his co-defendant, and the other Dom's older sister, Rosie. I could feel the frisson among the group, and knew from experience what sport Dom's friends would make of the trial, rising to their feet upon his inevitable conviction, and hurling swear words and outrage at us all.

Dominic and I sat opposite one another in one of the conference rooms. He had a frenetic energy to him, but there was a misplaced nobility about his face, as though it belonged to a time of aristocratic hedonism. He listened carefully as I went through the evidence and tested the version of events he had told the solicitors. His case was simple: it was the officers who had assaulted him, not the other way round. He had been drinking in town with some friends, celebrating his birthday. He heard a police officer call out to him, summoning him over, but instead of obliging he had run away, for no reason other than he did not want to be stopped and searched, again. The police had followed him, thrown him to the ground, then kicked and punched him. Caz had run after the police when they gave chase, and when she saw the officers on top of Dom she had tried to pull them off. When their attention turned to Caz, Dom had seen his moment and tried to escape. With handcuffed wrists still behind his back, he had soon been caught by the officers. They had put him on the ground again and sprayed CS gas straight into his face, before hustling him into a police van and arresting him for assault.

I glanced at my notebook and the chart that I had prepared of the officers' evidence, sighed, and warned Dom to prepare himself to be disbelieved. They were police officers and he was Dominic, and that was life. But Dom did not care. He did not care whether the police thought he was scum, or whether the magistrates were irritated by the cost in time and public money, and the taking of five officers off the streets to answer to someone like him. He did not even really care about the punishment he got. What he cared about, he told me, was pleading guilty to something he did not do. If he was found guilty then so be it, but he could not – would not – plead to it. Then he reached down and pulled a bundle of photographs from his bag. They had been taken by his sister, Rosie, after she collected him from the police station the day after the alleged offence, Dom said. The date and time were stamped on the pictures in red digits. Rosie would give evidence to say when she had taken the photographs and what his injuries had looked like. I paused, staring at the pictures, then pulled out the transcript of his police interview, skipping through to the last section. Dom knew well enough that simply alleging he had been injured by the officers would never be enough, so he had got the interviewing officers to confirm his injuries, on tape. I checked the interview against the photographs. Sure enough, the officers had agreed they could see red bruising and grazes to his ribs, his back and down the side of his face; cuts to the back of his hand; a lump and graze to his right temple; a lump and a cut to the middle of his forehead. The bruises had come out overnight and bloomed into green and purple welts, flashed by the camera into technicoloured glory.

I felt a sort of thrill, as the day began to shift. We left the room, and I sent Dom back to his friends as I went into court alone to show the prosecutor the photographs and tell her what she did not want to hear. We were going to have a trial.

I grew up in a cathedral city where the police were our protectors. If I was walking home from town at night and saw two on patrol, I would cross the road to go their way for as long as I could because it made me feel safer. I made them tea when we were burgled; pointed them in the right direction after one man laid a blow on another, then ran off. The only other contact I had with them was benign – teenage cider-drinking, the confiscation of a fake ID, my mother shouting 'Duck!' to the six children crammed on the back seat of our ancient car – and little trouble came from it. When I became a barrister, my voice and presentation guaranteed respectful treatment from the police, even when I was on the opposite side of the courtroom from them. It was only through defending that I began to see, and understand, why those I represented often viewed them so differently from me.

There are some police officers whom I rarely cross-examine. These ones are earnest and keen, view their job as a vocation, and strive to be fair. I have met a good number of them, but I rarely need to test their evidence in court for, most often, they tell the truth. Some are lazy and apparently without independent thought, but are not dishonest. Others are old hands who have seen their powers eroded and red tape strangle their investigations. They will break and bend rules and cut corners to ensure that – as they see it – justice is done, but they usually hover just on the right side of the line. As a defence barrister, my experience of challenging police in court usually involves a different type of officer. These are the ones who use their badge for no reason other than to legitimize their bullying, their brutality and their deception. In their witness statements they lie and exaggerate, which means that my client – who may well have done something wrong, just not the wrong of which they are accused – will cry 'No! That is not what happened!' So, rather than pleading guilty, we must come to court to admit the true parts and dispute the rest.

The police in Dominic's case were made up of this latter type of officer. And, on the second day of the trial, their evidence began to unravel.

The magistrates, as arbiters of Dominic's guilt, came into

court knowing nothing but his name and the charges he faced. They had not seen the police officers' witness statements before the trial because criminal evidence is what is said in court, under oath, and not what is written down beforehand. I, of course, had read them. In their statements, the police officers said they had suspected Dom of an offence, had approached him, and then chased him when he ran. When they caught up with him they took him to the ground, where he had then assaulted them. As a result, they had handcuffed him. Caz had tried to pull them off and, when they turned to deal with her, Dom had tried to run away, so they had sprayed him with gas and put him into the back of a police van. In evidence, however, the officers' attempts to minimize their own actions and exaggerate Dom's began to undo them. As each officer described a different version of events, I tried to keep up – circling the evidence in my notebook, attempting to keep track of who said what.

Then the final officer gave evidence. He was the one who had thundered into Dominic's side, taking him down. He was the one, Dom said, who had put his boot on Dominic's head and kept it there, crushing it into the ground, and who later sprayed gas into his face. He was the one who had got into the police van with Dom to finish him off. With every question I asked, the officer turned and addressed his answer to the magistrates with extravagant deference. It had the effect of aligning him with them as he stood, hands clasped before him, barely pretending to take my questions seriously.

'So, officer, am I right in suggesting that when you saw Dominic in the street, you immediately went over to him?'

'Yes, that's correct, Your Worships. Just before the defendant absconded and we pursued him.'

'You mean he ran off and you chased him?'

The officer stared at me, hard. There I was, a nice middle-class girl in a black suit with a smart accent. He must think that, surely, I should be on his side.

'In a manner of speaking, Your Worships.'

'And he seemed perfectly all right when you saw him? I mean, there were no marks or injuries to his face or hands, or elsewhere, that you could see?'

'None whatsoever.'

'When you caught up with the accused he was bent over, hand raised, at the end of the tunnel – is that correct?'

'I don't recall his position. My aim was to prevent his further escape.'

'By taking him to the ground?' I asked.

'Yes, Your Worships.'

'And, just outside the tunnel, there was a patch of grass. You say that was where you took him to the ground?'

'Indeed, Your Worships.'

I paused and looked at my notes. 'And tell us exactly, officer, how you detained him on the ground.'

'In a Home Office approved manner, Your Worships.'

'Right. And what is a Home Office approved manner?'

'It is a technique designed to prevent injury, Your Worships.'

'To you?'

'Yes, Your Worships.'

'And to the detained person?'

'Exactly, Your Worships.'

I had him. At last, I had him.

'I see. And was that, in part, why you detained him on the soft grass, rather than the hard pathway . . . ?'.

The officer turned to the magistrates, pleased with himself. 'Of course, Your Worships.'

I looked at the magistrates as I framed the next question. 'I see, officer. So, to be clear, using the Home Office approved manner on the grass would have protected both you and the defendant from any injuries – have I understood this?'

'Exactly.'

I slid my notebook off the photographs, and sensed the prosecutor twitch. I had shown them to her beforehand, but she could not have predicted that the officer's evidence would make their existence impossible. I held the pictures up, watching as the magistrates craned forward to look at the bruises, lumps and cuts in glossy close-up.

'So, officer – can you explain how my client got *these*, then?'

We sat in court in silence waiting for the magistrates to return, the clerk having summoned us from the waiting room. They had decided on their verdicts. I glanced quickly behind me at the dock where Dom stood, staring at the floor. Caz, next to him, looked up as the magistrates filed into court. The legal advisor, walking ahead of them, returned to her seat below their bench. She waited for everyone in the courtroom to sit, then asked Dom and Caz to stand once again, ready to hear their verdicts.

I spread the photographs out before me, even though they could make no difference now. The magistrates would not stop, midway through their verdict, and change their minds just because they caught sight of them. Perhaps, I thought, looking at Dom's bruised and cut flesh, I just wanted proof I was entitled to feel outraged.

The lead magistrate, seated in the centre of the three, leaned forward slightly. Like so many magistrates I have appeared before, she presented as a cliché: well-spoken, greying hair, small half-moon glasses pulled down to the end of her nose. She looked over them and at the dock as she spoke.

'We have listened carefully to the evidence from the five officers, the two defendants and their witness. We have also re-read the defendants' interviews and taken account of the advice given to us by our legal advisor. Firstly, Caroline Wood, you are accused of striking and kicking a police officer. You say you acted in defence of your co-defendant and denied that your actions were as described. We find you did make contact with the officer . . .'

I noted down her words and resisted the temptation to sigh.

'. . . but because of the conflicting stories given by the police officers and the evidence of the injuries to Dominic Parker, we find that your actions *were* in defence of another. We therefore find you not guilty.'

I held my breath. The magistrate adjusted her gaze.

'Dominic Parker, we have also listened carefully to the evidence against you. Firstly, you are charged with assaults on both PC Smith and PC Duncan. Because of the conflicting evidence, we find you not guilty, and find that any contact you made was accidental in the circumstances. Lastly, you are charged with an assault on PC Davis. We find that the spitting, which is the nature of the assault, did take place, but that this was as a result of the effect of the CS gas you had suffered, and was therefore also accidental. We therefore find you not guilty of all offences.'

I stood up, and hoped my voice was level. I had assumed that these three people, who were so different from those who appeared before them, could never have preferred a defendant's account over a police officer's. I had been wrong. I was embarrassed to have applied the same prejudices to them that I assumed they would apply to my client. The magistrates had not, of course, explicitly said the officers were lying. Over the following years I would never hear a magistrate accuse a police officer of poor practice, of lying or of planting evidence, even when the evidence suggested exactly this. The defendant's vindication had to lie in his acquittal. I glanced behind me to look at Dominic, and knew that, for him, that was enough.

'May the defendants be released, Madam?'

'Of course. Please unlock the dock.'

After our first victory, I went on to represent Dominic many times. His crimes were almost always theft, with occasional light violence and plenty of public disorder. He would target cash, alcohol and cigarettes, which he knew he could sell on fast, but which never made him sufficient money to survive on for long. He was not, I soon discovered, a good thief. His crimes were opportunist, usually unplanned, and often committed when he was too drunk to think about the trail of evidence he was leaving behind him like breadcrumbs.

Unfailingly, I would read the evidence against him and find myself laughing out loud. Once, climbing backwards out of an office window, he became stuck. Spotted by a passerby he had to wait, suspended in mid-air, for the police to come and arrest him. Another time he tore his bag on the way out of a window so that the bottles of alcohol he had just stolen fell and smashed, calling over curious witnesses to investigate the noise. In another drunken break-in, he left behind a tool covered in his fingerprints, and smears of blood from a cut to his hand. But my favourite piece of evidence was a letter, carefully placed on his pillow as though it were a love note, for the police to find when they raided his flat: 'Fuck You Pigs! Can't Catch Me! Ha Ha Ha Ha Ha. Dom xxx'. They did, of course.

I was involved in only one other trial in which Dom

refused to plead guilty. It involved a break-in at a local college and the evidence against him was slim, but the prosecution decided to charge him anyway. They knew that his previous convictions for burglary showed a propensity to commit the crime, and that this meant they were admissible by law into the trial. During his evidence, I asked Dom about his past, getting there before the prosecutor's cross-examination, hoping to deaden the punch.

'Dominic,' I said, as he stood in the witness box. 'You are twenty-one years old and you have twenty-three previous convictions for burglary.'

He clasped his hands in front of him, dropping his head. All we could see was his halo of dark hair.

'Yes, Miss, I have.'

'And how did you plead to those burglaries, Dominic?'

He looked back up and straight at me. 'Guilty, Miss, to every single one of them.'

'So Dominic, *why* aren't you pleading guilty to this one?'

'Because . . .' he said, turning to stare beseechingly at the magistrates, all of whom gazed back, '. . . I didn't do this one.'

As the not guilty verdict was read out and Dom skipped away from court with the friends who had been waiting for him, I found myself wondering whether I, like the magistrates, had just been deceived and, if so, whether I was glad he had got away with it.

The more I represented him, the more I began to understand something else. Dominic might be a terrible criminal, but he was not stupid. He would talk me through the evidence, what charges he thought we might persuade the prosecution to drop, which ones he should plead guilty to. He had a working knowledge of the sentencing guidelines, to which all courts are bound, and which predetermined his fate with a flow chart to his future. Dom would tell me which level of the guideline for his offence did, or did not, apply to him. He would point to details of the case which meant the judge could go below the sentence starting point. But his special skill was writing beautiful, heartfelt letters to the court, full of pleas and promises of reformation and his commitment to a life beyond crime, where, having never had one, he would hold down a job. He wrote with great charm; his spelling and syntax were better than most of the police statements that had imprisoned him, and more than one judge remarked how articulate they were, even if they rarely worked. He was canny enough to check which judge was sentencing him. 'Oh, right,' he once said, crunching his handwritten letter into a ball. 'He's had one of these before.'

Dom had so many court hearings that sometimes barely a week went by without my seeing him. I began to believe that he did not care about getting caught, nor about the consequences. Sometimes, on my way home from court, I would gaze out of the train window as dusk fell and lose myself in a fantasy where I took him from his life. I would help him find somewhere to live, get him a job, show him ways to focus his energy and rebellion and character. I would indulge myself in this daydreaming aware that it could surely never work, and that I would surely never try.

Some six years after I first met Dominic I found myself representing him for the last time, although I did not know it then.

I went into chambers, collected the case papers from my pigeonhole and started flicking through the evidence. Dom was due to appear in court to be sentenced for a burglary spree. He had set out into the autumn night with two friends, drunk and armed with a claw-hammer. The three of them had smashed their way into a row of local shops. A dry-cleaner: bottom pane of its door shattered, £15.23 of change stolen. A Tesco Express: door smashed, £320.21 of alcohol stolen. Next a newsagent: £500 of cigarettes and £26 of alcohol taken. Then an estate agent and a launderette, where, running out of energy, they left empty-handed, two splintered doors the only sign they had been there at all.

Dom knew he had to plead guilty. A fairytale trail of blood, fingerprints and DNA had led the police directly to him. However, twelve months earlier he had been sentenced for a different burglary. He had been released from prison halfway through this sentence, as the law required. Then he committed these new offences, with only a month left to go before that sentence expired. This meant that Dom was immediately sent back to prison, to serve out the rest of his existing sentence. When the month passed, we agreed there was little merit in asking a judge for bail. The guidelines said that the maximum sentence for this kind of burglary was fifty-one weeks' imprisonment. Dom had pleaded guilty, which meant he was entitled to one third off his sentence. We both knew, however, that any judge would look at the guidelines, and his previous convictions, and sentence him to the longest period he could. Dom might as well stay in prison and clock up some time, which would then be taken off his sentence as time he had already served.

Dominic was still in prison when his co-defendants were joined to his case. He was also still in prison when they pleaded not guilty and their trial date was set. Their trial was to be a 'floater'. It could begin on any day in a given week, but whether or not it actually began depended on another trial collapsing. If another defendant pleaded guilty, or a witness failed to attend court, or some other unexpected happening occurred which meant that a court became free, then this one would be waiting in the wings to take its place. If, however, no court became available and the week came to an end without the trial beginning, then everyone would be sent away to relive the experience months later.

Knowing that Dom had to wait until his co-defendants' trial was over before he could be sentenced, I persuaded the judge to grant him bail. By this point he had been back in prison for twenty weeks. Dom was in grave danger, I told the judge, of spending more time in prison waiting for his sentence than his eventual punishment could ever be. The judge agreed, and released him with a list of bail conditions, a requirement to report at the police station every day and a strict curfew monitored by an electronic tag.

On the first day of their trial, Dominic's co-defendants changed their pleas to guilty. I did not know why they had taken eight months to admit their crimes. I only wanted to make sure that Dom got credit for all the time he had spent abiding by his onerous conditions, waiting to receive his punishment. Every day of curtailed liberty spent on a tagged curfew, says the law, is worth half a day in prison. Preparing his case for his sentencing hearing, I wrote down the numbers in my notebook and circled them. Dom had spent 111 days on remand in custody on these offences, and 176 tagged on a curfew. Twenty-eight weeks in total, the same length of time he would have spent in prison had he been given a fifty-six-week sentence. He had already served a longer sentence than any judge was likely to pass.

I checked Dom's date of birth, printed at the top of his previous convictions. He had just turned twenty-four – only eight years younger than I was. The futility of it all, the inevitability of the cycle, crushed down on me. My fantasy of the life Dom could have, were he spirited away from his current one, seemed suddenly vain and absurd, and, as I packed the bundle of papers into my bag with my wig and gown, I felt embarrassed to have indulged in it.

In my hand I held Dom's pre-sentence report. This slim bundle of papers contained a probation officer's analysis of Dominic: an outline of his life, what remorse, if any, he felt about the crimes he had committed, and details of whatever sentence the probation officer recommended to the judge. I raised my head as the judge frowned down at me.

'But, Miss Langford, I have read the report. Your client professed to the probation officer to *want* a community sentence. He said he did not want to go back to prison yet again. He claimed he needed a chance to stop his quite frankly appalling offending and address his alcohol problem, and that he would be willing to undertake *any* community programme I might make?'

Dom's report had been written shortly after he had pleaded guilty, many months beforehand. He had used all his charm to persuade the probation officer that, despite breaching every other Community Order he had ever been given, this time it was different. He had done various food and hygiene courses in prison, he said. He'd learned to cook for himself when he was growing up, and now he wanted to train to be a chef, given the chance. He really thought he would be good at it. I could imagine how persuasive he had been, how charismatic. How the probation officer must have looked at the guideline starting point of eighteen weeks custody, then at this smiling young man before her, claiming he just needed a break, and remembered the reasons she had wanted to do this job. To help people, not to send them to prison. And she had gone back to her office and typed the words: 'Exceptionally, I recommend that this should be disposed of with a long community sentence'.

But when Dom had told her all this, he had no idea that he would, in effect, serve more than the maximum sentence for his crime while waiting for his sentence. Now, after many months in prison and even more on a tag, the prospect of spending the next year in weekly meetings with a probation officer, attending courses and doing unpaid work – even though he had already done his time – meant that he had, understandably, changed his mind.

I rolled the arguments around, weighing up the judge. He was a recorder: a barrister who sat as a judge for a limited number of days a year. His speciality was not, I knew, in criminal law, but in civil disputes. I tried again.

'Yes, I realize that my client *said* that, Your Honour. But, may I respectfully remind Your Honour once more of the sentencing guidelines for this matter? I fear the probation officer has been wildly optimistic in her recommendation. Your Honour will see that for a Category Two non-domestic burglary the starting point – regardless of plea or previous convictions – is a custodial sentence of eighteen weeks. Your Honour will also have noticed that the maximum sentence in this bracket is fifty-one weeks. My client has, therefore, already served a sentence in *excess* of the maximum, and that does not take into account the one-third discount he is entitled to for his early guilty plea. I respectfully *urge* the court to be careful that it does not pass a sentence which would prove . . . excessive.'

The judge looked down at the copy of the guidelines I had handed up. He paused, and I wondered whether I should push the point again. The sentencing guidelines were designed to create uniformity between courts, and had largely done so, but they also risked removing the skills and perception of the judge who has to decide an individual's fate. I thought of a maverick judge before whom I used to appear. He was once due to sentence my client, a man with a history of fighting who had meted out a number of injuries in a bar brawl and who should, according to the guidelines, have gone straight to prison. Instead this judge bellowed at him: 'Lay off the booze, stay out of trouble, get a bloody job, and come back here saying as much in a year's time or you will be going straight down for eighteen months. Now get out of my court.' A year later my client and I returned to show that he had faithfully obliged. He had new qualifications, a new job, a new home and a fiancée, and had kept out of trouble. Ever since I have been convinced that, in keeping him out of prison, that judge saved his life. But now, for Dominic, I needed the opposite. I looked at the judge, willing him to understand my plea, urging him to sentence Dom to prison so that he could walk free from court today.

'Yes, thank you, Miss Langford. Is there anything further?'

I hesitated, and confirmed there was not, then retook my seat. My two co-defending counsel then stood and, in turn, pleaded with the judge for leniency. Their clients had seen the inside of a prison cell before, their barristers implored, and knew that now was the time for change. It was their last chance. They urged the judge not to commit them to the cycle of custody with which the courts were all too familiar, and to enable them to swerve their future on to a different path.

The judge nodded. As he cleared his throat and looked towards the dock, I realized I was holding my breath.

'You are kidding?' My solicitor swore down the phone.

'No. I know,' I said. 'He gave him a Community Order. Twelve months of supervision to address his alcohol problem, an Enhanced Thinking Skills programme, and one hundred and twenty hours' unpaid work. The other two got pretty much the same.'

'Ridiculous. Didn't he see his record? Dom will never do it! We'll be back in court within weeks for a breach. It's just setting him up to fail . . .'

'I tried to say as much, but the judge didn't get it. He agreed it was a Category Two burglary. He agreed that it was aggravated by there being more than one break-in, and that they had gone prepared with a claw-hammer, at night, under the influence of alcohol. I mean, that *alone* should have meant an immediate custodial sentence. He was clearly on some sort of reformation mission – or maybe he thought he had to follow probation's recommendation, I don't know. He went through all of Dom's previous convictions and said that, despite the various remedies that had been applied – including prison – he had not learned his lesson and now was the time to do it.'

'But what about all the time he'd spent on remand – how could the judge just ignore it?'

'He didn't – he said he was not going to pass a prison sentence *because* of the time spent on remand. In effect, he used it as mitigation. I asked for permission to appeal, which, of course, he refused. Don't worry, I'll draft you an application to the Court of Appeal.' I paused. There was silence at the end of the line. 'The problem was that Dom had banged on to the probation officer about needing to change. He insisted that, although he had breached Community Orders in the past, he wanted the chance to try again – he knew this was the moment to really make a go of it, he said. The probation officer was convinced apparently; she went into some detail about his changed motivation.'

'I see.' My solicitor paused. 'I imagine that, by now, he is somewhat *less* motivated . . . ?'

I hesitated. 'You could put it like that.'

After we had come out of court I had stood in the corridor while Dom spat his fury at me. I understood why. The complaints he made were not new: the pointlessness of the brief appointments with the supervising probation officer crammed into an overloaded timetable, which offered just enough time to sign a name and ask a few questions but never enough to pull at the deep and secret thread that might undo the reasons for his offending. I watched Dom as he raged before me. He had put on weight in the last year, and the boyishness of his frame was giving way to slovenliness. Something else was different: there was a sullenness to him, a meanness and hardness I had not seen before. I looked at the other defendants, gathering in groups outside the courtroom doors, waiting for their turn, and realized that, for the first time, it was difficult to distinguish him from the rest of them.

My application to the Court of Appeal against Dom's sentence was refused. A few months later, I stood on the railway station platform after court and listened to a voicemail from my clerk. Dom had a hearing in court the day after tomorrow and his solicitor had asked if I could cover it. He had refused to go to his supervision appointments after the application for permission to appeal was refused, declaring them a waste of time. The court would be asked to find him in breach of his order and to sentence him for it. The voicemail reminded me that I already had another case in my diary for the same day. It was a civil case: a hopeless whiplash claim on behalf of a client who was, it was clear, part of a group of professional claimants who organized crashes for cash. Usually, I would have done anything to get out of it. I knew that as long as there was a competent, warm body in my place, the solicitors would not care who bore the judge's wrath towards my client on their behalf. I called my clerk back and, as he answered, I pictured Dominic the last time I had seen him.

'The thing is, I know I represented him at the sentence and that there should be continuity of counsel, but the other case *was* in my diary first so, technically, I have to do it.' I paused. 'I've also done loads of work on it. I won't get a penny if it goes to someone else and the breach hearing will barely cover my train fare to Oxford, right?'

All this was true. It was also irrelevant. A year or so before-hand, I would not have thought about it: I would have covered Dom's case. But the truth was I no longer wanted to witness his pointless and predictable lurch between prison and court, court and prison. I no longer wanted to watch the justice system fail to help him, and Dom fail to help himself. It not only made me feel impotent, it also made me feel complicit. I called the solicitor to explain why I couldn't cover the hearing and tried to ignore the gnawing of guilt in my gut. After that, although she asked me to cover other cases, the solicitor never again gave me one of Dom's. I never knew whether it was Dom himself who asked for someone else because, despite all the years of representing him, I, like others, had given up on him, and he would not forgive me for it.

A few years after I turned down Dominic's case, I was stay-ing in Oxford on another trial and went out for dinner with a friend to a bistro near her flat, slightly out of town, in an area I did not know well. It was relaxed and noisy, the staff and diners a collection of students. When we finished I walked over to the till to pay. Behind it was the door to the kitchen, swinging on its hinges as staff walked in and out carrying dishes full and empty. As I waited, a girl with a pile of plates walked past me and into the kitchen. I looked up, curious to see the action behind the door. There, balancing against a stainless-steel countertop, I saw – for two long seconds – a man who looked exactly like Dominic. He was wearing a white kitchen jacket and chequered trousers, and his face was in profile as he laughed at someone out of sight. The door swung shut.

I wondered about it for a long time afterwards. The next time I saw Dominic's solicitor I nearly asked her if I could be right, but fear stopped me. Fear that I had got it wrong; fear that I had seen another man – for I wanted, above all else, to believe I had seen Dom. I wanted to think that some unknown trigger – something someone said, something someone did – had made him want to change, want to stop. I wanted to believe the judge had been right to put someone else in charge of his life long enough to change it. I knew that this was not what the statistics told me and I knew it was wishful of me to think it, but I hoped that he – like others I had represented – had at last settled on a life that meant I would never see him again.

There are too many cases – too many faces – to remember them all. But sometimes, going through the many blue notebooks in which I wrote down all the evidence, a particular fact or name will bring my client and their case back to me so strongly I feel as though I am in the courtroom with them once again. These are the people who, for one reason or another, have touched my life. These are the people who will stay with me for ever. And Dominic was the first of them.

2

Derek

Newport Magistrates' Court,
Isle of Wight

Sexual Offences Act 2003
Section 71 – Sexual activity in a public lavatory

(1) A person commits an offence if—
(a) he is in a lavatory to which the public or a
section of the public has or is permitted to have
access, whether on payment or otherwise,
(b) he intentionally engages in an activity, and,
(c) the activity is sexual.

'POLICE, PLEASE.'

Ralph stumbled through the wood, his face burning. He pressed his mobile phone to his ear as he told the emergency operator his name, his number, where he was, why he was calling. Panting, he said that behind him on the edge of the wood was a public lavatory. In that lavatory there were three men. They were in there together; there among the damp smell of moss, the secret codes graffitied on to the walls and the lavatory partitions with holes cut at groin height. This was a place where men would close the door of their cubicle, unbutton their flies, and blindly invite pleasure from a stranger. The three men were all half-dressed, Ralph said, and performing acts upon one another which were disgusting, quite disgusting. And he would like an officer to go down there and clear them out, right now. Ralph gave the operator a description of each man, then hung up. He paused, catching his breath, and turned to look at the squat brick building, now half hidden by the trees. Then he walked away.

The police arrived shortly afterwards. They knew the building by its reputation. It sat at the edge of a small copse set back from the coastline on the Isle of Wight. As day-trippers ate ice-creams and, from the lawn of the yacht club, couples in brass-buttoned blazers and floral dresses watched boats race, here, in this infamous wood, men would meet for sex. When the police arrived they found not three but many men: chatting, smoking, hanging around outside the drab building. Inside it were two who fitted the descriptions Ralph had given. One gave his name as Michael. He was an accountant in his forties, conspicuous by his Scottish accent, moustache and air of assurance. The younger man was George. He was in his early thirties, slim, with a quiff of white-blond hair. He was new to the area, having just moved down from London for work. He was used to the easy bars and streets of the capital and had found it difficult in this tight-lipped place to find other men – not just for casual sex but also for companionship.

The police asked those still loitering outside whether they recognized the description of the third man. Late sixties. Tall and slim. Balding. Wearing brown corduroy trousers and a plaid shirt. 'Oh yes,' said one. 'That's Derek Pollard. He's here all the time.' That evening the police knocked on Derek's door. He was a gentle man with a quiet disposition. He had run the local post office until it closed down, and now filled his days with the allotment association, the church choir, fetes, teas, fundraisers, newsletters. A dependable volunteer; a local stalwart. He lived alone, unobtrusively, loved by those friends and neighbours alongside whom he had grown old. When he answered the door to the police Derek was wearing completely different clothes from those described by Ralph. Otherwise his appearance matched and, because he had no alibi for the afternoon, he found himself in the back of a police car being driven to the station for interview.

Whereas Derek and Michael chose to follow the advice of their newly instructed solicitors and answered 'No comment' to every interview question, George told the police everything. He did not need a lawyer, he said, for he was not guilty. The story was not right. That day he and Michael had been talking, smoking, hanging out. They had been fully clothed. Derek, he said, had not been there. It was true that he had seen Derek at other times, and that both he and George had used the place for the purpose that had earned it its reputation. But not that day. There *had* been another man there about the same age as Derek, who was also tall and bald. George had spoken to him briefly – he'd given him a cigarette. He didn't know his name. When the police arrived this man had melted away into the trees and when George was led from the building to the police car he could not see him. But Derek definitely was not there, George insisted, and none of them had done anything wrong.

If the men had admitted the offence, the police may have puffed their cheeks, cracked their knuckles and decided they could let them go with a caution. But all three denied their guilt and so the police were left to decide what to do. They looked at their evidence. They had a complainant – although not yet a victim, not until the word 'guilty' rang out in court – who was horrified by what he had seen and was prepared to come to court to say so. They had George's admission in interview that he and the others had been to the building for sex in the past. And if their witness had got it right about Michael and George, why not about Derek? They had enough. Enough for there to be a reasonable prospect of convicting all three men. Enough to believe that it was in the public interest to charge them. After all, there was an offence conceived for exactly this circumstance. Its purpose was to protect the public from witnessing the kind of acts George had just admitted to. The offence could be heard only in the magistrates' court, not being serious enough to find its way up to the crown court before a judge and jury. They made their decision. All three men would be charged.

It was only later, when the witness statement bearing Ralph's name made its way into his hands, that George worked it out. He had been inside the building talking to Michael that day – they were leaning against the wall, laughing, smoking, handing out cigarettes to those who asked – when a man walked in. George recognized him: he had had sex with him before, as had many of his friends. The man gave George a look George understood, walked into one of the cubicles, closed the door, unbuttoned his fly and put his penis through the hole cut for the purpose in the partition. But that day George was not interested. He ignored him. After a time the man flung the cubicle door open in rage and, buttoning up his fly, swore at the men. He stormed off through the wood as their laughter echoed off the building's tiles. After George read the statement, an internet search turned the name upon it into a face. Then it all fell into place. That man, George said, was Ralph.

It was then that George found a lawyer. She was a solicitor called Catherine, who practised from one of the small criminal defence firms left on the island, the others having turned their hand to more lucrative work or been driven out entirely by funding cuts. It was Catherine who stood in court as George confirmed his not guilty plea – echoed by Michael and Derek – and who noted down the date of their trial. And it was Catherine who then called me.

When Catherine rang I knew something was unusual. At that stage of my career my cases would most often arrive in silence. A solicitor would call the clerks in my chambers, who would then – depending on the date of the hearing and the type of case – offer up a list of barristers' names for them to choose from. If I was chosen, the case would be put into my diary and I would learn about it afterwards.

When Catherine told me of the charge, I laughed. *Sexual activity in a public lavatory.* I had not known that such an offence existed. I thought back to a conversation I had had with a barrister before I went to law school. 'How do you remember all the law?' I asked her, in wonder. She scoffed. 'You look it up! I have never, ever done a case where I haven't looked it up.' And so after Catherine's call I went and found the offence. It was buried in the middle of a statute passed only a few years before – a 200-page attempt to clear up the prejudice and homophobia in existing legislation. The Act had removed the offence of 'gross indecency' which had been used to persecute gay men throughout the century it had stood on the statute book. It claimed to put in its place something gender-neutral and non-discriminatory. But the new offence carried with it the legacy of the old, for it was used almost solely to target 'cottaging' – gay men meeting in public lavatories for sex. The wording of the offence applied only to a public toilet. If sexual activity took place in a shower cubicle in a campsite, a cluster of trees in a park, a changing room at a swimming pool, for example, this did not count. But if the sexual activity took place in a lavatory to which the public had access, then the offence had been committed. It did not matter whether or not the person was alone, whether or not he had caused anyone alarm or distress, nor what his intentions were. Most often, of course, there needed to be a witness to prove the crime had been committed. That witness was Ralph.

Ralph had identified all three defendants as the men he had seen in the public lavatory that day. In response, Catherine had asked the Crown Prosecution Service if she could use their identification suite to carry out her own procedure. She told them that a number of defence witnesses all claimed they had been intimately involved with Ralph and wanted their chance to point him out on a screen of photographs. Her letters were met first with a refusal and then with silence. Catherine was not deterred – she would conduct her own identification exercise.

One by one the men in her small waiting room came into her office and from a selection of similar-looking photographs they picked out Ralph. 'Yes!' they said, the man in that picture was a regular visitor to their secret club in the woods. They all knew him and he knew all of them.

The papers arrived in chambers on a Friday, some ten days before the trial, tied up in pink ribbon as they always were and left waiting in my pigeonhole for me to collect after I returned from court. I had grown used to first seeing case papers the day before the hearing. It was frustrating to spend time on cases that were later pulled from my diary without remuneration for the work I'd done – thwarted by a missing witness, an overfull court, an overrunning case – but I did not want to risk being unprepared. I took the papers to my room in chambers and began to read them through.

Catherine had agreed with the two co-defending solicitors that, because George's name was the first on the charge sheet, it fell to me to lead the defence. I began to comb through case law – trying to find a way to get Catherine's home-made identification of Ralph into evidence – and considered what joyous luck it was to have such easy, hard proof that a witness was lying. In the daily grind of the magistrates' court this was a rare thing. It made me think of a case I had seen when I was a very new pupil in chambers. I had been shadowing a barrister, Ivo, as he prosecuted a local gang leader, Terry, at Reading Crown Court. Among other brutal acts, Terry was accused of slicing a cut into the forehead of his girlfriend, Maria, with a knife. The blood would not stop coming and Terry realized that the wound was too deep. When they arrived at hospital Maria told the doctor she had fallen from a car. Now she was prepared to tell the truth.

All of us in court knew what a risk she was taking in doing so. If Terry were found not guilty he would surely kill her. Terry's evidence was full of denials that he had ever hurt Maria. When he had finished, his barrister stood and announced that he was calling a witness, Barry, to back up his client's story. Barry stood in the witness box, his eyes flicking from Terry's barrister to the dock at the back of court. I turned and looked at Terry. He sat in the dock in the middle of the row of seats. He was completely still, legs splayed, arms folded across his chest. His eyes, I noticed, did not move from Barry. Barry told the defence barrister that, yes, he had been at Terry's house that day. Maria had been so drunk, he said, that she had fallen out of the car and cut her head on the metal edge of the door on her way down. That was how she had done it. Terry hadn't touched her.

As Barry was giving his evidence I noticed two brief exchanges between Ivo and the police officer sitting behind him. The officer darted twice from the courtroom. The second time he returned holding a thin bundle of papers just as Ivo was beginning his cross-examination. Barry stood his ground in answer to Ivo's questions. No, he was not lying. He didn't even like Terry; he just couldn't see an innocent man go down for something he hadn't done.

Ivo glanced down at the paperwork the officer had just handed him and then back up at Barry. 'We can be sure of the date that Maria suffered her injury,' he said, 'because we have her hospital records which make it clear when she was admitted at A and E.'

'If you say so. I can't remember what date it was.' Barry waved his hand and looked away, uninterested.

'The problem, you see,' said Ivo calmly, 'is that on the twenty-eighth of November you were in police custody.'

I had never actually seen anyone turn white. The colour drained from Barry's face as literally as the cliché suggested it might.

'We have it you see – your custody record.' Ivo looked down at the paper in his hand. 'Arrested in the early hours of twenty-eighth November on suspicion of a public order offence. Solicitor arrived at two p.m.; detainee considered sober enough to be interviewed at four p.m. Released without charge just after eleven p.m. Which was approximately two hours *after* Maria was discharged from the hospital.'

The jury sat up in a collective shuffle, their attention fixed on the witness box, gripped. Barry stood completely still. He looked as if he might faint.

'No further questions, Your Honour.' Ivo sat down without flourish.

After watching the two officers waiting at the back of court arrest Barry for perjury, I hurried down the courthouse corridor after Ivo. He opened the robing-room door, taking his wig off as he did so. He paused, then turned to face me. The beginnings of a smile crept into the edges of his mouth. 'That,' he said softly, 'was manna from heaven. It hardly ever happens. Enjoy it when it does.'

It was late when I walked home from the tube station after reading through George's case, back to the house I rented with friends. I opened the door to a blast of warmth and smells and talk. The dinner party had started without me. I allowed myself to be waved into an empty chair next to someone I had met a few times before. It was not long before he asked the question I was becoming used to.

'So, what are you working on at the moment, then?'

Years earlier I would not have dared to believe that my answer could be so interesting.

My parents had never navigated the university system and so when I told them I was putting it off and heading around the world they had little choice but to acquiesce. At nineteen years old I travelled through five countries in ten months, then returned to start an English degree, knowing that, when it was over, I had to find a job I thought worthwhile, unpredictable, interesting and, most of all, where words were loved. Law seemed to offer everything I wanted, but without a top degree from the right kind of university, or at the very least some family connections, it seemed well beyond my reach. My grandmother – who had received no formal education of her own – had been a magistrate years earlier, but had returned to her role of tenant farmer's wife long before I left school and could not help. One day, towards the end of my degree, a friend sat me down and told me that I had, at least, to try. Buoyed up with new self-belief, I moved home and began to work out how to do it. I became a temporary legal secretary and spent my days filling out forms, typing letters and proofreading statements. In the evening I served drinks in my local pub and talked to the barristers staying in the rooms above while their cases were being heard in the local court. I found a few jobs taking notes for solicitors on trials they could not attend. One of these was a three-day lesbian abduction case in a small village in rural Wales. The defence barrister had a booming voice that you could hear three rooms away and red hair cut into a bowl shape with a blunt fringe. I loved her. She and I got drunk together in the bar of a tiny Welsh inn and she told me that I must become a barrister, that I could become a barrister and that I should become a barrister. So I took out a bank loan and studied three years of law in eight months on a law conversion course, astonishing myself by gaining a distinction.

Buffered by a scholarship from an Inn of Court, I then went on to Bar school and applied to a barrister's chambers in the city where I grew up. I nearly left my second interview with chambers before it started. The other candidates in the waiting room were men in tailored suits, who sat with legs confidently spread, looking only an inch or two away from middle age despite their youth. I fidgeted with the buttons of my H&M suit and wondered what I was doing there. But I stayed and got through it, and then they offered me a pupillage. During this year-long apprenticeship I began to understand that normal people did this job too. In fact, that can be what makes you good at it: being able to talk to your client, being able to talk to a jury – being able to say 'put yourself in his shoes – I can'. At the end of my year of pupillage the members of my chambers took a vote and decided I could join them, and that I could work from any of the five cities in which they had an annex. My name was engraved on a plaque, which was slotted into its groove outside chambers' door, rising as junior members joined beneath me.

I quickly found myself in the magistrates', county and criminal courts day after day, experiencing each case with all my senses. I turned my hand to whatever came my way: road traffic accidents, personal injury claims, accidents at work, inquests, courts martial, divorce, parental disputes over children. I was a hired mouthpiece, paid to lend my gifts of education and art to my clients, and to lead them, in all their shades of grey, through the black and white of the law. I was paid to tell their stories for them when they could not do so themselves. But the work I loved most – and the reason I had wanted to become a barrister – was crime. All life is there. Its courtrooms are filled with advocates navigating the kind of stories that others would struggle to believe. Rarely would a week pass without a case causing me to stifle my laughter with a fist, rage at the unfairness of life's lot, or send a cold chill of shock right through me.

Very often when I tell someone what I do a wistful look settles over them, and they declare that they 'always wanted to become a barrister'. I watch them imagining stone steps to ancient buildings, leather-backed chairs, wigs and gowns and gilded crests. I try to tell them of the 5 a.m. starts, the trains to towns they would never otherwise have cause to visit, the utilitarian courthouses of red brick and grey concrete; of the vending-machine lunches in windowless brick rooms, the interminable waiting, the clients who leave without an utterance of thanks, and the ever-decreasing rates of publicly funded pay. But often I do not press this, because I know that that is not what they want to imagine, even if the truth lies far from their fiction.

At the dinner table, nudged on by my neighbour's question, I took the wine offered, leaned back, and spoke of my newly discovered world of glory holes and the etiquette of homosexual sex with a stranger and the finer details of who goes where in an all-male threesome. Heads turned and voices dropped as the table rippled with laughter, shock and curiosity that I – a twenty-something girl with a nice accent, black suit and neatly crossed legs – lived in this world. I was aware of the contradiction between how I looked and the words I said. It was my circus trick and I loved performing it.

Over the weekend I began to prepare George's case. As I always did – even when technology made it obsolete – I opened the blue notebook all barristers once carried and wrote down the names of the people involved, the evidence found, the missing links, the law. Only when I had translated evidence to page would I begin to draft my questions. In court, the prosecution lawyer would stand before the magistrates and lay out the details of the crime with which the three men were charged. Then he would call his first witness. Ralph. The prosecutor would have to tease out the evidence without putting his own words into his witness's mouth. I planned to sit and bide my time, and allow Ralph to dig his way further into the pit he had created, unaware of my witnesses waiting outside the courtroom for their chance to expose him. I wondered whether, faced with the three men staring at him from the other side of the courtroom, he would crumble. Maybe he would try to go back on what he had said. Maybe he had just meant to scare them, humiliate them in revenge, not expecting the police to charge, not anticipating that he would ever actually have to go to court. I looked at the questions I had drafted and felt a surge of excitement.

I pulled the red leather-bound copy of my law book, Archbold, towards me. It was part of my duty to warn George what would happen if the magistrates didn't believe him and found him guilty. I needed to check the sentence he could face. I flipped through the pages to the law and winced. I would have to tell my client – when we met for the first time in those frantic moments outside court – that, however unlikely, if the magistrates wanted to they could send him to prison for up to six months.

I looked at Ralph's statement again. I had to consider the possibility that what he was saying might be true – that Ralph had seen what he claimed and that the real fallacy was his disgust. Maybe Derek *had* been there that day but some sense of foreboding had made him leave and, once safely home, he had changed the clothes that could identify him. Maybe George was lying to protect him, knowing how Derek's world would be undone if his secret life was uncovered? Until I was there in the courtroom – listening to the evidence, weighing it up – I would not know. I could only wait, and watch, and listen, and hope that the prosecution's evidence fell apart in my hands.

It was the evening before the trial. I had been away for the weekend and as I walked through the airport terminal on Sunday night, I turned on my phone. It came to life with a voicemail. It was from Catherine. I called her back, ambling slowly through the airport, aware of the excitement I felt at the prospect of the next day's case. I thought of the time I had sat opposite my gently baffled parents at the kitchen table and explained what I wanted to do. That it might take me a long time – years perhaps – but that I would get there in the end. And I had; and I loved it. And tomorrow I was going to start a case that I would surely win with a glorious exposé. With manna from heaven.

Catherine picked up the phone. Her voice was low. There had been a hearing, she explained, last Friday. I listened, wondering if she was about to tell me that the trial was off, that the prosecution had finally dropped the case. I felt prematurely disappointed, cheated of my drama. It was Derek, Catherine went on. He had asked for a hearing to try to persuade the magistrates to impose restrictions on any press reporting on the trial. He wanted an order which, if granted, would prevent them from putting his name in the paper. The idea of it pulled me up short. I hadn't thought about the press with their scribbling pens and cameras outside court. Of course they would be there. It was a story full of salacious detail which would thrill and titillate. I knew that, for I had told it. I imagined the bench in court where the reporters would sit and make notes of the trial and draw sketches of the defendants, locked into their dock, separated from the rest of us as though their criminality were catching. I felt a swell of anger on Derek's behalf. At the public humiliation of being revealed as the man he was, like this, in such an excruciating, shaming way.

Catherine told me that the magistrates had been silent as they listened to their legal advisor tell them of the rule of great exception, which applies to restrictions on reporting details of a trial. The unfairness most often lies in reporting a trial before it has concluded – the defendant's name is there for all to see, although the prosecution witnesses will not be known until they give evidence – but this application was for the trial itself. The magistrates were reminded of the principle of open court – that anyone can walk into a criminal court and listen to a trial. The evidence given is a matter of public record and, said the legal advisor, the principle of open justice must be fiercely protected. After the briefest of adjournments, Catherine said, the magistrates had filed back into court and refused Derek's desperate request for dignity. Afterwards the defendants' solicitors, having warned their clients to expect nothing less, had all shrugged their shoulders and waved each other off for the weekend.

And Derek, gripped with black dread, had gone home. He had sorted through his bureau, putting everything in order. He had written notes for all those he loved. He had pressed and folded his choir uniform and left it ready for its next wearer. And then he had killed himself.

On Monday morning the air felt mild and damp after a weekend of grey skies and showers. As the long journey from home to court took me, in sequence, on a train, a taxi, a ferry and a bus, I felt myself knot with nerves. I had no idea what would happen when I got to court. I just knew I was dreading it.

The magistrates' court is in the same large brick building as the crown court. The corridor outside the courtroom was quiet apart from a gathering of men standing bunched together, whispering, in the corner. I approached them, stopping just shy of their pack. I recognized George from the description in the witness statement and realized that those standing with him must be his witnesses. He turned when I called out his name and I noticed with shock that his eyes were puffy and pink-rimmed. I told him, quietly, how sorry I was and he nodded in acknowledgment. At a loss to know what to do, I said I should go into court to find the other lawyers, to work out what was going on. The mood had bled through to the courtroom, where I found Michael's barrister speaking to the legal advisor and Derek's barrister sitting alone at the advocates' bench. With proceedings due to start at 10 a.m., we waited, lurking, before the news filtered through. Ralph had failed to show up to court and was not answering calls. There would be no request for a witness summons to force him to come, or even a delay to see if he appeared. The prosecution was going to drop the case. It was over.

Later that morning, as wind whipped grey sea spray on to the windows of the ferry, I looked at what I had written on the page of my notebook:

R v George Clarke
10:10 a.m. *No evidence offered. Case dismissed.*

I did not know what to say to George afterwards. Unlike Derek, neither he nor I had grown up in the shadow of a law that made a man who loved another man a criminal. I knew only a little of chemical castration, of undergoing the cure, of undercover pretty police officers tasked with luring men behind bars. Even long after private homosexuality was decriminalized, a public gesture of affection – a hand held in the street, a kiss – could still mean an arrest for gross indecency. Derek had been almost thirty when the law had changed, by which time his fear of it was embedded. He had therefore lived a double life, keeping his nature a secret from all who knew him, terrified by the prospect of being uncovered. I was ashamed that this offence still existed. I was ashamed that the decision to drop the case had come too late. I was ashamed that the humiliation of exposure was, even now, worth more than someone's life. But I was also ashamed of something deeper: of my hubris, my delight in the details of the case, my thrill at the prospect of winning and my failure to remember the deeply felt pain that lay behind every life I rifled through. Behind the pages of the law and the court stamps lay secrets and histories, ruptured dreams and biting shame. The consequences of every case ripped far further than the courtroom. That, I thought as I pulled my wheelie case off the ferry, was something I would never forget again.

3

Saba

Reading Magistrates' Court

Children Act 1989
Section 8 – Child arrangements orders and other orders with respect to children

(1) In this Act 'child arrangements order' means an order regulating arrangements relating to any of the following—
   (a) with whom a child is to live, spend time or otherwise have contact, and,
   (b) when a child is to live, spend time or otherwise have contact with any person.

A MONTH BEFORE I first met Saba, I found myself at South-ampton Crown Court sitting opposite two men who were speaking at length to one another while successfully ignoring me. It did not matter how intently I watched them – followed the jabs of their hand gestures, the furrows of their brows, the rise and fall of their voices – I was unable to understand anything they said. Eventually I held up my hand to stop them.

'Please, Mr Khan, as I said before, your job is not to advise my client, nor discuss the evidence with him. Just tell me *exactly* what Mr Begum's answer is; no more, no less.'

The interpreter, Mr Khan, turned to me. He looked indignant. 'I trying, Madam, but he wants talk with me about its case,' he said, gesturing to my client, whose eyes flicked from him to me. I had been trying to extract the details of a fight outside a pub in which my Pakistani client – due to begin his trial for grievous bodily harm at any moment – had fractured a man's eye socket. The complainant's drunkenness and resulting concussion meant that he could barely remember a thing about it. The only witness willing to give a statement was a security guard who had been standing outside the pub, although he had been dealing with another fracas and had not seen the blow. My client's description of what had happened would, therefore, be largely unchallenged. He had every chance of being acquitted and walking free if only he were able to explain himself. If he could not do that and was convicted, then his life would be changed for ever. He would almost certainly be sent to prison, but he also then risked deportation back to the country of his birth after his sentence was over. I leaned across the table, urging him to look at me.

'Mr Begum. When the other man was shouting at you, how did you feel?'

Come on, I thought, willing him on. Give me the words I need to save you: *I was terrified. I didn't understand him. The man was much bigger than me and very aggressive, waving his arms around and shouting loudly. He came towards me. I thought he was going to hit me. I was trapped, there was nowhere for me to go. So to get him away from me, I hit him before he could hit me.*

If the jury decided that the cracking of Mr Begum's knuckles upon another man's face was a reasonable and proportionate defence against an oncoming attack then he was entirely within the law, no matter that his was the first fist to swing. But my client had to say the words himself – I could not give them to him, no matter how much I wanted to coax them out.

I watched helplessly as Mr Khan turned to my client, drew a breath, and spoke urgently and unintelligibly to him. The translation lasted a long time and required much gesticulation. Mr Begum began to speak, directing his answers at Mr Khan, who made grunting noises in response, nodding and shaking his head in turn. I cut in. I could hear the frustration in my voice but I no longer cared.

'Mr Khan, have you asked Mr Begum my question?'

Mr Khan turned and, imperiously, replied, 'I am just doing so, Madam—'

'It's just that your interpretation seems a great deal longer than my question. Can you please just tell me what he said – it is very important that I have his instructions.'

Mr Khan's face twitched. He swept his hand towards Mr Begum.

'He said, he hit the man.'

It was only the beginning of the week but already I wanted to close my eyes and rest my forehead on the cool tabletop. Before I could reply, Mr Begum's name blasted out of the tannoy, summoning us into court. I started to my feet, grabbed my wig and flipped it on to my head. This trial was going to start whether we were ready for it, or not.

I glanced up at the courtroom clock. It was already 4.30 p.m. and the prosecuting barrister was only now beginning his cross-examination of Mr Begum. There was every chance the trial would spill over into a third day. Mentally, I ran through my diary for the week. I would have to call the clerks on my way home and ask them to return the case I had on Wednesday to another barrister. There was still a chance we might finish Mr Begum's trial by tomorrow. If I returned Wednesday's matter now it would leave me out of work and pocket. But I couldn't risk it – the clerks needed to know now so they could find another barrister and get the papers to them in time. I tried to remember what Wednesday's case was. A hearing in a family matter – the father had applied for residence of his infant daughter. I was representing the mother. I remembered that the solicitor's letter had explained she was from Bangladesh and spoke little English. I looked up at the witness box as Mr Khan and Mr Begum were reminded by an irritated judge not to confer before the defendant answered questions, and felt weary at the prospect of taking on another case where I could not understand anything my client said.

Mr Begum's case did run into Wednesday, but only just. Word by painful word his evidence came out. I was therefore able to say, in my closing speech to the jury, that Mr Begum was the man under attack. The words were the ones Mr Khan had given us on Mr Begum's behalf, but in my order, with my emphasis and in my voice. By midday the jury had returned a sharp, short not guilty verdict. I left court relieved, and waited in the corridor. Mr Begum appeared, grinning.

'Thank you, Madam,' he said, grasping my hand. 'I am very thankful for everything you did.' It was the first time I had heard him speak English and, although his accent was pronounced, his grammar was perfect. Mr Khan appeared silently alongside him, proffering me his timesheet to sign, then the two men set off down the courthouse stairs together, chatting in their shared language. I watched as Mr Khan clapped my client on the back and laughed, and wondered, for a moment, if I had just been duped. And, maybe, whether the jury – who had been told they were bound by law to give Mr Begum the benefit of any doubts – had too. I walked back to the robing room, feeling uneasy. Had Mr Khan helped my client win by telling him to give evidence which he knew would help his case? Or had he simply tried to explain the nuances of each question, knowing that few direct translations could catch the secret meanings so often hidden within a word? I would never know, but I thought of all the others I had represented who had given evidence without a translator. Those clients who spoke in their native tongue and were assumed therefore to know the right words but, so often, did not. Was I, in some form or another, their interpreter? It was my job to find ways to draw from my clients what they needed to tell the jury, what they had thought, how they had felt. And then, at the end of the case, to wrap my client's words up in my own so that their story was told with a fluidity that theirs did not have. So maybe, I thought as I tapped the code into the robing room's keypad, that really made me no different from Mr Khan after all.

*

When Asif Choudhury led a procession of his relatives into Saba's house, the first thing she thought was that he looked like a pop star. He was older, tall, heavily built and exotic in his worldliness. His dark hair was thick and combed back. He smiled at her and she looked away, flushed with shyness. *This man is going to be my husband.* She said the mantra silently to herself, in case repetition could reinforce its truth. A few days later, when the marriage ceremony was over and their relatives had drifted away, Asif boarded an aeroplane back to England. Left alone with her family, Saba feared the whole thing might have been a dream.

Eight months later, Saba's uncle met her from the airport on the outskirts of London. The next day he drove her north to her new home, and her new husband. Saba's uncle was married to her mother's cousin and Saba did not know him well, but he and his wife were the only relatives she had here and she was grateful to them. Her belongings were to follow, so Saba arrived with only one bag of her most precious possessions. It was February, and a foreign grey chill seemed to penetrate through her as she and her uncle walked up the path of the modest terraced house. The front door opened to a pulse of artificial warmth, and Saba could smell cooking that seemed at once familiar and strange. Before her in the gloom of the hallway stood her new mother-in-law. Saba had met her before, of course, at their first introduction and then at the wedding, but away from the heat and light of Bangladesh and the encouragement of her parents, she seemed unrecognizable. Mrs Choudhury was slightly shorter than Saba, but her wide frame and authoritative air made her seem indomitable. After her uncle had left, Saba identified the sensation tugging at her since she arrived in the small house that was now her home. It was fear.

*

Asif's first act of unpredictable violence seemed to Saba afterwards so insignificant that, later, when her lawyers asked her to tell them everything, she almost left it out.

It was a few days after she had arrived in England. She and Asif were sitting beside one another on their bed, and Saba was absorbed in competing sensations of excitement and strangeness as she tried to grasp that this man was actually her husband. He was scrolling through music videos and Facebook profiles on his mobile phone as they tried to navigate and blend their different worlds. Saba, excited that they might share a love of music, darted across the room to her bag and came back with a book: an album of sorts, into which she had stuck pictures of Bollywood singers and actors she admired. Glued into the middle was a ticket. Saba and some friends had travelled to see their favourite singer in concert and, afterwards, they had waited until he appeared from backstage. With professional ease he had taken the ticket from the pretty, diminutive girls giggling in front of him and, turning it over, had written a note to them. He had signed it with a flourish of kisses underneath his name. As Asif flicked through her book, Saba felt glad that it might make him think her more worldly than she feared she was.

'What's this? Who wrote this?' he asked, tapping his large finger on the page with the ticket.

Saba dipped her head, coyly pleased. She began to tell the story, but before she could finish she realized that Asif was on his feet, shouting words in English that she did not understand. As she watched, he held her book up and began to rip pages from it. He tore out the ticket and shredded it; then he did the same to other pages, yelling, hurling the scraps of paper towards her. Saba watched him, frozen and confused, as the pieces floated impotently to the floor. She became aware of someone else in the room – Asif's mother – who rounded on her son and ushered him away down the stairs. As he left the room, Asif turned and ripped the spine of the book in two, flicking the pieces at Saba. She flinched away, and when she turned back he had gone. Scattered over the carpet were glossy scraps of colour and dancing limbs, and fragments of kisses on the back of a torn-up ticket.

Just over six months after arriving in England, Saba discovered that she was pregnant. Her daughter, Nazia, was born the following March as rain sluiced down the hospital window. In November the same year, Asif's mother took Saba to the doctor. The appointment had been booked to confirm that the pain and bleeding that had crippled Saba over the past two days had, as she suspected, been the end of a second pregnancy. It was a pregnancy she had not wanted, but she tried not to acknowledge her guilty relief that it was now over. The doctor handed Saba a plastic pot and waved her down the corridor to the lavatory.

Saba sat in the cubicle and looked at the back of the door. On it was a sign, laminated and in many languages, one of which was her own. It was not the first time she had seen it. Every time she had come for her antenatal appointments and afterwards with Nazia, the doctor had given her a plastic pot and sent her to this bathroom.

If you are the victim of domestic violence but cannot talk to us, tear off the strip on the label of your urine sample pot and we will get you help.

From the beginning of their marriage Asif had been violent, but once he saw his child growing inside her his physical abuse of Saba stopped. Instead he found other ways to wear her down. He found fault with her cooking, her cleaning, the way she did the family's chores. Her very presence seemed to irritate him.

Once Nazia was born the physical aggression returned, but because each individual act of his seemed to Saba to be somehow her fault, she tried to discount it. He pushed her off her prayer mat because she had not been listening to him. When she blocked his view of a football match on the television, he kicked her hard on her shins. He grabbed hold of her long, glossy black hair and pulled her back towards him if she turned away while he was shouting at her. After a time, pushes turned to punches, hair-pulling to dragging, a grip on the wrist to an arm pushed up behind her back. And at night she had to lie with him and allow her body to be used for his pleasure and her duty because, as he told her, she had not yet borne him a son and this was what a wife – his wife – needed to do.

Then, one shocking, shuddering day, while Nazia played on their living-room floor Asif held a kitchen knife to Saba's throat and she thought she was going to die. She knew then that if she didn't leave, he might kill her.

Whenever Saba left the house her husband, mother-in-law or another relative would go with her, explaining that she needed their interpretation. The front door was generally kept locked. She was able to speak to her parents and relatives only on a telephone kept in the downstairs hall next to the living room, to ensure minimal privacy. Asif refused to buy her a mobile phone, saying he could not see her need of it. His mother ruled over the family's finances. The trip that Saba was supposed to be making back to Bangladesh to introduce her infant daughter to her parents – fearing her elderly and unwell father might die without ever seeing Nazia – was continually postponed until, eventually, Saba stopped asking. In any event, even if she somehow found the money herself she would be unable to go – Asif had handed over her passport to his mother when she first arrived and she had not seen it since.

A few weeks after Asif threatened her with a knife, the postman rang for a signature on a parcel and Saba saw her chance. She answered the door with Nazia in her arms. As the postman climbed into his van and drove away, she walked swiftly down the path. Then, as she reached for the gate, she felt a burning pain in her scalp – it was someone grabbing her hair, pulling her back. She cried out and raised her hand, letting go of the gate, as her mother-in-law dragged her back towards the house and inside. Saba wept as she watched Mrs Choudhury lock the front door and take out the key. It was later that night that Saba began to bleed.

Now she stared at the perforated strip on the label of the sample pot in her hand. She caught the edge of the strip and pulled it free, folding it up and flushing it away with the contents of the bowl. She did not know that the urine sample was not needed, nor that the doctor who had watched her over the months – always flanked by her husband's family, who spoke on her behalf – had noticed the grip marks on her forearms and the shadows under her eyes, so had asked Saba to give a sample every time she came in the hope that she would read the sign on the back of the door. When Saba returned to the doctor's room, neither looked at the other as she handed over the pot, wrapped in a paper towel.

Things then seemed to happen so quickly that, afterwards, Saba's memories became confused. She remembered the doctor asking her mother-in-law to leave the room with Nazia, claiming that Saba needed to undress and be examined. Alone, in broken English, Saba told her: yes, she wanted the police to come and get her. She remembered the knock on the door of the house; being taken with Nazia to the police station in the back of their car. Somehow her uncle and aunt arrived and took her back to their house in the suburbs of Reading. Asif, she realized, must have called them. She found out afterwards that they had told the police that Saba did not want to press charges; she just wanted her husband to leave her alone.

For a time, things seemed to settle. There was no contact from Asif and, although her aunt and uncle's house was crowded, Saba began to feel as though it were her home. But then her aunt and uncle told her they had spoken to the community elders. Asif wanted a reconciliation. He wanted to see his daughter and he wanted his wife back, and they had agreed that she must try to work things out. Nazia's first birthday was coming up; Asif must see her then. After all, they reasoned, Asif had not been violent to Nazia, and he and Saba were still married. She was still his wife.

A few weeks later Saba found herself in her uncle and aunt's car, staring at newly budded trees silhouetted against a pewter March sky. Nazia slept in the car seat beside her. All Saba's senses warned her that she was heading towards danger, but her fear was masked by her sense of shame at her failure to make her marriage work. She reasoned that Asif was not a drunkard like some other husbands. He had a job and could provide for her. She felt the weight of the pressure to return to him and could barely breathe beneath it.

Saba stood on the doorstep behind her uncle and aunt, a sleeping Nazia in her arms. Asif opened the door, filling its frame, and, without acknowledging Saba, he went to take the child from her. Nazia woke and began to cry. She clung to Saba's neck, but Asif pulled her off, uncurling her small fingers one by one. Saba watched Nazia's terrified face disappear inside the house and wanted to go after her, but Mrs Choudhury stepped forward from the shadows of the hallway, talking loudly over Nazia's screams and blocking Saba's path. When Asif reappeared with the child Saba saw that she had snot smeared over one cheek and that her eyes were wide with fear.

Afterwards, when she described it to the police, Saba could not recall the order of events. She remembered moving forward, trying to take Nazia, but that Asif had pulled back. There was an argument between her uncle and aunt, Asif and his mother, the row flowing back and forth between the four of them. Asif flung out slurs – that he had a hundred women waiting to marry him, that Saba was a shameful wife and mother, that it would be better if he took the child and returned to Bangladesh to find a new wife to raise her properly. Then, somehow, he was walking towards his car. Saba ran after him, but the latch of the gate had caught when Asif slammed it. She saw him put Nazia in her seat before getting in to the car himself. *Had he planned this?* she wondered. Had he got Nazia's passport? Had he got his own? Was this the last time she would ever see her daughter? The latch on the gate finally gave way and Saba flew across the road, her aunt and uncle behind her. She reached the car and banged on the glass of the window with her open hand, over and over. Nazia, seeing her, reached out her arms. When the car began to move, Saba ran alongside it, her hand still on the window, but then it accelerated off and out of her reach, turned the corner and was gone.

The police found Asif two hours later, parked a few streets away. Saba never found out why. Maybe he had planned to go somewhere with Nazia but something had gone wrong – he never explained. Saba realized then that it would always be like this. She and Nazia were Asif's belongings, his chattels, to do with as he wished, and he had seen her this way since the day they married. The police decided to take no further action; it was a domestic matter and he had not broken the law, they said, but she should apply to the court for an order. Without it they could not guarantee that next time she would get her child back so quickly.

Saba's uncle and aunt stopped pressurizing her to return to Asif. His mother refused to give back her passport, so Saba and Nazia settled back into their home, for she had no other form of identification with which to apply for benefits or housing. Then one day a large manila envelope came through the door, filled with papers. Saba's uncle looked grave as he told Saba what it said. It was from Asif: he had made his own application to the court, asking it to take Nazia from Saba and place their daughter in his care.

Asif made his application in his local court, despite the fact that Saba and Nazia were living many miles away. It was months before the application came before a judge, who confirmed it had been made in the wrong place. Applications should be heard by the child's home court, he said, and sent the case south. And that was how Saba found herself in the corridor of Reading Magistrates' Court waiting for me and about to do the bravest thing she had ever done.

The fact I could not cover Saba's first hearing turned out not to matter. No interpreter had been booked for her and Asif failed to turn up at all. The directions hearing was adjourned for a further six weeks and, by the time I found myself walking over mulched leaves on the way to court, autumn had slipped into winter. Reading Magistrates' Court is an ugly, red-brick building, part of which is given over to the family court in which magistrates hear a variety of cases. I climbed up the handful of steps into the waiting room of the family court, which was empty except for Saba and a man whom the usher said was our interpreter. They were sitting apart from one another and it seemed they had not spoken. After introducing myself to Saba and showing her to a conference room, I went back to speak to him. He stood, gracefully. His hair was streaked with bolts of silver and his full moustache, combed and oiled and set upon a kind face, was greying. Later, in the conference room, I discovered he had the gift of quietness, of taking up no room. When he spoke his words seemed an extension of Saba's and the flow between them became so natural that, by the end of our conference, neither Saba nor I looked at him while we waited for his translation of her words.

Saba, possibly relieved at last to have found a way of speaking, told me everything. She talked about her marriage, arranged by both families, and her descent into invisibility in a country she did not know and was unable to understand. She told me how afraid she was of Asif's mother, who, as a widow, was entirely dependent on her only son. His sisters were married and had moved in with their husbands' families, so the burden of maintaining the family was Asif's alone.

When she had finished, I began to set out the court process for her. I watched her horror as she realized she must tell her story all over again in court. The words would be written down into a statement, I explained, and – because all family proceedings were in a civil court rather than a criminal one – the magistrates would treat this statement as her evidence. But then she would have to stand up, take her oath and be questioned on its contents in court. Tested, challenged, asked to give details and specifics, told that she was wrong, told that she was lying. And she would have to do all that with Asif in the room, watching her. She had not told her uncle and aunt everything that had happened, she said, nor her parents. They would say that these were private matters, to be dealt with in the community, not for the ears of strangers. She was terrified of the consequences of disgracing her husband in public and the impact of this dishonour. I understood, I said – thinking, *how could I?* – but the

Children and Family Court Advisory and Support Service (CAFCASS) officer had written a letter to the court saying that Saba had left her husband because of his violence. The officer, I told her, had made it clear that before the court could decide where Nazia should live it must determine whether or not this violence had taken place. This was the system, and there was no escaping it.

The CAFCASS officer was concerned about Asif's abduction of Nazia and had recommended that her passport be held by the court until the final decision was made, in light of the fact that Bangladesh was a non-Hague Convention country. What this meant, I explained as gently as I could, was that if Asif did take Nazia to Bangladesh, it could be very hard to get her back. I looked at Saba sitting opposite me in silence and thought how frail she seemed, like a trapped bird. We would go into court, I said, and I would tell the magistrates that Saba contested Asif's application and wanted Nazia to live with her. I would confirm that there had been no contact between father and daughter, as Saba was too frightened that Asif would try to take Nazia again. And I would tell them yes, Saba had made allegations of domestic violence, and yes, she wished to pursue them.

'If he disputes the allegations, the magistrates will order a finding of fact hearing,' I said carefully, sliding my file towards me. 'This is a hearing where we need to prove that what you allege is more likely to have happened than not. Then, after the contested hearing, the magistrate will order a full CAFCASS report to decide what impact the findings have on Asif's application.' I stood up, watching her. 'I know it's very, very difficult, but I promise I will try to make it as easy as I can. Lots of breaks and things.'

Lots of breaks, I thought, as I went to find Asif's barrister. What use was that? If this were a criminal case, any allegations of domestic abuse would have been given in a private room to a police officer carefully trained to deal with them. Saba's evidence would have been recorded and, during any ensuing trial, she would need never to be in the same room as Asif. The witness room is usually kept far away from the courtroom to ensure a complainant's and a defendant's paths cannot accidentally cross. Her cross-examination would take place via a video link or, if she wanted – as some complainants do – to see the jury and for the jury to see her, so that she can look them in the eye and say *Please believe me: I am telling the truth* – then a screen could be placed around the witness box, shielding her from Asif's view. This means that, unlike in a family case, when she gives evidence about the violence to which she says he subjected her, she does not have to see him glare, unblinking, at her, or silently run a finger across his throat.

So too, were this a criminal case involving a defendant accused of domestic abuse who was representing himself, all questions put to Saba in the courtroom would come through the mouth of a lawyer. Such a defendant is, by law, prohibited from asking the questions of his alleged victim himself. Instead a barrister is instructed by the court to cross-examine on his behalf. I know – because I have done it – that to be summoned to court by a judge to cross-examine a witness with questions that are not your own is an odd experience. But it is nothing next to the horror of watching, as I have also done, women in the family court forced to withstand questions that challenge their allegations of violence – physical, mental and sexual – asked by the very person they say has perpetrated it. Restrictions on legal aid have meant regularly arriving at the family court to find my opponent is a litigant in person – representing himself – and I then have to return to my conference room to warn my client gently that, if she wishes to pursue her allegations of domestic violence to a contested hearing, she must understand this will involve the unthinkable prospect of being cross-examined by the person she fears most in the world.

There is little practical difference between a fact-finding hearing in a family case and a criminal trial, except one. My family clients are not witnesses in their case; they are parties to it. They are parties even if they did not make the application or want to come to court. They are able and entitled to have a momentary shield for the purposes of giving evidence, but how can this help them when, in the time it takes to get to that point, they will have been forced to wait in the same queue into court, sit in the same waiting room, eat in the same canteen and sit in the same courtroom, along the same bench, from the person they accuse of abusing them? It may be that the only solace in this experience comes when the court believes their version over their abuser's. But when the judge or magistrates find my client's allegations proved and she folds herself into my arms like a child after a nightmare, or when I stand as a human shield as my opponent knocks over chairs, or throws jugs of water, or rages at the unfairness of it all, it can feel a hollow victory. It is all too easy for the law and lawyers to loop around and over a litigant in person, even when trying not to. Advocacy is not an art form; it can be learned, but too often in these cases I watch my opponent stumble through papers, emotion and frustration fogging their mind. Then they sit down, defeated and confused, knowing they will later remember all the questions they wished they'd asked. After it has finished I am left with the overwhelming sense that, even if I believe my client's evidence to be true, the hearing was not a just or equal one – and that, as far as I am concerned, means that everyone has lost.

*

I found Asif's barrister in the advocates' room, on her phone. She waved me over.

'Sorry, sorry, just on the phone to my sols. Client's not coming, I'm afraid.'

I weighed it up. This would be the second unsuccessful hearing in a row and the magistrates would not like it, but I also knew that any delay would work in Saba's favour. The longer the period since the last contact between Nazia and Asif, the more careful the court would be about reintroducing it. They were unlikely to find another hearing slot for many weeks and the time would enable Saba to regroup: to find her strength, to continue learning how to live alone. This would serve her well if, in many months' time, she were forced to convince a court that she could raise Nazia by herself.

'Any reason why not?' I asked, as she finished the call.

She looked embarrassed. 'He's buggered off to Bangladesh. A holiday, apparently. Obviously I read the solicitors the riot act for not telling him he couldn't go. They gave me his number, so I've spoken to him and have instructions. I've told him the court's not going to allow contact to start without a fact finding, given that he disputes everything your lady is saying. So – we might as well just go ahead and order statements and get it listed, agreed?'

I arched an eyebrow but said I did, then returned to the conference room to tell Saba that Asif was not coming and watched her shoulders drop in relief.

As the printer poured out hot pages, I fanned them out on the table. Saba and Asif had both filed witness statements, his in reply to hers, and behind each one lay another, translated into Bengali, its lyrical script jarring against the brutality of its subject. There was also a Scott Schedule: a table of columns listing Saba's allegations and Asif's response – a catalogue of suffering, boxed into black and white. The schedule ran over two pages and I scanned through it, realizing with irritation that Saba's unwieldy statement seemed to have been replicated verbatim within the schedule by the solicitors. There is no limit to the number of allegations a party can make against the other, but often solicitors will pick the most serious, taking the view that the court has limited time. That decision, however, is hard to explain to the person for whom all violations have felt far from minor. There is a temptation to put everything in and let the barrister in court field the temper of a furious judge who says they cannot possibly get through all the allegations in the time allocated – that they must be halved, there and then, much to the despair of a client who has prepared herself to face the lot.

I read through Asif's column in reverse order: *denied, denied, denied.* Then I got to the top, to the very first allegation. It was the smallest of them all: *Tore up the respondent mother's book.* Asif's response: *agreed.* In his witness statement he had given no explanation or account except that he did not like the fact that his wife had a note from another man. There was no repentance or regret: it seemed he had thought little of it. And in that moment I knew he could be caught. In that one casual admission Asif had betrayed what he thought about Saba. Her belongings, her past, her present and her future were his to do with as he wished – to control through violence and fear and, if he felt like it, to destroy. He knew he should not have beaten her, so he denied it, knowing it was her word against his. But for him the destruction of his wife's favourite thing was reasonable, given that it now belonged to him, because she did too and he saw no issue with admitting it. As I looked at the page I was furiously glad that the solicitors had not edited this allegation out as they so easily might have done, for Asif's admission would – I hoped – be the one that undid him.

Saba sat in the witness box, her eyes fixed somewhere beyond me in the corner of the room. The radiators clanked, trying to pump out heat, but the courtroom still felt cold. In the witness box Saba seemed even slighter than usual. I glanced to my right and looked at Asif sitting next to his barrister. His eyes were fixed on Saba. The interpreter stood silently beside the witness box, wearing his usual pressed tweed suit. I wondered if I should ask him to put the question to her again. *You have alleged that your husband raped you – when did this first start?* Then Saba looked straight at me, fixed me with large eyes, and began to cry. I glanced at the magistrates, wondering if I should urge a break, but was interrupted by the interpreter. His voice was strained.

'Your Worships, I must say this. I am finding it hard to exactly translate her answers.' He paused and drew from his breast pocket a handkerchief, which he passed quickly over his face. He looked towards the magistrates and I noticed his expression had changed. He seemed to be struggling for the right words. 'In truth, Your Worships, it is not in our culture for a woman to speak to a man of these things, to speak of these things to a stranger. I think she is finding it hard to tell me everything, to give the details she is being asked for.'

For the briefest moment he glanced at Asif and then away again, expressionless. I wondered what he thought. Did he condemn Asif for the way he was accused of treating his wife, or did he disapprove of Saba talking about such private things in public? He spoke again, breaking the silence. 'And there are also, you see, many things she has said which I cannot properly interpret. She has told us of being pulled from her prayer mat by her hair. But the word she has used to describe how she felt has no direct translation: she was ashamed, but also he broke her prayers and so she felt she had offended her god. The way he did it, by her hair, means more in our culture than yours.'

Before the magistrates could respond, Saba began to speak and, almost without pause, the interpreter switched back into her voice, drawing us into the horror of her marriage.

When she had finished her evidence it was Asif's turn. He was wearing dark blue jeans and his stomach bulged against the buttons of his white shirt. Together with his clothes, his accent – of Bradford, not Bangladesh – made him seem a world apart from Saba. Watching him give evidence after Saba I could see only the gulf between them, and his advantage over her.

In cross-examination his denials were short. Saba, he said, had simply made it all up. Then he added, almost as an after-thought, something that made me pause. Saba's family, he said, had told him many times that she wanted to return to him, but they kept pushing the date of a reconciliation back. And so instead he had decided he must come to court. And in that moment I saw what Asif's case was really about and rebuked myself for not having seen it before. Asif's application was not about his daughter – it was about Saba and his control over her. He could not, by law, force Saba to live with him, but he could ask the court to give him Nazia, knowing that, if it did, Saba would surely follow. She would not be without her child, and Asif knew it.

'Why did you rip up the book, Mr Choudhury?'

'It had a note in it, to my wife, from another man. Like, a love note. I wasn't going to have that.'

'The note was written before you met?'

'Yes. But she was my wife now, wasn't she?'

'And so when you married, what was hers became yours?'

'Yes. That's how it is in our culture.'

'To do with as you wished?'

'It's natural. She knows and I know what her role as a wife is.'

'A page of the book offended you, so you tore the whole thing up?'

'I've already admitted that, haven't I?'

'Her book, her possessions, her body, her freedom – they all belonged to you . . .'

'Look, it's different. Islamically, the wife has only duty for her husband, whether she does it willingly or not.'

Click. Got him.

I watched carefully as the magistrates filed back into the courtroom and took their seats. They had been deliberating for nearly two hours and I was nervous that my confidence had been misplaced. Unlike a jury, who are prone to scowl or nod and smile during a case, most magistrates have learned to adopt a mask of professional objectivity. Very rarely do they give any sign that they will find in your favour, but experience and observation have taught me that there is a silent language – a lightness to the face, a twitch, the slightest tip of a head to one side – which hints at agreement. There is one similarity I have found between juror and magistrate. If either is prepared to look at my client as they walk back into the courtroom to give their verdict – to meet their eyes with an open face – then I know we are safe. That afternoon, as the magistrates settled themselves in their chairs, they looked towards Saba and all three of them smiled.

After they had declared that they found each allegation proved, the lead magistrate looked directly at Saba. Saba

Choudhury, she said, had offered little independent evidence in support of her allegations. However, her cultural background, her lack of English, and the bullying and oppressive atmosphere in her family home would have made it exceedingly difficult to confide in anyone about the abuse she had suffered. When questioned at length about the allegations she had answered all that was asked of her, despite her obvious distress. The magistrates found that Saba had been brave and honest. Her evidence, and the way in which she had given it, ensured that they were more than satisfied she had told the truth about what she had been subjected to at the hands of her husband.

I glanced at Asif, but he was staring straight ahead. Later, after the hearing had finished, he strode from the courtroom. Saba, the interpreter and I then swung open the doors to discover Asif had already gone. Although I did not know it then, that day would be the last time I ever saw him.

Saba stood before me in the empty corridor as I checked that she had the date for the forthcoming directions hearing, at which the magistrates would decide what should happen next. She did not look at me as the interpreter translated my words, and I wondered if she understood what had just happened. Then, without warning, she staggered backwards on to a chair, put both hands over her face, and wept.

As I walked from court to the railway station in the late spring afternoon, I pictured the noble face of the interpreter and wondered what he felt, and then remembered the case of Mr Begum and Mr Khan. I wondered if I had been wrong. Maybe, in fact, the law is about more than words and language and weaving a clever argument from the pages of a law book. Maybe it is about more than being able to tell a good story. For, at its heart, the law is about humanity. It is about the thousand little flecks of perception and judgement that spin through the air in a courtroom, across language and class and gender. It is the reason we do not try cases on paper alone, but instead insist on holding up living, breathing flesh, and testing each side with equal strength. And, when we do that and we do it well, I believe that, more often than not, justice is done.

Six weeks later, I arrived at court for the directions hearing. It was, I realized, almost exactly two years since Saba had been rescued from her marriage. I saw Asif's barrister coming out of the advocates' room towards me, her face full of apology. She had just been told, she said, that her client had gone back to Bangladesh. She couldn't get to the bottom of it, nor could she get a date for Asif's return. She realized that without instructions she had to come off record. She would make the application and leave me to it. She raised both her hands, palms up, and rolled her eyes.

Saba and I sat alongside one another in a conference room. Over our shoulders the interpreter translated the new CAF-CASS letter, which had been filed with the court the day before. The letter was blunt. In light of the findings of fact, contact between Nazia and her father should remain suspended until a full CAFCASS report could be done. The court should strongly consider making a Residence Order in Saba's favour to ensure that she was protected in case Asif tried to take Nazia a second time. I put down the letter and told Saba not to worry – Asif was not coming today. He was back in Bangladesh.

Saba looked at me with an expression I could not read. 'He is in Bangladesh?' she asked, in English.

'Yes.'

'He want a divorce. He go to find a new wife,' she said, quietly.

I did not know what to say. If that were true then surely it was a good thing – now Asif would leave her alone. I looked up at the interpreter.

'She is ashamed, I think.' His voice was kind. 'She is afraid of embarrassing her family. She is afraid that no one else will want her now.'

I looked back to Saba, who held my gaze for a moment then reached down to her bag and drew out several large envelopes. They had been sent by Asif – pages from a sari catalogue, the women torn in two. In broken English and translated Bengali she explained that a torn sari represented dishonour. She had, by talking about their marriage, dishonoured Asif and he wanted her to know it. She had not thought he would come to court that day, nor that he would come any other day. He had been humiliated by her and had told her family she was no good. He did not want her any more. He wanted a divorce. She was worried about Nazia, about her not having a father, but feared that because she was a girl she mattered less to Asif than had she been his son. For him it was never about being a father; it was about owning them. If he couldn't then he was not interested. But if the court could force Asif's mother to release her passport, then Saba could start to build a new life for herself in this country with the support of her uncle and aunt. She could not go back to Bangladesh, not now. Not with the shame of divorce encircling her.

We went into court and I told the magistrates of Asif's request for a divorce, of his harassment of Saba, and of her suspicion about why he was now back in Bangladesh. The magistrates granted my request for a Residence Order in Saba's favour and decided that the onus to bring the matter back to court must now lie with Asif. If he did not do so within three months, his application would be dismissed. Saba's passport must, they said, be handed over to her solicitors immediately.

In the crowded waiting room outside court I said goodbye to Saba. Then I turned and shook the interpreter's hand, thanking him for his help, and noticed the slim elegance of his fingers, his skin smooth and cool. I felt suddenly overwhelmed with gratitude for what he had done and how he had done it. The two left the courthouse together as I packed up my bags, and I waved them goodbye, but I was walking to the station in the same direction and I soon caught up with them. They were winding their way through the weekday market, past the stalls full of early Christmas decorations. Something made me slow my pace and lag behind to watch. Saba's frame was slight against the swell of shoppers around her, but she seemed, despite her obvious difference from everyone else, entirely within herself in a way I had not noticed before. The interpreter was wearing the same tweed suit, immaculately pressed, with seams running down the front and back of his legs in the manner of my grandfather. I could see that they were talking by the way their heads inflected towards each other, and then I saw Saba turn to him in response to something he had said. There was something in the way she dipped her head that made me stop walking and leave them alone as they carried on without me, unaware I was watching them, until, eventually, they were swallowed by the crowd.

4

Raymond

Bournemouth Crown Court

Theft Act 1968
Section 9 – Burglary

(1) A person is guilty of burglary if—...
    *(b) having entered any building or part of a
    building as a trespasser he steals or attempts to
    steal anything in the building or that part of it or
    inflicts or attempts to inflict on any person
    therein any grievous bodily harm.*

M ANDY WHITE's breathing was noisy. She groaned and puffed as she bent her large bulk against the wheeled frame she was pushing. The usher hovered behind her, his arms slightly outstretched as though to catch her if she fell. In a moment of excruciating farce, the pair attempted to man-oeuvre the contraption around the corner of the bench where I and the prosecutor sat, trying not to look. Mandy White moved the frame forwards and backwards in slight increments within the narrow space, before a final rough shove allowed it to pass through. The usher then guided her to the chair which had been placed at the bottom of the witness box. Mandy White, we had already been told, would not be able to climb up the small steps to the witness box. She sat down heavily, letting go of the frame, and the usher, visibly relieved that the ordeal was over, pushed it to one side of the courtroom. Now she was seated before us, I allowed myself to study her properly for the first time. She was extremely large and her age was hard to guess – she could have been anything from forty to sixty, with a face that mapped life's hardships in its lines. Her skin was florid, worsened by the hennaed redness of her short-cropped hair. A roll of pallid flesh had escaped between her top and the waist of her leggings and I found myself transfixed by it. To reveal herself in this way seemed a painfully intimate thing to do and I wondered whether she was unaware of the exposure, or too embarrassed to readjust her clothing, or whether she simply did not care.

The judge leaned down over his bench and urged Mandy

to ask for breaks if she needed them or if she was uncomfortable. She stared back at him with an expression somewhere between nonchalance and surprise. I glanced to my right, watching the jury as they took her in. They had just heard the prosecutor's opening speech and were now able to fit Mandy's face into the silhouette of victim. Now they could imagine her fear as my twenty-one-year-old client, Raymond Baker, and his seventeen-year-old sister, Daniella, barged their way into Mandy's ground-floor flat on the estate where she lived. They could visualize how frightened she must have been when the intruders loomed over her, fists raised, yelling at her of gangs and guns and what they would do if she did not comply. They could picture her face as my client threw her mobile phone into the corner so she could not call for help; how terrified she must have looked as her flat was ransacked until, at last, they found something they wanted – a DVD player – and, with a violent warning, left. The jury could also now picture Mandy waiting helplessly until she was sure she was alone before slowly making her way across the floor to pick up her phone and call the police. I watched as a few of the jurors glanced to the back of the courtroom where my client sat in the dock, alone. The jury knew why he was sitting there without a co-defendant by his side, because the prosecutor had just told them. His sister and co-accused, Daniella, had already pleaded guilty to the charge of domestic burglary. She had admitted it and, in doing so, had admitted that the prosecution's case was true. When the jury heard this I had watched a shadow pass over their faces and known what they were thinking: if one of them has already admitted it how can the other possibly deny it? I knew this because, up until that morning, I had thought the same.

*

Bournemouth Crown Court is a large, long building with a lot of glass, slightly resembling a provincial airport. It was built within the unlikely triangle of a golf course, a regional hotel and a hospital, although the route to the court building, along bouncy tarmac with a row of mini-roundabouts, feels more like the entrance to a retail park. The cost of taking a train and taxi to this court is often equivalent to a hearing fee and so, enticed by the unusual privilege of a free car park, I usually drive instead. The six-hour round trip from London takes longer than the train, but I compensate for the loss of preparation time while on a motorway by rehearsing cross-examination and closing speeches out loud to the passing cars, scrawling corrections in my notebook in traffic jams and at red lights.

Four months before Raymond's trial began I was standing in Bournemouth Crown Court's robing room looking out of the window. It was mid-autumn. An Indian summer had stretched on long after the leaves had begun to fall and the weather was warm. The sky was mottled with clouds, puffy white against the blue, like a baby's mobile. On the table in front of me was the slim bundle of papers for Raymond's plea and case management hearing in court that morning. On top of them was the document I had prepared for the court setting out Raymond's defence, even though I doubted that the matter would ever get as far as a trial. The evidence against him was so strong that Raymond clearly had to plead guilty, I thought as I walked over to the mirror by the robing-room bathroom and took off my suit jacket. The courthouse heating appeared to be controlled by month rather than temperature and the robing room, busy with barristers getting ready for their cases, felt stale and close despite its size. Breaching unspoken protocol, I had worn a trouser rather than a skirt suit so that I did not have to suffer the heat of tights. My fitted T-shirt meant that the starched white collarette

I wore in court fitted far better than had I worn a shirt, but the act of undressing in front of everyone – of taking off my jacket to fix the bib into place – always felt exposing. I shot a look in the mirror at the collection of barristers, all men, strewn around the room and I wondered if any would watch as my arms reached upwards to fasten the Velcro at the back of my neck or, worse, whether any – as had happened one unbearable morning – would go so far as to offer unwanted help. I willed them to ignore me and made the motion as quick as I could before my jacket and gown restored my equality.

I had given Raymond and Daniella's case little thought that morning. I was due to appear in two other matters, all listed at the same time, all in different courts. As soon as I arrived I tried to find the clerk in each of the three courts – to beg leniency and to persuade them to check that I had finished in one case before they called the other on. One of the hearings was straightforward: a bail application by the defence, which I was prosecuting. I had already collected the papers from the Crown Prosecution's room on the way up to the robing room that morning and reasoned that, at least from what I had seen, the defence's application was a hopeless one. The defendant was a drug dealer. A week after his release from prison he was found on his usual corner by the police, who promptly chased him down the road. As he ran, small wraps of crack cocaine fell from his trouser leg in a narcotic paper-trail, but when he was caught the defendant improbably claimed he knew nothing of them. He said that the three pairs of underwear he was wearing were not, as the police suggested, to hide his drugs, but were in fact protection against the possibility of being kicked in the balls. My other case involved the defence of a client equally committed to his innocence in the face of overwhelming evidence against him. A middle-aged businessman accused of a complicated fraud, he was, I knew, determined to fight it all the way to trial. Like others I have represented charged with similar offences, he was difficult to deal with. Convinced of his superior intellect, it was clear he was sure he could outwit the court as he thought he had outwitted the police. He would slip and slide around my challenges with convoluted explanations and a smug confidence designed to deflect. It was an exhausting process and meant I would struggle to have enough time with Raymond. But, I reasoned, Raymond's was a straightforward burglary – a young guy and his sister, both with criminal records, up against a disabled middle-aged lady. They had no alibi for the afternoon. My client had been interviewed twice: once at home and afterwards at the police station, whereupon he changed his story – correcting his denial of ever going to Mandy's flat once he knew his fingerprints had been found all over it. He must surely see that he should plead guilty, I thought; it would be madness not to. Usually I would have sought out my co-defending barrister – worked out what she was doing – but she had not yet signed in and I had no time to go to find her. I reasoned I would catch her just before we went into court and hoped she felt the same.

I was trapped for most of the morning with my fraud client and so did not manage to meet Raymond until shortly before his hearing was due to start. He was sitting on one of the spongy blue chairs arranged along the corridor wall and raised his hand like a schoolboy in class when I called his name. I had not expected him to be so slight. His shoulders folded over into his chest and his legs were splayed at an awkward angle, as though his physicality was an inconvenience to him. He was, in truth, already barely visible. The sort of person easily missed, easily passed over. Had he knocked past you on the street, you would have been at a loss to describe him. Early twenties perhaps. Black-skinned, medium height, a slightly built boy with buzz-cut hair.

I sat beside him, perched on the edge of the seat so as not to sink into its soft middle, conscious that I appeared impatient. In truth, I needed him to be quick, to keep up. My other client was in a conference room opposite and was annoyed I had another case, seeing it as a mark of disrespect.

I went quickly through the offence. To make out that the crime was burglary, I explained, the prosecution needed to prove that Raymond had both trespassed and stolen goods. I summarized the evidence quickly, flicking through the statements and interview. Then I pulled out the defence case statement I had drafted. Was this *really* his defence, I asked him? That the two siblings had gone to Mandy's address because she had sent them a text message asking them to come, and she had simply offered up the DVD player in lieu of money she owed them? Raymond nodded.

'So, why did she owe you money?' I asked.

'My mum had lent it to her,' Raymond replied, 'and I was collecting it.'

'Great. Will your mother come to court to say that, then?'

Raymond puffed out his cheeks. 'No way. She doesn't like the law. I'm not likely to get her to come here.'

I hesitated, wondering whether to push the point but deciding it would be a waste of time. I flicked through the interview, finding the part I needed. 'Your fingerprints were found in the flat,' I said. 'And you say that's because your mum cleaned for Mandy sometimes and you went to help?'

'That's right,' Raymond replied.

'So why did you lie in your first interview and say you had never been to her flat before?' I glanced up at the court clock hanging on the corridor wall.

77

'I was scared,' he said, staring at his hands. 'I was at home and I didn't want the law to arrest me. I just wanted him to go. To leave me alone. It was stupid.'

'Scared? Why would you be scared? Because you thought you'd done something wrong?' I asked and he shrugged. I drew a breath.

'Do you still have your telephone – to prove that Mandy texted you, asked you to come over?' Raymond, still looking down, muttered that he'd lost it. I did not believe him. He was wasting my time, I thought, feeling the fury of my other client boring through the closed door opposite. Barristers burst through the courtroom's double doors as the tannoy boomed out Raymond's and Daniella's names. Too late, I thought, too late. We're on.

'Here, sign this.' I thrust the defence statement at him. Raymond took the pen I handed him and wrote his signature at the bottom of the page in a childish, looping script. I stood up and beckoned him to follow, rattling through my advice as we walked towards the doors. *Credit for a guilty plea: a third off any sentence. The closer to trial, the less credit you get. A disabled victim would be an aggravating factor. Not a good picture in court. Called the police straight afterwards. Plenty of evidence. Criminal record.* And so on, and so on. Raymond listened blankly, then, as we paused outside the court, he looked at me.

'I didn't take it. I didn't. She gave it to me. Honestly.'

Part of me was relieved. I hated the scramble of pressure, the lingering doubt over whether I had properly advised, properly listened. 'Fine,' I said. I pushed open the swinging doors and lowered my voice. 'You must only plead guilty to something you have done. If you say you haven't done it then we must have a trial. When they ask you for your plea you say "Not guilty." All right?'

As we walked into court I felt someone come in behind us.

It was Daniella with her barrister. The siblings acknowledged one another briefly as they waited for the dock officer. He ambled towards them, overweight and cheerful, unlocked the dock and motioned for them to take their seats as though he were showing them their way in a theatre. I turned towards Daniella's barrister, standing to my left.

'Sorry, I couldn't find you!' she said. 'Here – I've done a form.' With thanks, I took the long form we had to complete and hand in if our client intended to plead not guilty. 'Look,' she went on, 'I'm just covering the case for the trial barrister. She's going *not guilty* – for now, anyway. I haven't done a defence statement. I'll ask for time to file one, but let's just say I suspect she may soon have a change of heart . . .'

I nodded and hustled towards the front of the court, waiting for the barristers in the case before us to leave. The prosecutor had a stack of files on the bench in front of him and I watched him shuffle one set of papers to the bottom and reach for the next on the pile. Sensing I was watching him, he glanced over in my direction inquisitorially. 'Not guilty,' I mouthed and shook my head to reinforce the statement. He gave a nod of acknowledgment. I handed him a copy of my defence case statement and he scanned it, blankly. His involvement in the case was unlikely to go beyond today and he therefore needed to know only the minimum of detail. Squeezing behind him, I took my place on his right and began in haste to fill out my parts on the form my co-defendant counsel had handed me. Two sharp raps then sounded as the usher cried 'All rise!' and we scrambled to our feet as the judge strode in.

A month after the hearing an email appeared from Daniella's trial barrister. Not recognizing his name, I looked him up. He was older than me, dark-haired and smiling. He looked good fun: the sort of person it would be entertaining to do a trial alongside. The sort of person whose clients liked the easy assurance of the fact that he looked like, sounded like, acted like a legacy of criminal barristers they knew from page and screen. The email was friendly, polite, but I knew what he meant by it. He thought their account was ridiculous, laughable even, and he had arranged for his solicitor to meet his client, and her mother, and take some *sensible instructions*. It was a warning, I knew that much. Daniella was going to be told she should plead guilty. If she did, Raymond would be left to have a trial alone, and what hope did he have of convincing the jury that he had not committed the crime if his own sister had admitted they did it? I did not want to gain a reputation as someone who does not advise their client properly or tell them when the evidence against them is strong and they are likely to be convicted. The trial definitely wouldn't go ahead now, I thought, relieved I had been liberated from the humiliating prospect of calling a disabled woman a liar. I tapped my confident reply: all we needed was one of our clients to plead guilty first, and the other would surely follow.

A month after I sent my email, Daniella stood in court and changed her plea to guilty at a hearing listed for the purpose. She did so alone, for Raymond, my solicitors told me, had not changed his mind. And that was how, six weeks later, Raymond's name appeared alone on the screen outside court. He was going to have his trial, with or without Daniella by his side.

That morning I found Raymond waiting outside the courtroom. Several other hearings had been listed in front of our trial and so we had some time. I took him down to a quieter space at the end of the corridor, where we sat alongside one another and again went through the evidence. As he answered my questions, Raymond began to fill in his story with colour. He knew Mandy, he said. He and Daniella would go over to her flat, sometimes with his mum, sometimes not. Mandy had Raymond's phone number – she had texted Raymond asking him to come to the flat and take something in lieu of a debt she owed his mother. She had left the door open for them, invited them in, chatted to them. She showed them where the DVD player was kept and made sure they took the right cable to go with it. She even offered them a bag to carry it home. I frowned as I looked at the notes I had prepared for the trial. A DVD player was the oddest thing to have taken: cumbersome, heavy, not easy to get rid of, worth – should they sell it on – about £20. As well as this, they had found it in a cardboard box in Mandy White's wardrobe, in her bedroom right at the back of her flat. I looked at Raymond, trying to weigh him up. I could not shake the feeling that there was another story lying behind the one I was being told. This other story might just save him, if only I could work it out.

'Raymond,' I asked, 'if what you say is true, why did Daniella plead guilty?'

Raymond stared down at the blue carpet in the corridor. 'Her barrister told her she had to. Told her that the evidence was really strong. He said her record was so long that if she was convicted she'd definitely go down. Said this was the only way she'd stay out of prison, if she pleaded guilty, because she's still a youth and everything.'

I flushed. These were the words Daniella had repeated to Raymond and I doubted they were what the friendly dark-haired barrister had actually said, but the sense of it must have been there. And it was true. Daniella's record was far worse than Raymond's. Mostly petty theft, it was scattered with enough incidents of drug possession, light violence and public disorder to mean that a prison sentence was soon inevitable. Despite being four years older, Raymond had only one previous conviction: a shoplifting offence on 24 December a few years ago. Had I looked at the date properly before I asked him the details, I could have guessed his explanation and spared him the embarrassment of admitting that his mother had no money for a Christmas tree and so, for her, he had stolen one.

'Sarah Langford?'

The voice startled me. It was deep and assured, and I immediately recognized it as belonging to Stanley Sharp, the prosecutor. He stood over me as the court traffic of barristers and defendants and police flashed past behind him. He was one of a collection of well-known figures on circuit, part of a cohort of men who swelled the corridors and robing rooms with jokes and teasing and swagger. I knew him, of course, although he did not recognize me.

'Yes, hi, hello.' I rose and stood, matching him in height. I suspected from the unmarked papers under his arm, still neatly tied up in pink ribbon, that he had done little by way of preparation for the trial; that he had thought there was no need, such was the weight of evidence against my client. 'Can we have a word?' He motioned with his head in the direction of the robing room further down the corridor.

We did not go in. I stood alongside the keypad to the door as Stanley leaned back against the wall. His demeanour was of someone used to getting his own way, who knew his superior age and status was an advantage in a situation like this and was working out how hard he should press it. He did not want to waste three days on a petty burglary trial when he could be off doing weightier and better-paid matters. And we both knew it.

'Are we *really* going to have a trial on this?' Stanley asked conspiratorially. 'I mean, not to put too fine a point on it, your client's defence is a pile of shit. The sister's pleaded – you *did* know that, right?'

I nodded, conscious that there was little point in going through the weaknesses of the prosecution's case in response. At best I would just sound plaintive; at worst I would give Stanley a chance to work out how to mend the holes. But his confidence pressed on a nagging doubt. Maybe my sense that there was something to Raymond's story was entirely misplaced – nothing but naïve wishful thinking. Like most of those who are self-employed, I am required to learn to trust my judgement. In my first few years at the Bar I would spend journeys home from court running a case over in my mind like a film reel. Would someone else have lost? Would someone else have won? Would someone else have called that witness? Would someone else have asked that question? Experience had given me confidence and taught me assurance so that, by the time I represented Raymond, I did trust my instinct. But this did not mean that, faced with the displeasure of a senior barrister who was making it clear he thought I was being a fool, I did not doubt my decision and my abilities.

I knew I must continue to be affable and underwhelming, to flap my hands and roll my eyes at my client's stubbornness, for it was unhelpful to get a reputation as someone tricky, prickly or difficult. I assured Stanley I had tried everything, but that my client just *would not budge*. It would be a speedy trial, I said, over in a flash. I batted away the prospect of a legal argument about Daniella's guilty plea – of course I would *have* to resist his application to tell the jury, but I knew that the judge would almost certainly allow it in. Easier, then, just to get on with things. Better not to spend hours leaning on my client to get a guilty plea only for him to change his mind when it came to his sentence and protest his innocence to anyone who would listen. And so Stanley was left muttering that he had better go and make sure the court was ready for his witness, because of the walking frame, and the special chair, and the many breaks required for numerous different medications, and I returned to Raymond and said that we were ready. We were going to have our trial.

Stanley rose to begin questioning Mandy White. I could tell that his confidence in Raymond's guilt had been bolstered by the sight of her. The jury, surely, had convicted Raymond as soon as they had seen her laborious entrance into the courtroom. Stanley held her witness statement aloft, one hand on his hip, leaning nonchalantly against the flipped-up chair behind him.

'So, Miss White, had you met Raymond Baker before that day?'

'Oh yes, lots of times.' Mandy's tone was warm. 'I know his younger sister. Nice girl. Does some shopping for me. They've both popped in once or twice for coffee or a glass of wine.'

The image of this woman sitting down with the two young defendants for coffee or wine in a tableau of easy recreation was ludicrous and I saw Stanley stiffen slightly, although he remained in pose. I wrote down her evidence and drew 'XX' in the notebook's margin to remind me to ask her about it in cross-examination. Stanley paused, then clearly decided not to press her on it for fear of what else she might say. He moved quickly on.

'And tell us, please, how the defendant . . .' he moved his hand from his hip, sweeping it towards the dock at the back of court as the jury followed its arc with their gaze '. . . came to be in your flat that day?'

I looked at Mandy's witness statement in front of me and

read again the line describing how Raymond and Daniella had forced their way through her door with howls of threatened violence.

'Well,' said Mandy, contemplatively, 'the door was ajar, see? To let in the fresh air. And so I can get in and out. Don't want to lock myself in, do I? I had my back to it, and I heard some noise and turned round to see them standing there, saying "Hello, Mandy, you owe us some money."'

Stanley cleared his throat and pushed himself upright from the seat. Well, that's your trespass gone, I thought, glancing over at him. He did not look back. 'But had you given them *permission* to come in, Miss White?' he said, urging her to give him the right answer by his emphasis.

'Well, no, but I was turned away when they came in, like. He was being a bit confrontational, was Raymond. I didn't owe him any money, I said. Then his sister said I would be in big trouble if I didn't pay up, and they weren't leaving until I handed it over. And then they made the threats and stuff. Then they started ransacking my wardrobe. Raymond took my phone and called someone, saying he was going to give them my address. I don't know who it was though.'

Stanley leaned forward and began quickly skimming through Mandy's witness statement. I knew he must be looking for the paragraph where she claimed that Raymond had thrown her phone across the room, meaning she was unable to call for help while they were there. I watched him find the paragraph, confirm that it said what he remembered, and weigh up whether to challenge her new evidence. He decided to leave it. 'And, um, did they find anything in the wardrobe, Miss White?'

'Well, they pulled out my clothes, and then some electrical cables, and then they grabbed the box with the DVD player in it and plonked it down on the table. Then they calmed down a bit. And after that, they left. After talking to someone on the phone. Not sure who. They just scootched off. I yelled "Where's my phone?" at them and Raymond threw it back at me, and then I called the police.'

There was a pause. I could feel the jury looking at Stanley, waiting for him to ask the next question, wondering at his delay. 'And, so, Miss White, what would you estimate the value of the DVD player to be?'

She sucked air through her teeth. 'Oh nothing really, they're so cheap nowadays. Twenty, twenty-five pounds or so, I reckon.'

I watched Stanley carefully. His face remained expressionless, but I knew his confidence in what Mandy was going to say next must have evaporated. The witness statement he held in his hand was, clearly, no real help. He cleared his throat again, asked Mandy a few questions about how she felt about the offence, then sat down heavily, a brief wave of his hand in my direction indicating he was offering her up to me.

As I stood to cross-examine Mandy I tried to read her face. As with all witnesses, I needed to anticipate how she would respond when I questioned her. Some prosecution witnesses can only ever see the defence barrister as the enemy. They feel they have to deny any assertion I put to them and that they must take any opportunity to repeat their case, thinking that they must not give an inch. They do not realize that this can, in fact, make them seem far from objective and reliable. Mandy had every reason to be hostile towards me – I was, after all, about to call her a liar, even if I could not say why she had lied. Not yet. But when she looked at me her flushed, worn face remained passive and open, and it occurred to me that, maybe, she was not used to being the centre of attention. It was quite possible that Mandy was also unused to the courtesy and kindness people had shown her during this experience, and that she was quite enjoying it all.

We began with the layout of her flat. It was, she said, long and thin with the bedroom at the back and hard to find. Yes, she told the court, quite proudly, she owned a number of valuable items. A laptop, her phone, a handful of silver frames, a bit of jewellery, a camera. All smaller and more valuable, she agreed, than a DVD player. She flatly denied owing Raymond money, although, unprompted, she said she may previously have lent some to him. And, as it happened, this too was £20. There were, she said, looking at the ceiling, other *unmentionable issues* on which she would not be drawn because they were, she considered, *not relevant*. But yes, there had been other occasions when she had willingly asked the two defendants in. I pressed her to explain. Mandy glanced coyly at the jury. They had a *minor social arrangement*, she said. That night, for example, Raymond and his sister had come in while she was eating supper. Then they had all sat down together and she had offered them a glass of wine.

I looked up from writing down her evidence in my notebook. 'Sorry, Miss White. I just want to make sure my note of your evidence is correct. You said – you and Raymond and Daniella all sat down at your table, together, that night, and you offered them some wine?'

'Yes, that's right. I usually have a bottle open somewhere. And then, you know, I would have had a puff of whatever, which we would have passed around between us.' She let out a small cough and shifted slightly in her chair.

And with a snap the piece clicked into place. I could not believe it had taken me so long to see it. Raymond was Mandy White's drug dealer. These two young people were spending time with this odd and lonely woman because they were selling her weed. If they had sat down together at her table it was not because of some incongruous friendship, nor out of kindness or sympathy, but because she was buying their gear. The unmentionables were drugs and the debt was a drug debt. And I knew it by Mandy's words. I had heard the phrasing so many times. *I would have had a puff of whatever. We would have passed it round.* Making the action sound theoretical when it was not, was a way of creating distance between someone's actions and the resulting guilt they felt. That was why Raymond was hiding something; why I had glimpsed another story shimmering in between the one he had told me. For him to tell the truth, he would have to admit a crime with which he had not been charged. I thought how well he had done to get to twenty-one without any convictions for drug possession or supply. This is hard to do if that is how you make your living. I wondered whether, if he had had convictions for drugs, I might have spotted the link sooner.

I looked across at Stanley Sharp, wondering if he too had realized the truth. He was sitting forward, his pen in his hand, his notebook open, although he had made few notes in it. Mandy – apparently oblivious to the repercussions of her words – went on to describe Raymond bringing the cardboard box from her bedroom through to her table. She agreed that she then helped them find the right lead for the DVD player from the box of tangled cords, because, she said, she did not want them left lying around afterwards. At this Stanley flipped his notebook shut and sat back heavily in his seat. I wondered if he would have thrown down his pen but for the stares of the jury following his every move. He glanced up at the clock and it seemed the judge noticed too.

'Miss Langford, we are approaching the end of the day. Do you have much more?'

No, I confirmed, I had all I needed. The judge nodded and said we would break overnight. Warning the jury not to speak to anyone about the case, nor to discuss it among themselves, he allowed them to file out of court. The usher returned to deliver Mandy's frame back to her and help navigate her back through the courtroom. Packing up my papers, I turned to say something to Stanley, but he was already shoving open the courtroom's swing doors, his gown billowing with the speed of his exit. On the bench behind me sat the police officer in the case. I had not noticed her before; she must have come in when I started cross-examining, I thought. I smiled at her, partly in greeting, partly in challenge. She shook her head, as though in recognition of the prosecution's defeat. The dock officer began, loudly, to unlock the door of the dock and the noise made us both turn and watch as Raymond stepped out of it.

'He's not a bad kid that one, really. Especially, you know, given who his mum is,' she said, still watching Raymond.

I looked at the police officer without responding, and she turned to face me. I could see from her expression that she had thought I knew more than I did and was now embarrassed to have said it.

'Who's his mum?' I asked, not caring that she clearly thought I should already know.

She looked at me evenly. 'Biggest dealer on their estate. Record as long as her arm. Anyway, I'd better, you know, go and find Mr Sharp . . .' She nodded towards the court door, backing away. She turned and as she walked past Raymond, who was waiting for me at the back of court, I noticed the two share a look as if they knew one another; as if they knew something I did not. The warm feeling of victory that had wrapped itself around me evaporated as I realized that, in my haste and confidence, the real truth had completely eluded me. I picked up my papers and walked over to Raymond.

'Look, we'll take a theft.'

It was the following morning, and Stanley Sharp and I were again standing by the robing-room door as other barristers brushed past us on their way in and out. Stanley had spent the last minute or so blustering through a speech that had seemed more for his benefit than mine. Of the evidence against my client versus the disaster of Mandy; of the fact that, no matter how odd her account, Mandy had said there was a theft – she had been consistent in her claim that Raymond had taken the DVD player and denied she had given it to him. Stanley's face contorted as he lurched between needing to bolster his case and admit its failures. I could have, I supposed, hit back – pointed out the idiocy of Mandy's story and her veiled admissions, but I knew not only that he already knew this, but also that he could just carry on. He could leave it up to me to say to the judge, at the end of the prosecution's case, *There is no case to answer here – you must throw it out!* And, if the judge refused to do so, then my client would have to give evidence. If the jury then found my client not guilty, Stanley would be left with nothing, so he was trying to salvage what he could – to ensure he walked away with a conviction, even if it was as minor as a theft. A theft which, had Raymond originally been charged with it, was petty enough to have confined the case to the magistrates' court. I told Stanley I would put it to my client and went to find Raymond.

'Yeah. I'll take it. I'll take the theft.'

We were sitting opposite one another in a conference room and I had barely begun the speech I intended to give. I needed to warn him, I said, of the delicate balancing of knowns and unknowns that must be weighed and considered before the offer of an alternative offence should be accepted. A conviction for a dishonesty offence, even if minor, was still a blot. It could make it hard to find work or to convince a future employer that he could be trusted. Any Community Order to which he might be sentenced was likely to last some time and, if he missed any appointments, he would be convicted of being in breach of the order and punished for that as well. Most important of all, it was an acceptance of guilt. By saying he was guilty of theft he was saying he stole, and he could not afterwards claim otherwise.

Raymond listened, his face and body tense. He paused. I knew what he was thinking, because others had told me what it really felt like. To walk up the steps to the witness box whilst the jury stared and doubted you. To muddle your words and have them twisted by clever lawyers. To honour the frequent requests to keep your voice up, speak clearly, answer the question. But there was something else which I now knew Raymond feared: being asked to tell one story while he hid another. So instead, because of all this, he was going to plead to the theft. He was going to admit to something he didn't do.

His eyes fixed on me with an intensity that was almost overwhelming. It was all right for me, I thought, with my costume and the colour of my skin and my voice of confident authority, faked until it had become reality. When I stood up in court the worst a jury might think was *What's a nice girl like you doing in a place like this?* But Raymond had spent a lifetime trying to be invisible, to make no fuss, to be allowed to slip by without anyone noticing. Almost with a blow I was reminded how accident of birth, the tiny building blocks that made me and those numerous small twists of fate had meant that, when I stood up, the words I needed tumbled out and I was believed.

I thought how hard it must be to enter the witness box and know you will be doubted before you have said a word. I realized how much harder this was if the truth lay within a tale you could not tell.

Raymond and I left the conference room and went back into court. As I waited for the judge to come in I looked at the endorsement Raymond had just signed in my notebook, summarizing my advice, saying he was pleading of his own free will. *Always get an endorsement. Make sure you are protected. Save your own skin.* I stared at his signature underneath mine and could not help feeling that his plea was a sham, one in which I had colluded.

The judge, having been updated on our change of plea by his clerk, had not recalled the jury. Stanley Sharp stood and gave a brief explanation before asking for a new charge of theft to be put to Raymond. In a quiet voice, but without hesitation, Raymond then spoke, for the first and last time in his trial, to say one word. *Guilty.* Stanley said that this plea was acceptable to the Crown and he therefore wished to withdraw the burglary charge. The judge, confirming that the stance taken by both sides was *very proper*, agreed. He then adjourned the case to allow Daniella and her black-haired, red-faced barrister to come back to court another day and stand alongside us. He allowed Daniella to retract her guilty plea to burglary and re-enter one to theft, then sentenced both defendants to twelve-month Community Orders.

So, because Raymond could not find a way to tell his story, his story told him. I didn't ask him if he was collecting drug debts on behalf of his mother; whether the messages on his phone gave this away and this was why he could not use it to prove that Mandy had called him. I didn't ask if this was why he could be sure that his mother would never have come to court on his behalf. Nor did I ask whether he had lied in his first interview to protect her, or because she had been in the house when he was being interviewed and he had been afraid. And there was no one to ask why, if Mandy had given Raymond the DVD player in lieu of a drug debt, she had then called the police. Was it because she had assumed they had simply given her the drugs and felt aggrieved when they said she now had to pay for them? Or was it that she knew these two young people could not tell the truth about why they were at her flat without admitting another crime? Did she want to be able to claim compensation for the DVD player that they had taken, or was it actually because this case gave her a chance to be the object of sympathy rather than derision for a while? I did not know for sure, nor would I ever know. As with so many of my cases, I had to learn to live without a tidy ending.

After the sentencing hearing I drove slowly around the row of mini-roundabouts towards the motorway. I could not shake off a sense that I had forgotten one of the most important lessons my job had taught me. There was no one truth, there was no one story. Instead there were, behind every case, just webs of messy lives. To look for the truth in a case was to forget my role. It was my responsibility to guide those who came my way as best I could through the law and its systems, with humanity and empathy. It was my job to give them, as far as I was able, what they wanted. And I must try to do this even when what they wanted was not always, in the end, actually justice.

5

Rita

Salisbury Crown Court

Archbold Criminal Pleading Evidence and Practice
33–37 Spouses and civil partners
A husband and wife are not guilty of conspiracy if
they alone are parties to the agreement . . .
Where husband and wife are charged with
conspiring with another, the jury should be directed
to acquit the husband and wife if they are not
satisfied that there was another party to the
conspiracy . . .

NICK JOHNSON drew back his arm and, with controlled force, struck the pane of glass with the crowbar. Alongside him in the darkness stood Lee Poulter, his feet planted in the sodden earth of a flowerbed, trampling new green shoots. He held a felt blanket over the window to muffle the blow as the metal of the crowbar connected, catching glass splinters within its fabric which otherwise might have attached themselves to his clothes. Carefully, Nick tapped off the larger shards that had been left hanging like teeth in the frame. Lee climbed slowly through the opening, his gloved fingers carefully bearing his weight on the sill as he avoided the sharp edges. He took the rucksack that Nick passed through and started to unpack it – pillowcases, bleach, cloths. Nick then followed him through the window and into the room of the modest terraced house on Hawthorne Drive, his shoe leaving the ghost of an impression in the earth behind him.

It was not the first time that week, nor that night, that this routine had taken place. In the preceding days the two men had slipped their way into the homes and lives of twenty families. They had rifled through the memories and treasures of people they would never meet, pulling out the drawers they thought may hold what they wanted and scattering their contents in the hope of finding it. They filled pillowcases with DVD players, Xboxes, laptops, iPads. Cameras with pictures of holidays and newborn babies, Christmas and birthday presents, all tangled together. They took identities: credit cards, driving licences, passports, birth certificates. And when they could not find these they stole toy-car collections, cufflinks and tie pins, coins and stamps, engagement rings, engraved hip flasks, silver frames and trinket boxes etched with messages of love. Sometimes, as the men wordlessly demolished a home, its occupants were present. On one night a young girl and her father slept through the invasion until he, disturbed by something unidentifiable, woke and went downstairs to discover the fresh devastation. In another home a grandmother slept. When morning came and she wandered into her living room to find it unrecognizable, she feared the dementia she so dreaded had come for her at last.

But the house on Hawthorne Drive was deserted. Still holding the crowbar, Nick went into the bedroom, his path lit by the beam of his torch. Searching the wardrobe, he pushed aside shirts to reach into the dark corners where people so often hide their treasures. Unexpectedly, his fingers touched a large, sharp-cornered cabinet, standing as high as his waist, the coldness of the metal muted by the wool of his glove. He slid his hands over it, tracing where it was bolted through the back of the wardrobe to the wall behind. He felt the edge of a door and further down the lock that held it fast.

The two men wrestled with the cabinet for some time. They teased and banged the edge of the door, trying to prise it open with tools they found in the house. Finally, the metal wrenched and twisted and they were able to reach inside to lift out their reward. Guns. As he passed the weapons to Lee, Nick tried to weigh them up in the orange streetlight streaming through the window. His inexperienced eye failed to see any real difference between them: some with fine triggers and delicate engraving, the longer air rifles, the semi-automatic shotguns. Once the cabinet was empty, the men allowed themselves a pause to gaze at the weapons laid out on the carpet of the bedroom and a thrill passed between them.

*

Her mind elsewhere, Rita unlocked her front door and opened it. On her way home from the Job Centre it had begun to drizzle and thin strands of blonde hair clung to her face. She paused in the doorway, blinking, giving herself time for her eyes to adjust to the interior gloom. The narrow hallway was windowless and dark. Three rooms ran off it: a living room, a dining room and a small galley kitchen. All but the last were filled with bags and boxes, the curtains drawn, as they always were, despite the time of day. At the end was a small staircase, the varnished pine banister bearing the scuffs of the house's previous occupants. At the bottom of the stairs, their barrels leaning against the banister, were two shotguns.

Rita stared at them. She let the string bag she was carrying drop with a soft thud on to the doormat. Forgetting to close the door, she walked to the stairs. Reaching out, she touched the metal of one of the barrels with her fingertips. She was surprised at how cool and hard it was – much colder than she had expected. She felt sick.

'Mum?' It was Stevie calling from his bedroom. She could hear the muted noises of the game he was playing.

'Where's your dad? Where's Aimee?' Her throat felt tight and her voice sounded too high.

'Dad's asleep up here. Aimee's with Nan – she's dropping her off later. When's tea ready?'

Rita became aware of a chill and realized the front door was still open. 'Soon,' she called. She walked down the hallway, picked up the bag still slumped on the mat, closed the door, went to the kitchen and turned on the oven.

Around mid-afternoon the next day, Nick was playing computer games in his living room with Lee when a dozen plain-clothes police officers broke down their door. At first Rita was unsure whether it was the police or a gang coming to claim back their weapons and she found herself wondering, for a moment, which was worse. A pair of officers took Lee back to his own house three streets away. Rita and Nick sat in silence on the sofa, their two children between them, waiting for Rita's mother to come and collect them. Rita could barely bring herself to look at her mother when, escorted by the police officer who had opened the door, she came into the living room and took the overnight bag from her daughter's hand.

The night seemed to go on for ever. The police worked around Rita and Nick, emptying every cupboard and drawer in the house. The scene felt surreal to Rita, as though she and Nick were the victims. Sometimes an officer would ask what an item was, where it had come from, and she would force down her fear and try to focus on what they were showing her. A few times she became convinced that there was a receipt, somewhere in the chaos, and they let her sift through paperwork, standing behind her, watching her as she tried not to let panic blur the words on the slips of paper she was looking at.

Dawn began to break, pink streaks licking through the darkness, visible now that the curtains had at last been opened. A pair of officers took Rita from her home and went with her in a police car down to the station. Nick was taken too, in a separate car. The police interviewed Rita over the next two days, question after question, for hours and hours, as the duty solicitor sat silently beside her. She wondered whether she should answer 'No comment', as both her husband and Lee did, but she hoped that if she cooperated then they might let her go. Instead, at last, they charged her. Conspiracy to burgle and possession of firearms – offences so serious, the duty solicitor explained, that they could only be heard in a crown court. He told her it was irrelevant that she was not the one wearing the balaclava, prising open the windows, slipping into the houses. The prosecution said there had been a plan, an agreement to burgle the houses, and that she was part of it. And if a jury agreed, then there was no doubt: they would all go to prison for a very long time.

The two medieval wooden gates into Temple are almost hidden among sandwich bars and cafés and shops lining Fleet Street. Cut into one of the gates is a small door, which opens on to a cobbled lane leading down to Middle Temple Hall. Flanking the courtyards that run off the lane are rows of barristers' chambers, each using their address for their name. These courtyards are separated by a web of cloisters and tunnels and small pathways. The sensation of walking through them feels like tumbling back in time to some secret, long-forgotten kingdom.

It was early evening on a Tuesday. With a sigh, summer had slipped into autumn, and leaves lined the path, catching in the wheels of my case. I stopped under the streetlight to shake them off, then heaved the case up my chambers' stone steps, aware of a familiar sensation in the pit of my stomach. When I know a case is waiting for me apprehension and anticipation fuse together, almost indistinguishable. The phone call had come earlier that afternoon, when I was still in Portsmouth County Court in the middle of an all-day final hearing in a family case. By the time I had rung my clerk back on my way to the railway station the trial was already in my diary. There would be no way of changing it now, even if I had wanted to.

My clerk had told me what I needed to know. A burglary conspiracy, which had been 'floating' – waiting for a court to become free – had just been called on at Salisbury Crown Court and the barrister who had held the brief was stuck in a different trial. A guilty plea, a missing witness or some other unexpected happening had meant that another trial had collapsed, so this one could begin. Tomorrow. It was due to take a week. Rita – my new client – had pleaded not guilty to all the charges. She had been in prison waiting for her trial to start for six months. Then last week, unexpectedly, she had been granted bail, as though the judge wished to tease her with one final shot of freedom. The papers were no more than an A4 file's worth, my clerk re-assured me, and were waiting on the marble mantelpiece in chambers. I was not to worry; there were other hearings listed for the next morning so there would be more than enough time to meet the client and prepare the trial.

I took the papers home and began to read them on the nearly empty tube. There was little information from the bar-rister whose case it had been, just the endorsement on the brief, a flourish of blue ink recording Rita's not guilty plea and her remand into custody. The statements were unmarked and unordered, the most recent ones simply filed on top as they had been sent through from the solicitors. I imagined he had sus-pected that his current trial would run on and did not want to waste time preparing a case for which he would not be paid.

Once home, I read through statement after statement of anger and violation from those whose lives had been filleted of their treasures. The burglaries had been so prolific that when the police had spread out the haul in a large room and asked the victims to come to identify their belongings, some saw objects they had not even realized had been stolen, lighting on them with exclamations of astonishment. Almost all the stolen pos-sessions had been found at Nick and Rita's home. As I cross-checked the items lost against the items seized, I noticed something. I checked again, just to be sure. Out of the guns listed as stolen, only three had been found. Two at Nick and Rita's, and one at Lee's. I grimaced. There was nothing more likely to anger a judge than a stolen shotgun which then goes missing, slipped into the darkness of the underworld until, months or years later, it reappears, sawn off at the barrel, used to rob, to threaten, or to kill.

In my notebook I began to chart the small pieces of forensic evidence. The burglars had been careful. All the houses had been cleaned, with no fingerprints or physical traces left. There were only snatches of evidence: a glove lift from a frame, tool marks on the edge of an unlocked window, the smallest thread hanging off a shard of glass. Footprints from the same pair of shoes had been found underneath a window sill, on a leather sofa, on kitchen worktops – although the shoes themselves had not been found. But then, at last, they had slipped. Underneath one of the windows, forgotten in the escape, was a screwdriver. At least three people's DNA had been found on its handle. One of those people was Rita. A second fingerprint had been found on one of the guns in Rita's house, and that too was hers. I winced as I wrote it down.

I sifted through the statements again, trying to find the evidence against Lee, matching exhibit numbers with my list of stolen property. The police had searched every room in his house, but the haul was modest. A laptop, a camera, an Xbox. And a gun – an air rifle – stolen from the house on Hawthorne Drive. I sat back and looked at the chart I had made, links and arrows joining the dots, making sure I could trace the path between theft, seizure and identification. There was no doubting it: the evidence was very strong. Surely, I thought, the two men – when faced with the prospect of a trial in reality rather than in abstract – would relent and admit their part, lured by the discount the judge was obliged to apply to their sentence. But I could not count on this and so, glancing at the clock and working out how long I had before exhaustion set in, I switched on my laptop and began to prepare.

I double-checked the order of names on the indictment. For some reason Rita was first. This was unhelpful. It meant I would be the first barrister to cross-examine the prosecution witnesses, Rita would be the first defendant to give evidence, and I would be the first defence advocate to make a closing speech. Coming second – or even better, last – held a huge advantage in a case like this. It meant being able to see what the prosecution witnesses were like in evidence, and where their weaknesses lay. It meant knowing if there were gaps in the evidence, missed by the barristers who had gone before me. It meant being the last voice of persuasion in the closing speeches that the jury heard before they went to their room to decide upon the defendants' guilt. Going first meant I had to cover everything, for fear that those who followed may not notice – or care – about that part of the evidence. But, more importantly, going first gave the wrong impression to the jury. What I wanted was to be almost invisible throughout the trial, for the focus to be entirely on the men until right at the end when Rita, terrified, stood in the witness box and everyone looked faintly surprised, having almost forgotten she was there. It was a powerful tool, but now, simply because whoever had written the indictment had chosen to include her first, I was unable to use it. Instead of being at the back of the fray, watching and listening, she was going to be the first person from whom everyone in the courtroom would hear, and it could cost her dearly.

'Oh, well, this is just *excellent* news . . .'

The robing room at Salisbury Crown Court was busy and it

was hard not to feel a blush of pleasure as Leo bellowed his delight. He was representing Nick – we were going to be in the same trial. 'I mean it's hopeless, *hopeless*. Don't know why they've bothered with your girl, mind you, given that they never arrested Lee's missus. But the boys are *buggered*.' He paused, considering. 'I just hope Nick knows we're buggered. He should do, given how many times he's been buggered before.'

'I haven't seen your guy's previous, Leo. Can I have a look?'

'Of course, my dear, whatever you want. Here – have my copy.'

I could tell from the weight of the paper that Leo was right. Nick had nearly forty previous convictions going back decades – burglaries, thefts, assaults, affrays. The only pauses in criminality had been forced by spells in prison.

'Guess who *this* one was with . . .' Leo's short, plump frame pressed against the table as he leaned over to gesture at a burglary conviction dating back more than ten years, circled in red on the printout. 'Yup. The pair of them at it again. I mean, if you've been nicked together once, why on earth would you do it again?'

He turned as Fred walked over, swinging his robe bag from his shoulder and shrugging off his overcoat. He was a few years older than me: thin and wiry, with a kind face and retreating hairline. 'Did you know that, Freddie? That our guys have been at it before? Although then they only got twelve months. Not so lucky this time, I imagine.'

'You are kidding . . . !' Fred came over to the table and peered at the closely typed page as Leo stabbed at the circle of red ink.

'But remember, they didn't do it this time . . .' Leo sat down heavily on one of the chairs at the table, drawing a fat finger down the side of his nose. 'This time it was all *Harry*.'

Fred looked at him. 'Oh God. Who the hell is Harry?'

'It was all Harry, you see. It was Harry who broke in. It was Harry who stole the loot. It was Harry who used our house as a storeroom because he had nowhere else to put it. We'd plead to a handling, though, of course. Who's prosecuting?'

'Matthew Finch.' I had signed in already – typed my name into the computer in the robing room set up for the purpose and seen Matthew's name entered as prosecution counsel. Leo brightened. 'Ah well, then I reckon I might have a crack. Although you're in with a better chance, Fred – not nearly so much stash at your guy's place as at mine. What are you saying, anyway, about where it all came from?' He gestured at Fred, who was now trying to attach his starched white court band to his shirt, his chin stretched upwards.

'What do you think? We bought it all at a car boot a few days before the house was searched, didn't we? Must have been sold it by Harry, by the sounds of it.'

'Oh bloody hell!' Leo snorted. He turned to me. 'So what do you think, Miss Langford? Shall we all go and lean on Matthew together? Or will that just scare him?'

I stood up, sliding my file off the table, my wig balanced on top. 'I'll leave that to you, I think, Leo. I'm going to go and find my girl.'

'Ah yes, you got bail didn't you.' Leo tugged on his cloak, his stomach straining against the buttons of his waistcoat. 'Well, at least you'll have some time to take instructions. Bet Serco won't bother bringing our two along until the afternoon. Cuppa, Fred?'

The two men, confident in their prediction that the van from the prison would be late, as it so often was, set off to the small café on the ground floor of the courthouse which served burning tea from white polystyrene cups. I followed them down the stairs and turned left into the busy court corridor, searching until I saw a small woman with frizzy blonde hair. Her face was without expression and she was standing completely still in the crowd outside the locked doors to the courtroom. I walked over, knowing she must be Rita.

'They're not really interested in her,' said Matthew. He was sitting at his computer, looking at me as I leaned against the door frame. He motioned at his desk. 'Your copy is in there, by the way.' I took the distinctive beige, slippery-thin paper, stapled in the top corner. More disclosure, this time an attempt to link the footprints found in the case with a burglary of which Nick had been convicted years earlier involving a footprint with the same markings. I stood behind Matthew, scanning through the papers. I wondered if I should make a fuss, demanding an explanation for why I was seeing it for the first time on the day of trial, but decided against it. Matthew's weariness suggested that Leo and Fred had been to see him while I was with my client and already said as much. There was no point sabotaging the possibility of any kindness towards my client by attacking him further.

Perhaps sensing my judgement, he began to speak. 'Look, if we got guilty pleas from the other two, then I'm sure we could come up with something for you. Handling stolen goods, something like that. They might even be persuaded to drop it completely. But without their guilty pleas it's a full house, I'm afraid.' He paused. 'It's the guns you see. The police hate missing shotguns.' I nodded, tempted to share my frustration that the men had not yet admitted their guilt, but something pulled me back. A possibility that I was wrong? A fear, creeping in year by year, that I was becoming too sure of a defendant's guilt before I had seen or heard them? A nagging possibility that, despite everyone assuming otherwise, maybe their story could be true?

I sat with Rita in a corner of the corridor for most of the morning, only partially sheltered from the tussle of barristers, defendants and police all waiting for their turn. I took her through the evidence and interviews, trying to pull out answers to my questions. I told her that, if the other two pleaded guilty, then she would be able to walk away, possibly without charge. She hesitated, and I wondered what she was thinking – of her children, her family, her life? The moment passed. I realized the idea that she would deliver up her husband and his best friend to the prosecution by admitting their crimes because they would not was unthinkable. If they were not going to crack, then she could not crack for them, even if doing so could save her. I had to try another way. So, after lunch, with the trial finally about to start, I went up to Leo and Fred, chatting to one another as Leo leaned his bulk against the locked court door, waiting for the usher to open it.

'Come on, Leo. You can't really be running this? They'd let her walk, you know. If your guy did the right thing—'

Leo cut me off. 'You're not entirely off the hook, you know. Remember,' he pushed himself off the door and leaned towards me with a smile, 'the only forensics in the whole case are yours. On the bloody tool and on the bloody gun. Ha!'

'Oh come off it, Leo. I mean, what are they saying? That she packed his burglary backpack for him? Popped in the screwdriver along with a sandwich and a Scotch egg? She may, at some point over the years, have touched it, but that doesn't mean she used it to lever her way into these houses. Your guys did that, and everybody knows it.'

'And the print on the gun? You can see it, can't you? He

walks in the door, she's cleared a space for the next load of loot, he passes her the bag of guns, she helps unpack them . . .'

'Or—'

He cut me off with a wave of his hand, starting to lose his humour. 'Sorry, my dear, I've given him my advice, got my endorsement. If he wants a trial, he wants a trial.' He turned as the key rattled in the courtroom doors. 'And there's not a lot any of us can do about it.'

It was a boring beginning for the jury. The defence did not – could not – dispute that any of the burglaries had actually happened; just who had carried them out. And so all the evidence of smashed-up lives, sleepless nights and fear was delivered not by tearful, trembling witnesses, but in statements and lists read without expression by Matthew. I could see the jury's interest waning. It is always hard not to look at them when they first file in, their names chosen at random by the court ushers, their turn to do their civic duty decided by a courtroom lottery. Even if they are resentful that they cannot escape, most are curious about the case that lies ahead of them, secretly thrilled by the possibility of blood and murder, lies and deception. This time, though, as the days passed and the prosecution evidence grew no more exciting than a police officer describing searches and forensic evidence, I watched the jurors fight heavy heads. For the time being the fireworks were reserved for us. The jury were protected from our lawyer's arguments about whether they should be told of Nick's old footprint, or of a recorded telephone call from prison to Lee's wife giving instructions to get rid of a pair of shoes, or of the defendants' long list of previous burglary convictions, or of all the other secret evidence about which they would never know.

*

'I'm going to have a go, I think.' Fred looked almost apologetic.

'Up to you, Fred. It's your call.' I wondered if I would have done the same: made a submission of no case to answer to the judge at the end of the prosecution's case. If the judge agreed with Fred and decided that there was not enough evidence against Lee for a jury safely to convict him, then he would simply direct the jury to enter a not guilty verdict and end the case against him. If the judge did not agree, however, then Fred could risk looking like a fool, having annoyed him with a hopeless argument and wasting precious court time.

It was the morning of the fourth day of the trial and the judge strode into court. He wore the purple robe and red sash of the circuit judge – a full-time crown court judge who had made his way from the Bar up to the judicial bench long ago. Some such judges have been made bored, impatient and bullish by their years on the bench, but not this one. He was kind without being sentimental, authoritative but without the desire to interfere in a case – trusting instead that those who appeared before him would act as he expected them to. He walked in and nodded without ceremony as we bowed to him and sat down.

Fred's submission was short, at least. 'It's a matter of knowledge and control, Your Honour,' he said slowly. 'My client asserts that in respect of the belongings found at the home of Mr and Mrs Johnson he had neither, and that the items found at his home had been legitimately bought by him at a car boot sale. No receipts, of course. But there is, I again repeat, no forensic evidence against my client whatsoever. The case is wholly circumstantial.'

The judge stayed silent. I watched him, trying to read his face. He turned towards the prosecutor. 'You, of course, oppose this application, Mr Finch?'

'Yes, yes, Your Honour. The prosecution say—'

'No need, no need.' The judge waved him back down into his seat and looked at Fred. 'I'm not with you, Mr Barrow. The property taken, which includes, lest we forget, various shotguns, was found in close proximity to your client's home, at the home of the co-defendant. I concede there's no scientific evidence, but this has got to be seen in that context. That is to say, he *was* in recent possession of the items soon after the burglary, which is ample circumstantial evidence. He was also found at his co-defendant's house the day after the final burglary. There has got to be the inference that the three were in it together. The application is refused.' Fred nodded and sat down, slowly. The judge turned towards me. 'So, shall we have your client, Miss Langford?'

As Rita walked up the steps and into the witness box, I willed her to remember the speech I had given her that morning. Keep calm and listen. Answer what you've been asked and not what you think they want to know. Be polite to the prosecutor – don't disagree with him for the sake of it. And remember, when you walk into the witness box your case will be at its weakest. The jury have only heard from the prosecution and they want to hear your side of the story. Tell it to them; tell them your story.

She was good, better than I thought she would be. Stronger than I thought she could be. She told the court about her life with Nick; her cash-in-hand job in a bar, six nights a week, stacking glasses and cleaning ashtrays while Nick watched their two children. She said she did not know about the burglaries, had never seen most of the stuff the police showed to her, and claimed that what she had seen was hers even if she could not prove it. She spoke about arriving home and seeing the guns – reaching out, touching the metal with her fingertips so she could be sure they were real. She told the court about her husband's friend, Harry. That she didn't like him, wouldn't allow him in the house. That he was trouble. I watched her for a flinch or some sign that betrayed her lie, knowing that the Harry she tried to blame had been arrested and released, having produced an alibi, but I could not see any. I glanced down at my notes and flicked briefly to the single sheet that listed her previous convictions. One for possession of cannabis, punished by a fine; the other for assaulting a police officer some years ago. The jury knew nothing about them, as they knew nothing about Nick's or Lee's twenty-year criminal careers. A defendant walks into the dock as a blank slate. The jury may look at his tattoos, at his broken nose, at his shaved head, but they will not know if all their prejudices are confirmed, not unless the judge has given the prosecution permission to tell them, and even then they will be told only about the offences relevant to the case.

I glanced to my right and watched the jury, who were looking at Rita as she gripped the edge of the dock and gave her answers. They were fascinated. I knew why: they had watched the three defendants sitting silently in their dock for days, and now, finally, they were going to get to hear them speak. There was something of the zoo about it: as though she were an animal they had been watching, waiting for her to perform a trick. I tried to encourage her with the tone of my voice, tried to pull her along the slow pathway of her evidence until, suddenly, we had reached the end, and I had to sit down and deliver her to the other barristers.

'No further questions, Your Honour.'

Leo and Fred then stood in turn and asked Rita a handful of questions each. Rita then looked at Matthew as he rose to his feet and I could see her fight her contempt. I wondered if he saw it, if he knew he could push her to reveal it. It would work well with the jury: disrespect for the prosecutor, disrespect for the police. Over and over again Matthew went through the detail of the day before her house was searched. Rita stuck to her story. She reiterated the minutiae of what she had eaten for breakfast, the route she had taken to the Job Centre, what bus she had caught back in the rain, how she had felt when she saw the guns brazenly laid out by the stairs. She gave evidence for most of the morning and I could see her beginning to tire. I found myself willing her on and glanced at Matthew, trying to work out where he was going. He seemed to sense it, drawing himself up, reaching his crescendo. 'And when, Mrs Johnson, you had confirmed, as you say, that the guns *were* real, tell us why you did not immediately contact the police?'

'I didn't know what to do.' Her face was hard to read. 'It's my husband . . . Something's obviously happened, but I didn't know what. I didn't know what was going on.'

'But it *is* your house?'

'Yes, but . . .' She paused. When she spoke, it was as if she was talking to herself. 'Every day, I think I should have called the police.'

She would never have called the police. I knew that and Matthew knew that. I wondered if the jury knew it too. Rita carried on. 'But the police kept going on about loads of guns and I had only seen two and I didn't know what to think. I didn't know. Look . . .' her voice faltered and I looked up from my notes. 'I was taken away from my kids for six months – for all of their school holidays, for both their birthdays – because I didn't know where some guns were. I am being punished for not knowing. I would have told them if I'd known, but I didn't.'

She looked down and I felt Matthew hesitate. 'No further questions, Your Honour.' He sat down, carefully. And then it was over. I glanced at the clock, only now aware of the tension in my stomach and shoulders. The judge followed my gaze and, rising, adjourned us all for lunch.

*

112

As Nick walked up the steps into the witness box I realized I had not yet really looked at him, not properly. He was short, a stocky man, with chaotic blond hair. Broken veins on his cheeks and nose gave away a drinking habit, although I imagined he probably looked better now after six months' drying-out in prison. I found myself wondering about their two children; whether they looked like him or Rita. As Leo rose slowly to take Nick through his evidence, his notebook held in a steady hand, he let out a barely audible sigh.

Nick's evidence was terrible. Apparently keen to be precise, he confused himself and Leo with contradictions and mixed-up dates, tangling himself in meandering sentences. The judge had to stop him, ask him to pause, to repeat the evidence, only to get a different answer. I could feel Fred sinking lower in the seat next to Leo, wondering whether he could undo the mess in his cross-examination. I tried to keep up, noting down what Nick said in my book. Every now and then, at a particularly bad point, I would write expletives in capital letters in the margin. I wondered, seeing Leo's expression, whether this was the first time he had heard this version. Undeterred, Nick ploughed on. It was his friend, he said, not really a friend, an acquaintance, really, called Harry, someone whom he'd known for a while. Harry had phoned Nick and said that his mum was kicking him out – he'd been staying with her for a bit and had nowhere else to go, had split from his girlfriend, was sofa-surfing, that sort of thing. He had said to Nick – could he leave his stuff at his while he sorted something out? Nick had agreed, thinking it was a bag or two, some boxes maybe, but then Harry had turned up in the early hours of the morning with tons of stuff. Pillowcases filled with things and boxes and bags and a massive sports bag. They'd argued about it and Harry had promised that it would all be gone by the next day. Then Lee had come over and they'd played some games and watched a film. Then they'd wanted to see what was in the sports bag, so they unzipped it and in the middle were some guns. And that's when he got really worried, but it was too late because then the police turned up and raided the house, and he was arrested and that was that. As Nick reached his final sentence, the court appeared to exhale in relief. Leo looked down at his notebook, then sat down with a mutter, gesturing to Matthew.

Lee was like Nick in build, but that was where the similarity ended. He was not wearing a suit, but someone had brought him a shirt and trousers and his dark hair was neatly combed. Fred warmed him up, asking him about himself. The jurors liking him was the best chance he had. Lee began to explain where each of the items had come from, which car boot sale he had got them from. He'd found the air rifle at a car boot sale too, he said, and bought it for his son. He wanted to get him into the cadets; wanted to make sure he had a hobby so he didn't find himself with too much time on his hands and getting into trouble. He shot a conspiratorial glance at the jury, with a smile. With painstaking precision, Fred then took Lee through all the benefits Lee and his family received. The point was not a new one – Fred was trying to build a picture of someone who did not need to sell off other people's treasures to put food on the table. It was going quite well. Lee was trying too hard, but you could forgive him that. Until, apparently without realizing it, he undid all Fred's hard work in a moment.

'Bloody Disneyland!' Fred threw his wig down on to the robing-room table. 'I mean, why say it? Three thousand pounds for a holiday, and after all that evidence about the wife's bad back and agoraphobia and how he couldn't get a job because someone has to look after the children. Then he bangs on about the holiday they're missing because of the trial? I haven't been on holiday for two years, for God's sake. And this guy feels hard done by because he's lost his deposit. Did you see the jury's faces: that bloke in the front row was fuming. He'd probably just done his tax return. Oh, I give up . . .' He slumped into the frayed armchair by the window in the robing room and gazed outside, the springs in the seat letting out a low whine.

As I walked the route from the railway station across the cobbles of the cathedral city on the last day of the trial, I noticed how soothing I had begun to find the routine. Getting up at the same time, buying coffee from the same stall on the station platform, sitting in the same carriage on the same train, seeing the same people and being able to continue the jokes and teasing. The rhythm was restful, a relief from the unpredictability of my usual practice. I wondered, not for the first time, how I would manage this job if, one day, I had to be home by a certain time; with a fridge filled with food and clothes cleaned for others; when I found myself in charge of small people's lives as well as my own. I checked myself. I had, after all, sought out a job which meant I never knew how my day would unfold. A life in which I could ride the adrenaline from the pitches and curves dealt by the unexpected, and experience the instant hit of success when it was gloriously close.

As I carried my case up the steps to the courthouse's doors, I was reminded of something else. To be a legitimate voyeur into people's lives, within a machine both ancient and modern, which tries to represent and uphold the values that underpin the country in which we live – that is an extraordinary privilege. It is not one which, no matter how hard the work or difficult the case, I have ever taken for granted.

Later that day, about an hour before lunch, I sat on the court bench, dangling my shoes from the end of my toes, waiting for the judge to return. The atmosphere in the courtroom now all the evidence was finished and all the closing speeches given was one of tangible relief, almost bordering on cheerfulness. I could not suppress a feeling that, if I lay low and held firm, Rita and I would be released back into the grey autumn day, hearts thudding at our escape. All we needed now was for the judge to give his summary of the evidence. Then the jury would be sent out and there would be nothing left to do but wait.

The usher thundered 'Court rise!' as our judge strode in from his secret door at the back of court and took his seat, raised above the rest of us. He was carrying his copy of Archbold and I watched him flick open the rice-paper pages to the one he wanted.

'Counsel, before I start the summing-up I thought it helpful to clarify exactly what directions of law everyone wanted me to explain to the jury?'

When I was very junior, I wondered whether the law bent too heavily in favour of the defence. The judge's legal directions to the jury – instructions on the law and how they should treat the evidence they had heard – were only part of it. I wondered whether the rules of court and evidence did too. The convention that defence counsel sat nearest the jury; the rules that always gave the defence the last word; the prohibition on disclosing a defendant's past lest the jury be prejudiced against them – all were dutifully followed. I wondered whether it was disproportionate for an entire trial to collapse, weeks of work and expense come to nothing, because a juror had conducted their own research, or been told something that the law said they should not know. I was sometimes frustrated by the rules of questioning and the bar on speaking about the case to witnesses, lest their

evidence was affected, which everyone observed with strict
solemnity. But then, when I saw twelve eyes turn and gaze upon
the silent defendant locked away in the dock, I started to realize
how hard it was to walk into the courtroom an innocent man. I
began to understand why a judge would be so concerned that, no
matter how delicate the balance, the jury should not take into
their hallowed room anything that was not evidence given in
open court. And I began to understand that it was not enough for
justice to be done. It must also be seen to be done. This sense of
fairness is with us from the beginning of our understanding
about the world and we carry it with us into adulthood. Time and
time again my clients remark that all they want, really, is their
day in court and a fair hearing. Accepting an unwanted decision
is infinitely harder if it is accompanied by a sense of injustice.

The judge paused. 'Something occurred to me which has
yet to be raised, and which may become relevant during the
jury's deliberations. It is still the law, is it not, that a husband
cannot conspire with a wife . . . ?'

I looked up, sharply. I thought I knew all the law on conspiracy. *To be a conspiracy there needs to be two or more people.*
I had looked it up again in the late hours of preparation the
night before the trial began. I had scanned through a few of the
cases in the pages of my law book. All familiar, all straightforward. I had looked through the book that set out the possible
directions relevant for our case. I had not found this exception
within either of them. Now my hands flew out and flipped my
Archbold open to the pages I needed. I traced my finger over
the tiny print explaining the lengthy precedents on the law. I
was aware of the other barristers next to me nodding their
agreement, suggesting that the judge was quite right. Then I
found it, a short paragraph right at the back of the chapter, near
the end of the section to do with parties in the case: the

anachronistic legal fiction from common law that a husband cannot conspire with a wife because they are believed to be of one mind, of one will. The judge must therefore advise the jury that Rita could not, in law, conspire with Nick. A conspiracy must involve two or more people and, in law, Nick and Rita only counted as one. If the jury therefore found Lee not guilty of conspiracy, then they must acquit Nick and Rita too. I looked up, aware that the voices in court had stilled. The judge was looking down on me.

'Um, yes, Your Honour. Your Honour is, um . . .' I looked back down at the paragraph, '. . . quite right. It is still law.'

I looked across at my co-defendants. The frustration I had felt that their clients could not accept their part – and that they were prepared to take Rita down with them – grew to anger. The law encouraged the jury to think of Rita as indistinguishable from Nick; to find her guilty by association. Even though it was possible for the jury to convict the two men alone and find her not guilty, this outdated principle placed her in danger. Far from distancing her from the criminality of her husband, the judge was going to ask the jury to believe that, as far as the law was concerned, she had no independent will of her own. So much so that, had she wanted to conspire with him, the law would not have allowed her to do so.

The judge nodded, closing his law book. 'Very good. Well, if there's nothing further, can we have the jury in, please? I shall start my summing-up.'

It is true that, at a glance, the most important people in a court-room might appear to be the ones in costume: the judge, a deity raised high above us all on his great throne; the barristers, with their ancient uniform so instantly recognizable; or the clerks and ushers, who run the courts in their own black gowns with varying expressions of ennui. But it is, of course, the twelve members of the jury, in jeans and T-shirts and floral dresses, who decide my client's fate. I know nothing of them except their names, read out by the clerk at the beginning of the trial. Throughout the rest of the proceedings it is impossible not to watch a jury and try to work out who they are. Which one is the oppressive bore, who the libertarian, who the reactionary longing to send someone to prison? Which alliances have formed? Who is on your side? In a sense it is a pointless game because I will never know – no one will, except the jurors themselves. The way in which the jurors decide the fate of the person they have been staring at in the dock is so secret that, before they leave the courtroom to deliberate, an usher takes an oath, before everyone in court, to protect and maintain this secrecy. Even after the verdict you will not know what went on in the sacred space of the jury room. Only occasionally, when I watch a jury file in to deliver their verdict, do I find a jury member glancing towards the dock. I have come to learn that this often means they are about to set the defendant free. Sometimes they will flash a grin, knowing the victory they are about to hand me. More often it is a cautious smile as I try to hide my own. Sometimes I have been met with a hard stare, other times a curious one. And, every now and then, I leave court after a trial and realize – as I buy a coffee, slip into a nearby shop or wait for my train on the station platform – that I am standing next to a juror. Sometimes they do a double take, as though astonished that my life could be as pedestrian as theirs. Although several have acknowledged me with a greeting and a grin, only once has one approached me. She gripped my arm and breathed into my face, 'We knew he was lying, that other man,' before beaming and setting off down the street.

And now this representation of society – twelve of Rita's peers – was to decide her fate.

Leo threw open the door to the robing room where Fred and I were waiting and his black gown billowed in the backdraught. 'Jury's back,' he barked. Fred and I stood urgently but Leo held up his hand. 'A question, only a question.'

The judge had already been passed the jury's question by the usher before we got into court. In the jury's absence, he unfolded it carefully, read it aloud, then passed it down for us to see.

Please can the judge repeat the direction about husbands and wives?

Leo and I glanced at one another. Sometimes a jury's question can lead to hours of agonizing. It can show that they are clearly on the right track, or the wrong one. It can show they have grasped, or wildly misunderstood, the law. But this question felt like a punch. Did it mean that they wanted to acquit Rita, but were not sure if they could? Did it mean that they wanted to acquit Lee, but were unsure whether that really meant they then had to find Rita and Nick not guilty too? Or did it just mean that they also could not quite believe that this extraordinary doctrine was still part of modern law?

As the jurors came back into court to hear their answer, the judge repeated the law in exactly the same words he had already used. Being a man of brevity, the direction was short and to the point. He was careful to use the same phrase: neither more nor less, as he was required to do.

An hour later the jury had made their decision.

The atmosphere in a courtroom when a verdict is read out is unlike any other. It creates a tension so heightened that, even if you are an interloper waiting for your hearing to be called on afterwards and with no idea of the evidence or the charge, you feel giddy, like a tightrope walker, knowing you are about to fall off on one side or the other.

The jury filed into court and I tried as hard as I could to resist the temptation to look at them. I realized I was holding my breath. As the final juror took her place I could last no longer and looked up. Most of the jury were staring straight ahead at the judge or down into their laps. I ran through the things I had said earlier to Rita, encouraging her to prepare herself. But, despite my words, I had been sure they would acquit her. I thought they must have seen that she had little choice but to accept her husband's way of life and had understood the domestic trap she was in.

'Guilty. Guilty. Guilty.'

The word rang out, over and over again, to every count, for each defendant. The air in the court seemed heavy and I could not bring myself to turn round and look at the dock for fear of the expression on Rita's face.

We returned to Salisbury Crown Court for the sentencing hearing a few weeks later. It was just before Christmas. In the pre-sentence reports prepared on their behalf, Nick and Lee admitted carrying out all of the burglaries. Both men also tried to exonerate Rita in the same document, finally maintaining that she was not part of it, that she knew nothing of their plan and had had no say in it. It was, of course, far too late for that.

It was a sentencing day and the courtroom was full of broken-hearted friends and families in other cases, filling the seats of the public gallery. After the hearing was over, I walked down the corridor to the cells to see Rita. A woman came up to me and it was only then that I recognized her from the front of the public gallery in court. She introduced herself as Rita's mother. Her face bore little resemblance to her daughter's, but then time had been cruel to it. She was almost ageless, the blows and knocks of life etched out in deep lines and shadows.

'It's a long time, four years. She's never been inside before. She'll find it hard,' she said to me, without emotion. 'Tell her we were watching and will tell the kids. And tell her to get a Visiting Order as soon as she gets there so we can come and see her for Christmas. If she asks about the social coming round, tell her not to worry about it. I will sort it.' She was completely calm.

'Of course,' I replied. And then, 'I'm so sorry. The jury must have disbelieved her. They clearly didn't believe the other two. They must have thought that she was part of it as well. Unless . . .' I trailed off. Unless the law had confused them, I thought. Unless they had misunderstood it and – having been told that the law considered Nick and Rita as inseparable, of one mind – had thought they could not convict him without also convicting her. I would never really know.

'That Nick, he was always like that, you know.' She looked at me as if she were weighing up my worldliness. 'I know it's hard. My old man was always up to it, like hers. Was in and out of prison when she was a child. She saw it all. And I do know. I know what it is to feel the back of their hand. But you know what, my old man would never have done this. If you were stupid enough to get caught, he used to say, then you faced it. And he would never, never have taken me down with him.' Her face shifted and I wondered whether, when she got home, she would let herself cry. Tears for her daughter, and for herself, and for the same desperate cycle beginning all over again.

As I walked away from court later that afternoon, I thought of her words and began to wonder whether I had been wrong and the law had been right. For years I believed that marriage did not mean a thing: a stamped piece of paper, as easily torn up as made; an outmoded ritual that has no place in modernity. But then I began to listen to and think about the vows of marriage. The words were the biggest promises a person could make, and I began to notice among the friends I heard say them the subtlest of shifts in how the world viewed them afterwards; of their place in it together, as one unit. Maybe this antiquated rule just reflected a truth – that marriage did bind you together in a way nothing else could. Maybe, in marrying a liar and a thief and staying with him knowing what he was, Rita had become one too. For better, or for worse.

A week after the trial my grandfather died. My great oak of a grandfather, with his war-moustache and six-foot-four frame, who had spent a lifetime harvesting fields and feeding cattle and watching the seasons flow past him. He spent the day before he died chopping wood, enough to last all winter, as though he knew death was coming for him. He woke up, dressed himself in the tweed suit he always wore, and let his dog out of the bungalow where he and my grandmother lived. Then some premonition drove him back to his bed and he lay down, arms folded across his chest, and died. His dog jumped into his arms and that was how he was when my grandmother found him soon afterwards. Still warm, but with life gone.

Over the winter after the trial I went back to my grandparents' farm – back to my childhood place of woodland hideouts and secret bush caves. I stayed the night with my grandmother, drinking sherry, looking at photographs and trying to keep the loneliness from her door. While my grandfather had spent long days in the fields, she had been at home: cooking, cleaning, caring for four children. As dementia followed its cruel course, she found herself in the past: not in the years of family life, but almost always reliving the war when she had served as a Wren. Defying her pastor father, she had signed up at eighteen, and her stories were always of friendships and adventures. Then, soon after her freedom had begun, she met my grandfather and one form of service was replaced with another.

The morning after I stayed the night, I went into his room. It was completely ordered – just as he had always been. I looked towards the window and noticed a shotgun leaning up against it. For some reason, that day it was not locked in the cabinet where he had always secured it. It had been his habit to wake in the early morning and spend a happy hour shooting rabbits in the garden from his bedroom window – my grandmother claimed this as the reason for their separate rooms. I walked towards the gun, reached out and touched its barrel, my fingers tracing the lines of the metal. In that moment I thought of Rita, and of my grandmother, and of all the generations of other women who had remained silently loyal to their husbands and, in doing so, had sacrificed themselves. And I thought how the law had helped them do it.

6

Maggie

Medway County Court

Children Act 1989
Section 31 – Care and Supervision

*(1) On the application of any local authority or
authorised person, the court may make an order—*
   *(a) placing the child with respect to whom the
   application is made in the care of a designated
   local authority; or*
   *(b) putting him under the supervision of a
   designated local authority*

*(2) A court may only make a care order or supervi-
sion order if it is satisfied—*
   *(a) that the child concerned is suffering, or is
   likely to suffer, significant harm; and*
   *(b) that the harm, or likelihood of harm, is
   attributable to—*
      *(i) the care given to the child, or likely to be
      given to him if the order were not made, not
      being what it would be reasonable to expect a
      parent to give to him; or*
      (ii) the child's being beyond parental control.

THE PAPERS for Maggie's case arrived a few days before the hearing. They were already voluminous. I scanned through the brief and the chronology, trying to get a picture of the case. Maggie was a young mother, so poorly parented herself that the local authority did not consider she was able to look after either the daughter they had already removed three years beforehand or her new baby son. I found her date of birth. She was twenty-two.

I wondered when this set of facts had become so typical to me. It had not always been the case. I can still remember the first young mother I represented whose baby was removed by the state. It was in Basingstoke Magistrates' Court, years before Maggie's case, long before I really understood how the system of family public law worked. It was also long before I understood the power of a social worker over the outcome of a case. In the years to come, experience taught me that effective social workers worked well enough with parents to steer the case away from a contested court hearing so that I did not become involved and rarely met them. But I had not yet learned this and arrived on that first case to find my young client in the waiting room, sitting next to her social worker. 'Cabbage leaves,' the social worker was saying to her kindly, maternally. 'That's what you need. Not just any cabbage, though. It has to be Savoy. Just pop a leaf or two in your bra. Helps with the aching. It's worked for all my other mums.'

All her other mums.

Those women she saw, week in and out, who discovered they need only think of their newborn's scent or mewling cry to trigger some ancient part of themselves they hadn't known existed, as the milk drew through their newly hard breasts as sharp as the slice of a knife. Those women who, even if they did not want it, or still could not comprehend it, found themselves mothers. When she saw me, the social worker gave me a half-smile, then got up and walked over to join a group of women on the opposite side of the waiting room. They were, I was later to realize, the team that always outflanks my clients in number and resources, made up of the local authority's barrister, solicitor and social worker, the guardian – the independent social worker there to represent the interests of the child – and the guardian's barrister. As I led my young client to a conference room, I listened as this group laughed with easy familiarity about some weekend mishap and noticed that they all held takeaway cups from the same café.

I knew that my client had already agreed not to return to hospital and her week-old daughter. Instead she would go back, alone, to her room in the house she shared with strangers. An order, the contents of which had already been agreed by all the parties, was due to be signed off that morning by the magistrates. Then the social worker could go to the hospital, take my client's baby from the transparent cot in which she slept, and give her to a foster mother.

My client and I sat in the conference room, facing one another. It was only then that I understood the reason for the social worker's advice. On this new mother's sweatshirt two wide dark circles of leaking milk had formed. I watched her embarrassment at her inability to control this instinct to nurture, and I felt ill-equipped, unprepared. Not on the law – I knew the law. I knew what to say inside court, just not outside it. This girl, whose body now promised her that she was a mother, was being told by us all – the social worker, the solicitor, me – that what she was doing was brave and right. That what she was doing was for the best. For the baby. For her. For everyone.

I may not have known what to say to someone about to lose their child, but I knew what I felt coming from her in pulsing waves. Doubt. Fear. Powerlessness. 'This must, you know, be *your* decision,' I said, hesitantly. Her eyes remained fixed on the floor. 'Section Twenty is about your consent, your informed consent. They cannot just take the baby without it. They need an order from the court to do that.'

I felt her shift and then, in a low monologue, she began to speak. She told me of the classes she had found, the projects she had been told about. The anger-management course. The drug and alcohol groups she was going to join. She paused. 'I would do it all. I would do anything to keep her.'

I walked over to the other parties and could tell that one of them was telling an anecdote. The others were leaning in, waiting for the punchline, readying themselves to laugh. It made me hesitate. When you are the youngest professional in the room and your suit is cheap and the soles of your shoes are made of plastic, and everyone else appears to have been doing this job for as long as you have lived, it is hard to interrupt. The joke came. I stepped forward into their laughter and told them my client had changed her mind. They looked at me blankly, falling silent. I repeated the statement. She had withdrawn her consent. She understood the local authority's concerns, but she did not want to give her baby up. She wanted to fight for her, even though she knew she might lose. Their expressions changed. It was clear what they were thinking. *What are you doing? Why are you creating problems? Agreement is the best way – the least painful. We know that, and you should too.*

The other parties and the furious legal advisor made calls

to cancel hearings and meetings and stared irritably out of the window at the spring sun. In an instant, the ten minutes in court that we had anticipated became three hours of evidence, cross-examination and judgment. I paid the price in court through their unremitting criticism of this new mother and their determination to prove how strong the evidence against her was. Proof, as if it were needed, that they thought this contested hearing a futile and avoidable charade.

After the evidence and speeches were over, the magistrates filed back into court to give their decision. The lead magistrate – a man in his sixties – read out the judgment in a flat tone. The court, he said, adopted the reasons given by the social worker in her application and oral evidence. The legal threshold for the bringing of the proceedings had been met: the local authority had proved that this baby was at serious risk of significant harm. It was in the child's best interest that an Interim Care Order be made placing the baby in the local authority's care while they prepared their case. He approved the social worker's recommendation that contact between the mother and the child should be ninety minutes, three times a week. In a state-ment that seemed to me extraordinary at the time, he agreed that this supervised contact was at a sensible and sufficient level to enable assessment and bonding between mother and child at this stage in the child's life.

He looked up and past me, fixing on my client. It was the first time he had really looked at her. When he spoke, his tone had softened. He wanted to remind the mother, he said, that this *was not a done deal*. There would be a parenting assess-ment and if she engaged then the local authority would look to see whether they could place the baby back with her. *This was not the end of the line*. I noticed his vocabulary. I would grow used to it. The baby, not her baby. The mother. The father.

Ownership had been claimed, individuality removed. Was it easier to make a decision that way, I wondered? I looked up at him and he gave me a small beneficent smile. Only later would I understand how hollow his words were and learn that, nine times out of ten, once a baby is removed it will never go back. Nor did I know then that, by losing her first child, this new mother had quadrupled the prospect of the same happening to her next baby. I could imagine how, when my client went home to sit alone and stare at unworn baby clothes and wait for her body to realize no baby needed it, she would yearn to fill its void. I did not know then how regularly I would find myself in court discussing a mother's baggy clothes and denials of another pregnancy, or how often I would watch a client's plea to be allowed to parent the child already born over the swelling bulk of her next baby. But, although wretched, I never found it surprising. To be declared an unfit mother pulls at some primal part of womanhood. It is, still, one of the worst things to be accused of. I understand this overwhelming desire to try again – to prove the existence of maternal instinct and to fill a vacuum of self-love with someone who is predesigned to love you back.

After speaking to my client, the magistrate turned to my opponent and asked her to email the court a list of their facts and reasons to attach to the order, as usual. I glanced over, unsure how this could be allowed – surely it must be the magistrates' words, not the local authority's, which supported their decision – but the lead magistrate ignored my frown. When the document was sent through, the reasons listed seemed to me, at the time, overwhelming in their gravity. I knew that judges of the highest courts said that the removal of a child against the wishes of the parent was one of the greatest interventions the state can make. I understood it must be done only as a last resort, when all else has failed, after everything possible has been attempted to maintain the relationship and rebuild the family. And yet, reading that order, I admitted my relief that this tiny innocent would not suffer the experiment of whether her mother could parent or not. But in the years that followed I would tire of the regularity with which I heard the same phrases. Mother's own background of poor parenting and spells in care. A chaotic lifestyle. Low IQ. A history of domestic abuse. Drug and alcohol misuse. Self-harm. Not engaging openly and honestly with professionals. Lacking insight into difficulties. Minimizing matters of importance. Reasons by rote, in a tick-list of censure.

Over time, I, like others in the family courts, felt the swelling panic among social workers that they too might find themselves on the front page of a newspaper next to the heart-stopping picture of a dead boy whose blue eyes matched his jumper. The odds are high. Two children a month are killed by those who are supposed to care for them. No one can claim that this numbing statistic is completely preventable, but the news cycle dictates that blame must be apportioned and that social workers should bear it. In the year in which my first care client's baby girl was born, some 800 were also removed from their parents. Five years later the number had more than doubled to over 2,000, more than in any other country in western Europe.

I began to find the process wearing. I would watch a parent stand in the witness box and swear to a statement in a file that they often could not independently read, as they poured out their good intentions. Hope, I learned, even when manifested in miniature, is potent. I watched it survive up until the point when the magistrates filed into the courtroom and read out swathes of the social worker's report regurgitated as their judgment. I understood why: it took considerable courage to question a social worker's or a guardian's recommendation. They were, after all, the ones who had access beyond the parental promises of change. They had come to know what daily life within this family really looked like, and had found it untenable. Even so, I began to think it near cruelty to say to a mother and father, as some did, that if they skipped and jumped through the hoops set out for them then all would be well. In reality, by the time they reached court, there was often little they could do or promise that might sway a social worker's or guardian's opinion. I also knew, from a confession which haunted the teller, that the pressure upon magistrates to grant the local authority its application can be overwhelming. Even in a case where they might consider there is a prospect of hope, a legal advisor interrupting their deliberations to ask, with exasperation, what could be taking so long – *this case is a no-brainer* – would ensure a seal upon the order before the day was out.

But I was troubled by how often a local authority was prepared to spend money on experts to prove a mother couldn't parent, rather than on helping her learn how to do so, and by how often a guardian would simply turn and agree with them. I began to learn that it took something greater than bravery to overcome the fear of leaving a child with a parent who may cause them harm. Few, understandably, felt able to take this risk.

The occupants of the high rise flats in which Maggie lived were often transient, although a small number of them had lived there all their lives. Maggie was one of them. She had grown up there with her mother, Shelly, through a childhood marked by turmoil and danger. There were spells of time with her grandmother, Pauline, who lived with her partner, Tommy, in her own flat a few floors down. Sometimes Maggie went to foster carers – a respite, a chance for Shelly to get her life together. On occasion, Shelly did. But then the social workers would stop coming, and her slide back into chaos seemed faster every time.

Maggie was ten when she told the social workers knocking on her mother's door that she refused to go with them again. That she would not leave Shelly by herself. That she would run away, again and again, until they gave up. Shelly was her mother. She was her mum. Nothing was stronger than Maggie's knowledge and understanding of what this word meant. When she was born her infant brain had, by instinct and design, sought out the smells and sounds and sight of her mother above everyone else. The shouting and fighting and broken glass to which she had listened, as she lay deceptively impassive in her cot, were absorbed by her brain, defining its pathways and, in turn, her future. Maggie had learned how to read her mother's face, the smell in the air, the frequencies that flowed off her as though she were a satellite. She had learned she must not confuse these changing signals: that she must anticipate when she would be hugged, or shouted at, or hit. Her mother had unknowingly trained her daughter's nervous system to cope with the shattering terror of living with her. To Maggie, this was her normal.

There were other children – Maggie's brothers and sisters – but when they left the flat they did not come back. Maggie decided upon her own rules about social workers: they smiled and said they were there to help you, then they took your babies. When she turned twelve another of her new siblings was removed, but this one seemed to break Shelly in a way the others had not. Maggie watched her mother escape into a pretend world on the cold, bright screen of her laptop until, one day, saying she had found true love with a faceless stranger,

Shelly took Maggie to her grandmother's flat in the middle of the night and banged on the door. Maggie, holding the shopping bags of clothes Shelly had packed for her, knew by her mother's energy, humming and fizzing, not to say anything. She watched her walk away. She would not see her again for seven years.

When Shelly came back, Maggie was nineteen. Pauline and Tommy tried to stop Maggie being won over by Shelly's promises of a new life, a fresh start, but could not do so. Maggie was an adult now. And even if she had been a child, they had no parental responsibility for her – a legal power granted to a mother even if her actions defy the meaning of the words. All they could do was stay nearby and try to help. So it was that, after a time, the men who came to visit Shelly in the middle of the night, shouting and brawling and drinking, began to notice Maggie. It was Pauline who first saw the strain of her granddaughter's stomach on her tiny frame and realized, with a lurching sadness, that it was all about to begin again.

Three years later, a social worker called Andrea knocked on the door of the flat Maggie still shared with Shelly. She was there because Maggie, she had been told, was pregnant again. The last time she had seen Maggie was over two years ago, in court. A panel of magistrates had agreed with Andrea that this young girl had barely been parented herself; how could she possibly parent anyone else? Maggie's first baby, placed in foster care since her birth, had failed to bond with her mother. If she was not asleep during the short permitted visits, then she would often fail to recognize Maggie and would cry when she picked her up. Maggie began to hate the contact sessions and started to miss them to avoid the humiliation of her tiny daughter's rejection. There had been one last visit – a final goodbye – at which Maggie was under firm instructions not to weep or frighten her child by holding her too tight or against her will. And then she was gone.

It was an odd logic to send Andrea back to knock on Maggie's door two years later, but one I would see in practice time and time again. It was true that Andrea knew the background of the case, that she had done the work and had a pre-existing relationship with Maggie. It was also true that this relationship was, by now, toxic. When Maggie showed Andrea into the flat that day and pointed to the changes she had made ready for this second baby now growing inside her, Andrea's approach and tone seemed hauntingly familiar. Andrea said she was there to help, but Maggie feared her visit was only to gather evidence to use for the report that would, eventually, say that this baby should be removed as well.

The baby was born weeks after Andrea's one visit to see Maggie's home. As dawn broke, animal pain took over Maggie's body and she thought for a moment that she might not survive it. But then came Aaron. Baby Aaron, blinking with eyes like the father he would never meet into the medical light. A few miles away, Andrea, hearing news of the birth from the hospital, printed off the pre-prepared form enabling her to issue the proceedings designed to take him away.

What happened next changed everything. The court form was sent off, but Andrea contacted a woman who agreed to take vulnerable mothers with new babies into her home. And so, unlike the last time, Maggie left the hospital with this baby in her arms. She did not return to her flat but by agreement took her baby to a semidetached house in a modest cul-de-sac on the outskirts of town, where she met the foster carer who would teach her how to be Aaron's mother.

A week after she arrived at the mother and baby placement, an Interim Care Order was granted by the magistrates'
court. This gave the local authority control of Aaron, albeit that
he could stay in his placement with Maggie. Maggie did not
fight it; she would do anything they asked if it meant she could
keep her baby. The local authority then immediately began
their parenting assessment. At the first meeting, when Aaron
was ten days old, Maggie found herself surrounded by social
workers and professionals, their titles, laminated on cords
around their necks, confirming their power as they talked over
her about her future. By the time Aaron was twelve weeks old,
the local authority's report was finished. Maggie was doing
well in the mother and baby foster placement, it conceded.
The foster mother had reported a good bond between Maggie
and Aaron. But Maggie's own childhood had been marked by
severe physical and emotional neglect and she had never
learned how to parent. Her baby would be at potential risk of
serious harm if placed in the community with his mother. She
was compulsively compliant: she found it hard to stand up to
dangerous individuals because, so often, these people were her
only form of support and shelter. She could not see the threat
Shelly posed, and although she had promised to cut off contact
with her mother, no one believed she could. She would need a
lot of help to be a parent, both physical and emotional. And,
most importantly, Maggie herself had already conceded she
could not parent when her first child was removed. Not her
fault, of course: just history repeating itself. There was nothing
to be done.

The first time I met Maggie was at her interim resolution hearing, some nine months after Aaron was born. The solicitor

instructing me had represented her at every other hearing that had taken place in the magistrates' court. There had been delays – putative fathers needing to be ruled out, hearings adjourned, expert reports ordered. A decision had been made that the issues had become too complex for the magistrates and the case needed to go before a judge. That was how Maggie came to find herself sitting alone, in the atrium of Medway County Court on a cold morning in January, waiting for me.

Medway County Court is an ugly red-brick building. It loomed ahead of me, depressing in the grey winter light, as I wheeled my case up the winding slope and over the grey concrete bridge towards its entrance. I was late. Snow had paralysed the trains leaving London and I was over-hot from running from the station wrapped in winter layers. Once inside the courthouse I looked for the other parties, but it was almost empty. With a rush of panic, I wondered if the hearing had started without me. Then I saw a girl sitting alone on one of the flip-up chairs in the waiting area, and knew she must be Maggie.

I signed in and at the same time checked which judge we were before. Judge Nicholas. I frowned. He had been a family district judge for many years, but had only recently moved into public law. Maggie's case was to be, I discovered later that morning, his first care case. I had appeared before him many times. He could be a difficult judge, for no other reason than that he felt too many lawyers fell below his high standards of precision and preparation. I knew that the local authority's failure to send through the documents they were supposed to have provided for the hearing would already have aggravated him. Their lateness was likely to tip him over the edge.

Eventually, in a hustle of coats, the local authority solicitor and her barrister, Pippa, arrived, with loud complaints of snow and gridlock on a journey that should have taken under half an hour. Shortly after them came the social worker, then the guardian's solicitor with a message to say the guardian, Deborah, was ill. A cold. She was not going to make it.

Judge Nicholas strode into court and flung his fury across the desk. The two lever-arch files for the case, which he was supposed to have read for that morning's hearing, had, he said, been sent through only yesterday and were now lost in the court office. Pippa, stumbling for an explanation, said that she had forgotten to prepare the required documents, then immediately regretted this confession when Judge Nicholas's face turned puce. It was *just not good enough*, he said. He was going to adjourn the hearing and expected to see everyone back there again in two days' time. He wanted the practice direction documents by the end of the day without excuse. Five minutes later we found ourselves outside court, admonished. I waved off Maggie and called my solicitor. 'I think,' I said, kicking brown wet mush off the wheels of my case, 'that Judge Nicholas is actually going to be quite good at this.'

Maggie and I were again the first to arrive at court two days later, the other parties turning up just as the hearing was due to begin. Deborah, the guardian, was still unwell and was not, in spite of the judge's wrath, at court. Pippa handed out copies of the 'Case Summary and Chronology' she had emailed two days earlier. They were inelegantly done: every order made in the case so far had simply been cut and pasted in its entirety and I flinched at what the judge would say.

Judge Nicholas fumed at the documents the local authority had sent through but knew that we had to get on with the hearing. The purpose of an interim resolution hearing is to try, as far as possible, to resolve outstanding issues by agreement. If all works well, a final hearing can be averted. *No*, Pippa said. The local authority was making no changes to its plan, nor offering any concessions or alternative suggestions. It wished to place the baby with a foster carer as soon as possible; too much time had already passed. The social worker was already twin-tracking – looking for adoptive parents who might take Aaron when the court sealed the order they expected it to make. Judge Nicholas turned to the guardian's solicitor, standing alone at the end of the bench. Yes, she said in response to his question, Deborah was in complete agreement with the local authority. Judge Nicholas looked at the solicitor long enough to see her flush, then turned to me. *Yes*, I confirmed, the mother still very much contested the application.

The judge turned to Pippa. 'And the author of the psychological report – she is, I presume, warned to attend the final hearing and give evidence?' he asked. I looked at him with curiosity. Dr Dymphna was a clinical psychologist who had assessed Maggie many months before my involvement, at the request of all the parties. Her report had been filed and thereafter little had been said of it. Barely any mention was made of her findings in the social worker's evidence and, when I had read her report, I understood why. Dr Dymphna had been highly critical of the local authority's failure to help Maggie above and beyond securing her a mother-and-baby foster placement. This was a mother damned by her heritage, she had said, but until Maggie's ability to change was tested there was no way of knowing whether she could break from her past and mould her own future. There was every indication that she might be able to do so, given her demonstrated abilities so far, albeit that they were acquired only recently and in the cocoon of her placement. But there were several areas of therapy and practical help which the local authority should try before they could say for certain that the risk of leaving the baby in Maggie's care was too great, or that the case was as hopeless as they considered it.

'Yes,' Pippa confirmed, 'the expert has been warned to attend on the first day.'

'Good, good,' replied the judge, nodding slowly. He looked, for a moment, as if he were absorbed in a plan. 'I would like her called first, please. Right then.' He snapped the file shut in front of him. 'Then there is nothing for it: we must have our final hearing.' And with that he stood, causing the rest of us to start to our feet, and marched out of his door at the back of court.

The final hearing began two weeks later. I sat in court with Maggie behind me as Dr Dymphna stood in the witness box and swore her oath. She wore a boxy navy suit and round, black-framed glasses. Like many of the experts I cross-examine, she had the lightly contemptuous air of someone convinced of their superior intellect. Her answers to the questions that followed were clipped, peppered with the jargon of psychological theory, but delivered in a way that made it sound as though she was entirely uninterested in the actual outcome. I wondered if this was deliberate: nonchalance designed to add objectivity and, therefore, weight.

She spoke of Maggie without warmth or affection. Maggie's reading and writing ability was that of a child's, she said, but she did not suffer the kind of cognitive dysfunction the social worker had initially suspected. Quite the opposite, in fact. Maggie excelled in some areas, indicating a higher than average aptitude for understanding new problems if they were explained to her well. There had been a number of assumptions made by the local authority and an anticipation of failure, with heavy reliance on the removal of the previous child, but without subjecting Maggie to any real test. Dr Dymphna found that

Maggie was open, compliant, able to cooperate. She had managed to work as well as she was able with a social worker she greatly mistrusted. Maggie was able to form long and sustained attachments, and was able to prioritize her son if she was given clear guidelines on how to do so. Dr Dymphna could not, she concluded, comment on whether Maggie was able to shift her ability to think objectively about risk, because she had not been assessed while living alone in the community. The psychologist paused, as though she hoped everyone was listening. Shortly after she delivered her report, she said, there had been a meeting with all the professionals at which she had set out all the work that could be done with Maggie. And, to be plain, if the local authority had done it, she would now be able to tell the court whether or not Maggie presented a sufficient risk to justify her baby's removal. As no such work had been done, she was unable to give the court a determined view.

Direct criticism of social workers, or criticism of a local authority's approach, is most often confined to the comment columns, misleading tabloid articles and vitriolic websites, and, occasionally, the appeal courts. The bite-back to accusations of failure is often political: it was not their fault – they are underfunded, services have been cut, they are poorly paid and overworked. This is, of course, true, but does not explain why some local authorities do what others do not, or succeed where others fail, despite the same challenges and budget. In reality, those who choose to do difficult jobs for modest remuneration do so for a multitude of complex reasons. Among them, almost always, is a desire to do good, to make things better, to help. This desire does not always equate to ability. But some feel the boast of a good heart and the right intentions should excuse poor performance, and I wondered whether it was this which lay behind the expressions on the faces of social workers I cross-examined in court who objected to such scrutiny, as though their title alone were proof of their rightness.

I watched Judge Nicholas listen, carefully, as all the barristers cross-examined Dr Dymphna in turn. Then he leaned forward. 'Dr Dymphna, the level of work you are recommending with the mother is intensive. You have suggested that, were she to move from her placement into the community, you would expect daily visits for some period and close supervision for at least a year. The local authority and guardian have raised two objections to your plan. Firstly, the high level of resources required. Secondly, the consequential delay for the child if the work is undertaken and fails. You are aware that we are now required to conclude these kinds of proceedings within twenty-six weeks – a timescale that we have already missed. Can you help us, please, as to why this further delay and intervention is necessary?'

Dr Dymphna turned to look directly at the judge and he stared back at her in silence. Before she spoke, I thought I heard her give a sigh. 'The mother is young,' she replied. 'She is at the beginning of her reproductive career. She will almost certainly go on to have more children and, if this child is removed, a pregnancy is statistically likely to happen relatively quickly, as has already been the case. The child this court is concerned with is the fourth generation of his family who has had contact with social services. At some point the opportunity to break the cycle should be seized. I am aware of a study currently being undertaken to examine birth mothers in recurrent care proceedings. Records held by the Children and Family Court Advisory and Support Service suggest that one quarter of all children in care proceedings are from vulnerable mothers aged under twenty-five who have had successive children removed. Of the women studied, the average number of children removed was three. This mother,' she swept her hand towards Maggie without looking at her, 'is at very high risk of becoming one such statistic. If we don't act now, there is every reason to believe we will be back in this courtroom in a few years' time.'

I looked at her words in my handwriting in my notebook. A flow of faces passed through my memory. The young mothers and fathers I had represented. The ones I had represented more than once. All the unseen, silent children.

'I know, Sir,' Dr Dymphna continued, 'that you must complete a balancing act. On the one hand, I would say that the current timetable of twenty-six weeks imposed by the legal framework is completely unrealistic in terms of enabling and testing long-term change in a mother who has been assessed as presenting a potential significant risk to her child. I also understand that the court has no influence on the local authority's monetary distribution. However, the court should remember that the cost of a foster placement is, on average, between twenty-nine and thirty-three thousand pounds each year. The average total cost of removing a child from its mother is between two and three hundred thousand pounds, depending on what kind of placement is undertaken. I am unsure about the cost of instructing an independent social worker, and therapist, to undertake the work I have recommended in this area . . .' she waved her hand dismissively towards the window, towards the concrete car park beyond, where rain pattered listlessly into sad grey puddles, 'but I would expect it to be around a few thousand pounds.' She paused. 'Quite simply, failing to teach this mother to parent could cost this local authority significantly more than doing so.'

Dr Dymphna looked down at her report, which remained unopened in the file in front of her. 'I feel I *should* say that, in my professional experience, the success of an outcome depends in large part on the approach taken by the local authority. Where the court has gone *against* a local authority and the local authority is still not minded to get on board, then any intervention is, frankly, unlikely to succeed. Bearing this in mind, if this baby is to be placed for adoption it should be sooner rather than later. The prospects for adoption are, quite simply, better for younger children. There is an emerging body of work which suggests that emotional impact becomes encoded at a younger age than was previously thought. Placement failure is higher for children after six or seven. I should say, though, from the child's point of view, I cannot see why he cannot stay in his current placement with the mother until the adoptive parent is found. I see no difference between this and placing him with another foster carer, or several different carers, before his final move.'

I wanted to turn around, to reach and put my hand over Maggie's. I wanted to offer her something – although I did not know what, for I could not reassure her that what had been said was either irrelevant, or untrue.

Maggie gave evidence the following day. She described what it had felt like when Andrea arrived at the placement without warning '*with the adoption lady*'. How Maggie had sat in silence as they took photographs of Aaron and asked questions about him to put in his booklet. His advertisement for a new family. I glanced to my left to check that Andrea was listening to Maggie's evidence but saw that instead she was whispering to her manager, who was sitting beside her with a hand of reassurance on her back. She had given evidence just before Maggie. It had not gone well.

'They got into *such* a panic,' I said to my solicitor, on the way home after court, as I leaned against the wall of the train corridor and looked out of the window at a world already in winter darkness flashing past. 'We were halfway through my cross-examination of Andrea. She stuck to what she said in her statement – pretty much ignored all of the expert's evidence, just said Maggie's history was too much of a risk, the fact she'd already failed once and so on. Even when I put to her all the programmes Maggie had gone on – off her own bat – she just said that there was no way of *really* knowing that Maggie *wanted* to do them, or that she had actually *understood* what they had taught her. That Maggie was the sort of personality to exhibit *disguised compliance.* Damned if you do, damned if you don't, that sort of answer. She conceded, just, that there might be an argument for delaying adoption to test Maggie's parenting but that to do so was not *within the timescales of the child.* Anyway, I was asking her why she had cherry-picked a handful of notes from the foster carer to attach to her statement – the only ones which could be read as critical of Maggie. It was only then that the judge realized he hadn't got the full set of foster carer notes. He had never received the updated index and so he hadn't noticed they were missing. He was furious. Andrea had to admit that the rest of the notes were all positive, even though there was no mention of them in her statement. Pippa then tried to blame the LA's admin staff – said it was their fault, not hers. You can imagine how well that went down . . .'

I rang off with a promise to call the following day, then returned to my seat on the fugged-up train to go over my notes and prepare for my cross-examination of the guardian. The next morning, Deborah, the guardian, stood in the witness box and swore the oath. It was the first time I had studied her properly, for she had not come to any of the earlier hearings. She was in her late fifties, with a bush of wiry grey hair and an anxiously mobile face. Around her neck, on a rainbow-coloured cord, she wore half-moon glasses which rested over a brown linen jacket. Her statement was now many weeks old and, as she gave her evidence, I listened for a sign that she would retreat from her blanket approval of the local authority's case. A guardian volte-face was not unusual in circumstances where a judge appeared to doubt the local authority's approach, and Dr Dymphna's evidence had given her ample reason. I knew that the skill was less about attacking her failure to give an independent examination of the evidence, and more about showing her the way out. I needed to offer her an excuse to say she had reassessed her recommendation – point her towards fresh evidence or refer her to the progress made by Maggie since she wrote her statement. Deborah blustered and stalled, but ultimately stuck to her view. No, she said, based on her many years of experience she was quite sure that Maggie's problems were too entrenched, the challenges too hard, the support she required too great. She did not consider that leaving Aaron in the care of his mother without the constant supervision of foster carers would do anything other than place him at significant risk. I watched the judge, but he just looked carefully at her and made a note in his book.

It was late in the afternoon by the time the evidence had all finished and our closing speeches given. As the judge rose, causing us to do so in response, he looked weary. He would give his judgment tomorrow, he said, but he wanted the morning to deliberate. We need not be at court before 2 p.m. As the door swung shut behind him, I wondered how any person could possibly bear the weight of the decision the judge was being asked to make.

I stood waiting for my train at the station, unable to push away a sensation of resignation. I had been here so many times: cases where I had felt, at individual moments throughout the hearing, that my client was in with a chance. That the judge must understand the strength of the child's bond with their parent; that he must see the efforts they had made. The father had explained away the bruises. The mother had said they were not her empty bottles. They had promised there would be no more violence, no more police call-outs; they would do anything if it meant they could keep their children. My job is to fashion a crystal ball from evidence and ask the judge to decide whether he or she can see far enough within it to feel able to take the risk. But, at this point, when the decision cannot be influenced and I no longer need to believe, doubt creeps in. This must be the same fear which bears down on every social worker who has no agenda other than the protection of the child: that it must surely be the definitive act of selfishness to risk a baby's future with an experiment in which they might pay a lifelong – or the ultimate – price. The train arrived at the platform and I climbed on and took my seat, trying to push the thought away.

Six months later, in the city heat of midsummer, I stood on a tube train into Temple. I had taken off my jacket, which now lay limply over the extended handle of my wheelie case, and leaned against the end of the carriageway near an open window, allowing the strange warm gust of wind that rushes through London's bowels to cool the sweat on my neck. It was teatime and I was returning to chambers to drop off my files. Maggie's files. For that day was the last time I would ever see her.

At the end of the final hearing the previous winter, Judge Nicholas had come into court and declared he was not going to make a decision after all. He wanted there to be an assessment of Maggie's parenting in the community, at the level and intensity suggested by Dr Dymphna, and he wanted the local authority to pay for it. He found as a fact that as soon as the initial parenting assessment of Maggie had been negative they had closed their minds to the possibility of any other outcome but adoption. They had done, he said, no work with Maggie at all, even though there was much that could be done. Work that might just break a generational cycle; that might allow Aaron to be brought up by his family – and, very possibly, future children also. He would give the local authority a week to put a plan into place and if they had not done so then he would have no choice but to dismiss their application and remove their legal power over Aaron.

And so, over the coming months, Maggie moved into her own council flat in a converted house in the suburbs. The foster mother from her placement came to see her often. She was to have help with budgeting, problem-solving, parenting and life skills. And she was to have her own therapy, which might begin to loosen the complicated knots within her.

I thought of her often over the months that passed. I wondered how alone she must have felt arriving in the darkness of winter at a place she did not know. I wondered how hard it was to refuse Shelly's calls; to have the humiliated social worker visit her home, look in her fridge and cupboards and bedrooms, and wait for her to fail.

But Maggie had not failed. And so, on a bright and sunny August day, Judge Nicholas had made his final decision. There would be a Supervision Order requiring the local authority to support and monitor Maggie for a further year. There was still potential for significant risk, he said; he could not ignore it, but it was insufficient to separate this mother from her child or to give the local authority care of him. His decision was clear. Maggie would keep her son.

As I walked through the stone archway leading away from Temple Church towards chambers, I suddenly felt overwhelmed by the white-stoned gravity of the place. I knew that the risk for Aaron was great. I knew I would be unable to overcome a desire to search for Maggie's name on Google or Facebook, looking for clues as to whether she had made it. Waiting for the image that would reassure me: her face in a photograph, grinning, pressed up against the cheek of a toddler with a crop of brown hair and slanting green eyes. And that only then would I be able to admit how relieved I was; how grateful that this little boy was smiling up at me from the bright screen on my desk and not from the front page of a newspaper.

7

Peter

Inner London Crown Court

The Protection of Children Act 1978
Section 1– Indecent photographs of children

*(1) Subject to sections 1A and 1B, it is an offence for
a person—*
> *(a) to take, or permit to be taken or to make, any
> indecent photograph or pseudo-photograph of a
> child; or*
> *(b) to distribute or show such indecent photo-
> graphs or pseudo-photographs . . .*

**Archbold Criminal Pleading Evidence and
Practice, Chapter 31 – Offences against Public
Morals and Policy**
'Making' includes opening an attachment to an
email containing an image, downloading an image
from a website on to a computer screen, storing an
image in a directory on a computer and accessing a
website in which images appeared by way of
automatic 'pop-up' mechanism.

I USED TO think that I could spot a paedophile.

In my first few years as a barrister I began to believe that people conformed to stereotypes more often than they disproved them. That belief was only strengthened by the sex offenders I encountered, who so often cleaved to a type: the dysfunctional youth volunteer with the greasy stain of otherness; the pock-marked school caretaker; the reedy-moustached tyrant teacher, all using their careers as cover for their abuse. I discovered that these men – for they were mainly men – were marked out not only by their life on the fringes and their lack of social inclusion, but also by a predictable refusal to admit their crimes.

I once covered an early hearing for a barrister whose client, Mr Bunn, had been accused by a man in his twenties of abusing him many years earlier. The statements I read the night before the hearing contained the kind of horror that makes representing someone charged with these crimes so conflicting. The shock of the story left me light-headed, as though I had watched a deep wound being inflicted, someone's muscle pulled back from their bone. In the years afterwards I discovered that, although I never forgot the images that the words created in my head, their power lessened. Familiarity brought with it desensitization. Repetition reduced their impact. Torment and suffering were turned into text within a statement as human horror morphed into cold evidence. Rape. Penetration. Fissure. Bruising. Blood. Abuse. Someone else's hell translated into tomorrow's job.

When I was asked to cover Mr Bunn's hearing, though, I was still a pupil and the evidence against him made hard reading. The complainant recalled how, as a boy, he was raped by Mr Bunn on his childhood bed, which was reflected in a mirror in the hallway. He spoke of how he would watch in this mirror the moment when, upon ejaculation, Mr Bunn would fling back his long, oily hair. It was vivid and memorable and, therefore, entirely believable. When I read the papers, I was relieved that Mr Bunn's guilt or innocence was not my concern – my only duty was to represent him in a hearing about diary-juggling. All I had to do was offer no resistance to the prosecution's application to postpone the trial date by a month. My terror at being in a grown-up court, dressed in a barely worn wig and gown, was mitigated only by the knowledge that I would have to say fewer than five words. The task was to get in and get out without disruption or intervention.

Early the following morning, I walked along the corridor of Guildford Crown Court. It was busy. The blocks of seats flanking the wall opposite the courtrooms were filled with huddled conferences between barristers and their clients, uneasy eyes and twitching jaws. Without my pupil master to follow, I worried how I would identify my client. I walked to the courtroom door where the hearing was listed and scanned the people hanging around outside. Then I noticed a man sitting alone, a few feet away, staring straight ahead and past me. He was wearing bottle-bottom glasses and a soiled navy-blue anorak. In his hand he held a folded-up piece of paper and I could see from where I stood that his fingernails were stained yellow and overlong. His hair, receding at the front, was tied with an elastic band into a thin, limp ponytail.

'Is there a Mr Bunn here?' I called over the throng of people, surprised at the assurance of my voice. The man with the ponytail looked up and stood, then walked over and extended his hand for me to shake it.

After the hearing I went to the bathroom in the robing room and, even though I felt embarrassed doing so, I washed my hands three times. From then on, if I represented a paedophile, I usually did not need to call out their name. I would know who they were from a sweep of the room.

But then I met Peter. Peter had curls of strawberry blond hair, streaked with summer light. His face seemed angular, as though it were waiting for age to fill it out. Its childlike milkiness was marked with tiny freckles which ran over the bridge of his nose, upon which sat an oversize pair of rectangular tortoiseshell glasses. He wore a well-intentioned cheap black suit on his willowy frame, and smelled of soap and fear. He had just turned eighteen.

On Peter's computer were over two hundred images of child abuse.

It was the man tasked with repairing water damage on Peter's laptop who first called the police. When the two officers were shown into Peter's home by his pale-faced mother, he admitted his guilt immediately. He led the police to his bedroom, where they found his walls and shelves filled with the relics and mementos of childhood. In the corner of the room was a computer, and on it was a drive with more of the forbidden pictures stored upon it. Peter took the police straight to it. He said he wanted to show them everything he had, to draw a line and never step into this rabbit hole again.

Later that day Peter waited in the foreign land of the police station with his mother, frozen into silence by the wailing drunks and junkies with whom they shared their bench. The policemen were nice to him and he told them everything. How he had been posting pictures of himself online since he was thirteen, sending them to other boys who had asked him to do so and who had sent him pictures of themselves in return. He agreed with the officers' questions: no, he didn't know for sure that the people he was messaging were also boys; yes, he supposed they could have been men. He was quite good at computers, he told them, adept at wiping and rebooting. This was why none of those images of him on the cusp of adolescence survived on his computer. And so, after it had all begun, he had found himself straying into those corners of the internet where he should not have been. Folders of images had sprung up in surprise invitation and he had downloaded them. There they had waited, dormant, ready for the moment in the early hours of the morning when curiosity and something darker pulled him towards the glowing monitor in the corner of his room. He hadn't looked at all of them, he insisted; there were too many for that. After the interview, he repeated his confession to the two police officers separately, as though he was glad that his time of click click clicking late into the night had been ended for him – although both officers knew what kind of searching Peter must have done to have been invited into the world he had joined. They also knew that the court would not care whether or not he had looked at the hundreds of images within each file, nor whether he had taken his own kind of pleasure in them. He knew they were there and what they were, and that was enough for the law to prove his guilt.

The policemen were young and kind and told him that, maybe, this could be dealt with by way of a caution: a legal slap on the wrist. Not really a conviction, more a *you made a mistake but all this shall pass* kind of resolution. But it wasn't up to them. They filled out their forms and wrote up their statements and ticked off their boxes, then gave the whole bundle of bureaucracy over to someone from the Crown Prosecution Service. It was this unknown person, sitting in an office, who would decide Peter's fate.

The CPS solicitor looked at the file and, of course, saw only the evidence. Two hundred and fifty still photographs and thirty-eight films: innocence and violation and exploitation divided by the law into levels of perversion. The majority of the pictures were at Level 1: nude or erotic poses, but no sexual activity – the stuff of Greek antiquity and art-house exhibitions. But there were nearly fifty images and some twenty films at Level 2, showing some sort of sexual activity between children or solo masturbation by a child. And then they found the pictures and the fifteen films at Level 4: the penetration of a child by a child, or of a child by an adult. I can guess at their relief not to find the final level, Level 5: the unimaginable, reduced to the legal descriptive of 'sadism'.

The sentencing guidelines were clear. If a large number of the upper category of images had been downloaded for personal use, but not shared with others, any sentence should start at twelve months' imprisonment. It could be reduced for a guilty plea and other mitigation, but not below six months, or if the judge thought the case serious enough it could be increased up to a maximum of two years in prison. Peter was seventeen when he was reported to the police, but it had taken some five months for the CPS to work through the evidence, in which time his joyless eighteenth birthday had come and gone. And so, now officially an adult and therefore to be treated in law as such, the CPS solicitor decided his fate. Peter was going to be charged.

The papers arrived in chambers the day before the hearing, spouting out of the printer in hot bursts. I was representing Peter. Peter the paedophile.

Peter's solicitors had represented him when he entered his guilty plea at the magistrates' court at the first hearing. The magistrates, inevitably deciding the case was too serious for them to hear, had sent it up to the crown court and so a barrister was instructed. This barrister's trial had overrun and so now – the evening before Peter's sentencing hearing – the solicitors were passing Peter on to me. I scanned their cover letter. It gave a short, cold summary of what had happened. As I read it, I felt a guilty surge of relief. The solicitors acknowledged that it was too late to arrange an appointment for me to view the secret CD of all the indecent images in the case. I would therefore have to take it from them that they had been through the evidence and agreed with the prosecution's categorization. I thought of my old pupil master. *You must always view the images*, he had said. *You can never trust that the prosecution will have done so thoroughly or properly, or that their decisions are correct. Besides, this is your client and it is your duty to look at all the evidence, however horrible.* He was right, of course. But while I had represented people charged with possessing indecent images before, for whatever auspicious reason the pictures themselves kept eluding me. They were like kryptonite; the CDs that contained them were kept by the police to be viewed by the defence by appointment only, and shown to the judge only in his room in court, on a laptop kept specially for the purpose. This, inevitably, led to a limitless number of bureaucratic breakdowns, which had, so far, enabled me to avoid the gruesome obligation of my job. Reading the letter, I realized with guilty relief that my luck was going to continue.

Usually when I read a case I imagine it as though it is a film playing out in my head. It helps me remember it; helps me put myself into the shoes of the defendant, the victim, the witnesses. It helps my speech to the jury, as I pull them into this world and ask for their judgement. Of course, this sometimes means looking at morbid evidence: photographs of a room decorated with a man's blood; cigarette burns on flesh; brain or bone fragments; a long serrated knife with a dead woman's blood dried on its blade; CCTV of punches, punches, punches, before a final, lethal stamp to the head. I do not forget them, but by treating them cinematically I play the role of director, distancing myself behind the camera. But there was something different about indecent images of children, as though I had drawn an invisible line for myself that I refused to cross. I had appeared in child abuse cases in the family courts – I had seen photographs of welts and teeth marks and read statements about maggots in mattresses and cruel punishments in dark wardrobes. Why, I debated with myself, were sexual abuse images different? Why did I want to maintain that thin shield of innocence between myself and those obscure corners of the web that I knew existed but had never seen? I reasoned it was because I knew the seen could not be unseen and I feared being haunted by the images. And so, if I could get away with not looking, then I wouldn't look. But what I had not considered – not until Peter – was how my not seeing the pictures would make it impossible to represent someone properly who took their perverse pleasure from them.

I began to read through the bundle of papers on my way back on the train and it was only then that I realized what a mess they were in. Once home, I spent several hours attempting to chart how the prosecution had come to the eleven charges they were bringing; trying to work out whether the continuity – the gossamer thread stretching between the evidence and the eventual charge – was all in place. In truth, without the images and a schedule detailing which picture went with which charge, it was a maze without end. In the early hours of the morning I decided that, as Peter had already pleaded guilty to all the charges, there was nothing to be done. I would just have to get to court early and hope that the prosecutor was in the mood to be helpful. At least, I thought, the hearing was at Inner London Crown Court, a tube ride away from home. I wondered whether, if all went well, I would make it back by lunch.

Inner London Crown Court casts a stately presence over the block in which it stands, flanked by tenements and council housing and tired, polluted streets. Its black iron railings, white Portland stone and grey slated roof do not entirely prepare you for its entrance hall. Once you have climbed the steps and walked under the broad stone pediment, you find yourself in a vast, double-height hall with a barrel-vaulted roof, its walls panelled in dark timber. Above you a *piano nobile* is marked off by a wooden gallery and, were you to turn and look back at the entrance you have just passed through, you would see three large windows, set into the stone and filtering light on to the stone-flagged floor. It smells of polish and dust and, although built a year before the First World War ended, the ghosts of the Sessions House it replaced, which had stood on the site for well over a hundred years, seem to whistle down the corridors. I can only imagine the fear that leapt into Peter's throat as he crossed its threshold and took it all in.

Once at court, I went to the advocates' room and dressed in my robes. Unable to find my prosecutor, John More, who had not yet signed in, I went to collect Peter's pre-sentence report. It painted a sympathetic portrait and, with a written shrug, confessed that the probation officer wasn't exactly sure what useful work could be done with Peter to address whatever issue he had with his sexuality. At the end of the report she had suggested that, if custody was inevitable, could the judge consider imposing it *at the lower end*?

I waited outside the courtroom until Peter arrived, alone. It was the first time we had met. He stood out among the tracksuits and jeans and bravado, one of only a few wearing a suit and a face fixed with tension, failing in his effort to appear more grown up than he was. He had the habit of pushing his glasses back on to his nose when their heavy frame made them slip, and the tick gave him the air of a juvenile academic.

We sat in the corridor outside the double doors to court. Peter spoke at length and with animation about his life, finding relief, it seemed, in describing his normality. He told me about his job in a shop, the diploma he had just completed with distinction, the university place waiting for him in September. He talked about the break-up of his parents' marriage; how hard it had been for him and his two older brothers. He described the solace he had found with his local youth organization – how he would spend his weekends volunteering for them, running clubs, organizing camps. He said how proud he was to wear their lanyard with his name on it, confirming his position and his status in black and white.

I nodded and smiled and wrote it all down, then flicked to the end of the probation officer's report, tapping at the paragraph with my finger. Right at the end was a line that suggested a Criminal Records Bureau request had recently been made by Peter to the youth organization for a paid job. As they were obliged to do, given that the role involved working with children, they had asked the police whether he had a criminal record. The probation officer explained that the information had reached her after her interview with Peter, so she had not been able to ask him about it, but that she thought the court should know. It was odd, she said, that he should have applied for such a role given the charges he faced. It showed perhaps both a lack of insight into the offence he had committed and the risk he might pose to children. Peter denied it, furiously. He had not applied for the job, he insisted; why would he, knowing all this was coming up?

And then I asked him about the offence. He stopped talking and stared between his knees at the floor. I paused, at a loss how to reach him. I took out the indictment and explained that on that piece of paper were written eleven separate charges, each one called a 'specimen count', each one representing a different type of image or film. The judge would know that many images and films belonged to each count, but this was how the prosecution could capture the various levels without charging each image individually. Peter nodded his understanding, staring impassively at the black capital letters on the whiteness of the page. I paused. My voice was gentle. *I need to talk to you about prison.* He had to understand, I said, that the judge was bound by the sentencing guidelines, even if I could persuade her that Peter's circumstances were unusual in that he had been lured into this way of life by others. She would have to find a very good reason not to follow the guidelines, and if she did not then the sentence could be challenged. It was inflexible and sometimes unfair, I agreed, but that was the way it was. It might be that I could persuade the judge that the probation officer was right – that this was not a case for custody; that Peter was too young to have his life shattered by a prison sentence; and that the circumstances of his initial involvement in this world were that of a victim, not a predator. But he must prepare himself for the very real possibility that I could not and that, at the end of today, he would leave the court in a prison van. Some, faced with the possibility of prison, rail angrily at the unfairness of it all. They say they won't go; they say they'll run. Peter wasn't like that. I wondered whether, if I softened my voice and put my arm around him, he might start to cry. When Peter finally looked at me, fear had frozen his face into a mask. 'I can't do it,' he whispered, 'I just can't.' I nodded, but knew that my understanding of his fear could not prevent it. I knew too that there would be worse problems waiting for him – the prisoners alongside whom he would be incarcerated, the vigilantes who would seek their own form of restorative justice, and, even when he was released, the constant fear that people would find out, and what they would do when they did – all were more frightening than the sound of a key in the door of his cell.

I told Peter that the prosecution would probably apply for a Sexual Offences Prevention Order – a list of restrictions that would haunt his movements even after his sentence had come to an end. As well as this, for the rest of his life he would have to notify the police of his details every year. If he changed his name or moved, or even went away for a certain period, he must tell the police within three days. If he failed to do so, then he would be in breach of the order and would be brought back to court for the judge to punish the breach. He would, of course, be barred from working with children, which in turn meant that his voluntary work would have to end. I stopped talking and watched him as he slowly realized that his world, and his future, had fallen apart.

Leaving Peter within his silence, I went to find John More. He was someone I liked and respected, without particular style or flair but competent and capable, with a ghost of the overworked, careworn sigh that many of the prosecutors employed by the Crown Prosecution Service carry with them. I eventually found him in court – he was covering all the hearings that morning, some twelve cases, all listed to start at 10 a.m. There was little chance of being able to talk before we were called into court, or of being able to work out where we agreed and disagreed so that we were not left floundering in front of the judge.

The morning's progress was slow. Our sentence was still waiting to go on when the court stopped for lunch and, in the brief hour that he was free, John handed me his hastily drafted application for a Sexual Offences Prevention Order for me to agree its terms.

Eventually, just after lunch, we were called in. John smiled a greeting sideways at me as I hustled to my place, the retreating barrister before me still collecting his papers from the bench. John tried to whisper something to me, but it was too late: we were off.

We both stood as our judge walked in. I knew her well. Outside court she was quick-witted and charming. Within it, she was terrifying: bad-tempered, quick to anger and impatient. As the years slipped by and I found myself in the same collection of courts, day in, day out, it was inevitable that I would come to know the judges, the other barristers, the staff. It was also inevitable that I found myself in courtrooms opposite and in front of friends. I often wondered – as the barristers laughed and gossiped before the arrival of the judge or jury hushed them – what the clients thought of this, as they watched from the dock or the bench. How they must wonder at the split of personality required in these people to be friends one minute and foes the next. Having appeared in front of Peter's judge before, I was under no illusion that her relaxed and irreverent nature out of court bore scant resemblance to the frown darkening her face as she sat in the judge's chair, glaring down upon us.

Peter had been separated from me at the door and ushered into the large, glass-slatted dock at the back of court, into which he was locked away from the rest of us. When asked by the clerk to confirm his name and address, he did so in a thin voice. I was expecting the usual process of sentencing to unfold. John would introduce both barristers to the judge by name, with nods and slight smiles, followed by confirmation that the defendant had pleaded guilty and was here to be sentenced. He would then go on briefly to outline the charges and the facts, before handing over to me. I, rising, would take the judge through the probation officer's report, before saying something sensitive about my client's circumstances and his remorse. I would then go through the sentencing guidelines, pointing out where I conceded any aggravating factors and suggested any mitigating factors in respect of the offence itself. Finally, I would make a plea for leniency. And sit down. And wait.

Instead, our judge roared. This, from the evidence she had seen, was clearly a case of distribution of images, so why had it been charged as the lesser offence – mere possession? As John stumbled to his feet, my stomach lurched. I had not expected this, nor did I know how John would respond – whether he would fold under the wrath of the judge and agree that the more serious charge should be preferred. That would mean an immediate and lengthy prison sentence was guaranteed. I stared at my Archbold book on the bench in front of me as though hoping it might fly open and deliver up a way to stop this happening. I wondered if I should start leafing through it, or whether, anticipating my attempt to halt her, this might enrage the judge even more. John began to speak, hesitantly, but the judge barked over his reply. She was going to put this matter back until the end of the day so that the prosecution could get an answer. The court clerk called the next case. Admonished, we left, as the barristers in the case behind us eagerly filled our seats.

And so, hours later, we were called back in to court, the last case of the day. The matter had not been charged as distribution, John explained, because the defendant, by his own admission, had rebooted the computer some years before. This meant that there was little evidence of distribution, only possession. The judge scowled and stared at him, weighing up how far to go. I looked down, feeling the heat of her frustration, irritated by John's words. It was the prosecution's job to find the evidence and to charge the offence accordingly, but he had now created a suspicion in the judge's mind that Peter's proficiency had allowed him to get away with something more serious – a suspicion it would be impossible to dispel.

Before the judge could protest further, John moved on in haste, setting out the rest of the facts. Twenty-four per cent of the still images were of children under thirteen, fifty-seven per cent of the films were children under thirteen. The Level 4 films were of children aged ten to fifteen. I stared at the notes I had made and wondered whether the reduction of images to a percentage made them more, or less, shocking. John ventured, cautiously, as though worried he may be inviting further criticism, that none of the children was under ten. They were not, he said, *very small children*. The judge murmured and looked back down at her papers. It seemed the chapter of the alternative charge had been closed. I exhaled, realizing I had been holding my breath.

Without raising her head, the judge spoke into the silence. What she really wanted to know about, she said, was the requested CRB check. I sat up straight, ready to rise and mount Peter's protest. John looked pained and admitted that he had been unable to find out. The information had come from the police officer in charge of the case, who had told the probation officer about the CRB request after her interview with the defendant. No, he apologized, he didn't have a copy of the CRB application.

'Well, where is he, your police officer?' asked the judge, brusquely. In a resigned tone, John replied that he was not working that day and, no, he had not been able to reach him. Yes, the allegation that the defendant had applied for a job working with children was something, he believed, that was contested. The judge exploded. She could not possibly carry on without this information, she thundered. This man had a sexual interest in young children, which had, for now, manifested itself only in looking at images, but it was perfectly possible to suggest that it might evidence itself in other ways. It was impossible for her, she said, to put this alleged application out of her mind. Was it innocent, or predatory? She needed to know. It was now the end of the court day so she had little choice but to send everyone away and call us all back in a week's time. Without a pause she rose – as did we in a reverential wave – nodded curtly into the middle distance and swept through the door behind her. It swung shut with a bang.

And so, a week later, we all returned to court. The case was eventually called on just before lunch. The terror painted upon Peter's face was now clear to everyone, his attempt at assumed adulthood forgotten as he watched his fate balance before him. The judge, looking at her papers, remarked impatiently – as though reminding herself of the fact – that the case was a shambles. She paused, then looked up at John. 'I want to see one,' she said. John rose quickly to his feet, but remained silent. I sensed both his relief that the judge appeared to have forgotten the CRB check and his concern about what had just been proposed. The judge looked straight at the dock. 'Before I sentence this man, I want to see an example of each of the images, in particular a Level Four film and a still image. I will adjourn this matter to enable this to be facilitated. Counsel should come into my chambers when all is ready.'

And so I found myself staring at a shabby laptop screen in the judge's room, John More next to me, the judge on my other side, a police officer fumbling at a keyboard in front of us. It felt supremely odd to be standing together so intimately, avoiding one another's eyes, all still wearing our protective uniforms of robes and wigs and badges as we waited for the misery that was about to appear before us. Now the decision had been made for me I felt numb to it, ready for it, unwilling to imagine what the pictures might look like but not resisting, waiting for them to flash up and wash into me. The police officer, thick-fingered, clicked on the keyboard. Nothing happened. Panicking, he took the CD out and tried to replay it, several times. Still nothing happened. He carried on, fear disabling his efforts, the process – the CD's exit from the computer, the wiping of its disc, the replacing – all painfully slow. After the third attempt the judge's frustration brought the spectacle to an end. The officer, wincing under her gaze, confirmed that there was no other way to play the CD. The judge looked down, as though trying to compose herself. She would, she said, just have to carry on without seeing the images.

We returned to the safety of the courtroom and before we resumed our places I had seconds with Peter to explain in a half-breath what had happened. The judge came in moments afterwards and as I stood I realized I felt light-headed. I had almost no idea what she would do.

'Stand up, Peter.' The judge's voice sounded weary. 'I am sentencing you for possession of eleven indecent images. These kinds of pictures and films are disgusting. You should be ashamed of yourself, in particular of those at Level Four. This is a worrying case. You are eighteen years old and have had some disruption in your upbringing. You have denied that you applied for a job within a youth organization. The police are not able to obtain a copy of the CRB form, but on the face of it the evidence appears to suggest that you did. This means that you showed an interest in applying for a job with children and all this would entail, and then lied about it when found out. Sentencing someone like you is always of concern. Your case, however, falls squarely into the guidelines. You have amply satisfied me that the threshold for custody has been crossed. I sentence you to one year. Had you not pleaded guilty at the earliest opportunity, you would have got eighteen months.'

I felt the moisture leave my mouth. I stared straight down at my notepad and the words I had just written: *1 year custody.* I did not look back towards the dock to see Peter's face; I could not.

'However . . .' continued the judge, and my stomach plunged. 'In light of your circumstances I am prepared to suspend this sentence for two years. You need help to deal with your offending. You will spend eighteen months of this period completing a Supervision Requirement where you will be asked to attend a programme. Any breaches will be referred to me and I will not look lightly upon them. I also entirely approve of the prosecution's application for a Sexual Offences Prevention Order, which I shall make to last for seven years in the terms which were agreed before today.' She paused, and I looked up at her, willing her to finish and let us go. The judge stared straight past me and into the dock. When she spoke, her voice was thick. 'You should consider yourself lucky not to be heading immediately through those doors behind you and to prison.' And then, without saying anything further, she rose, nodded at us all, turned, and left.

Afterwards I stood with Peter in the corridor outside the courtroom doors. I noticed not only that he was shaking, but that I was too. It had been too close. I was but a hair's breadth from sitting opposite him in a cell, trying to discover which prison he would be sent to, writing down his parents' phone numbers before the guards came and led him away. I was also aware that, by some serendipitous twist, a faulty CD had kept me behind the line I had drawn for myself. As we stood there, my relief became mixed with confusion. With every verbal assault on Peter by the judge I had felt indignant; with every assumption that a man who had looked was one who might go on to touch, with every comment that he was a predator and that the world's children were at risk from him, I had felt resentment on Peter's behalf. This was not, I thought, the young man who stood before me, whom I had spent time with, talked to, whose vulnerability was so clear. But there was no point in saying all this now. Our stunned silence was interrupted by the court usher, her keys rattling loudly in the lock as she closed the court for lunch, sounding out an echo of what might have been.

I walked down the wide gum-stained pavement and around the corner of the court building as stationary traffic coughed out fumes, and thought, was that all about luck? Very bad luck. Bad luck that Peter hadn't been born twenty years earlier, when camera phones for all and portable internet were the stuff of fantasy. Bad luck that the lonely men who prowled the dark corners of the internet had found him as a confused thirteen-year-old and reeled him in. Bad luck that he had spilled his drink on his laptop. Bad luck that the delay between his arrest and his guilty plea in court had spanned that crucial birthday, which meant he faced an adult rather than a youth court. I was angry on his behalf at a system that had punished Peter rather than protected him; that saw him in the same frame as the middle-aged man who does more than look at those pictures – who creates them. I was angry at this system that had taken a young person's hopes and prospects and potential, and squeezed them until they were a pinprick.

As I approached the underground station, I noticed there was someone begging just outside it. This was not unusual; I had seen different people in the same spot before, their faces appearing, after a time, tragically homogeneous. This time it was a woman, relatively young, hunched within the shroud of an unzipped sleeping bag, worn like a cape. I stopped near her and began to scrabble in my handbag for my Oyster card. The woman raised her head and spoke. 'Please?' she said. Her voice sounded clear above the traffic noise. It was a plea, but did not sound pleading. It sounded reasonable, firm, as though she were negotiating with a child. She held out her hand towards me, the cuff of her coat sliding back to reveal the inside of an arm covered with shiny, pinkish lines, stretching as far as I could see, like a musical score of her pain. Without thinking or speaking I took my purse from my bag and gave her the only note within it, before walking quickly into the station, through the barriers, down the steps and on to the platform. I did not look back.

I stood, waiting for the strange warm rush of air that warned of the train's approach, feeling confused. I did not give money to beggars, for a variety of reasons which I felt were reasoned ones. I could not understand why I had just done that. Was it the marks on her arm? Seeing the physical manifestation of her suffering was different, I realized, from imagining it. Being confronted with the shocking reality of what she had done to herself, meant, in turn, that I was unable to avoid seeing her. And then I thought of the judge and I understood. She had seen indecent images before, that judge. She knew more than I did: more than the theory, more than the narrative. She knew, in pixelated moving colour, what it looked like – the violation by an adult of a child. But I did not. I had read descriptions of it and I had spoken to and met the victims of it. But I had not seen it. And then I wondered whether my sympathy towards Peter – my conviction that this was a contemporary crime being dealt with in a pointlessly old-fashioned way, my belief that he was a world away from the squalid men I had represented in the past – was enabled only by the fact that I had not seen those pictures that moved him in ways I would never understand. My outrage that the judge had assumed Peter to be a predator could be entirely misplaced. Maybe Peter had, as the judge suspected, told lies about the missing job application; maybe he had intentionally destroyed the material that would have seen him beginning his adult life behind bars; maybe in time, if left unchecked, he would go on to act upon those late-night fantasies. Was that why my old pupil master had been so insistent that I must look at all the evidence: not only because it was my duty to, but because only when I had seen it for myself would I truly be able to understand my client? Only then would I really be able to comprehend the crime I was defending, in the way that the judge understood the crime she was punishing. Then, having unveiled the monster, I must continue to fight for him using all my skills and abilities and gifts, because that was the job I had chosen to do and that was the system I believed in. That was the test. I realized that what had stopped me looking at these images, what had prevented me viewing the horror that took place in that dark world and then seeing it again and again and again, was not the fear that I would be haunted by it but the fear that, eventually, I would not be. That I might become desensitized to this kind of evidence as well. That I might *stop* being moved by it. And that this was the only way I would truly be able to pass the test and become what I professed to be: an instrument of the law.

Hot wind plunged down the claustrophobic tunnel. Stepping forward, I pulled my wheelie case to the platform's yellow line. Today was over. Another day, another case. I got on the train, thinking of the papers waiting to be picked up in chambers for tomorrow's case, as the tube train doors closed tightly behind me.

8

Daniel

Winchester Crown Court

Sexual Offences Act 2003
Section 75 – Evidential presumptions about consent

(1) If in proceedings for an offence to which this
section applies it is proved—
   (a) that the defendant did the relevant act . . .
   the complainant is to be taken not to have
   consented to the relevant act unless sufficient
   evidence is adduced to raise an issue as to
   whether he consented, and the defendant is to be
   taken not to have reasonably believed that the
   complainant consented unless sufficient evidence
   is adduced to raise an issue as to whether he
   reasonably believed it.

I T WAS Christmas and my sister and I were standing in a long queue in the Winchester post office. 'So . . .' she said, killing time, 'what case have you got on at the moment, then?' My family will not always ask this question. Not because they don't care, but because this world in which I half-live seems sometimes, from other people's points of view, foreign and unreal. I find myself increasingly desensitized to blood and pain and suffering, but for others the subjects can seem large and unwieldy, and so removed from normal life that I wonder whether their reticence is simply due to a desire not to talk about such things.

'Actually, I've just been given a really big case,' I said, as the queue edged forwards. 'There are five defendants. The judge decided there was so much evidence that each barrister should have a junior to help them go through it all, and I'm one of them. It's starting in a few months' time. My client's been in prison for *over a year* already waiting for the trial to start . . .'

'Hmmmmm,' she responded, so I didn't press the point that this was a very long time to wait for a trial. The law tries to prevent accused defendants languishing in prison by imposing strict time limits on how long they can be held in custody waiting for their guilt to be proved. The judge had overruled these limits to enable all the evidence to be gathered. Not just the phone records, text messages, site maps, CCTV – files and files of it – but also tracking down witnesses and persuading them to come to court. As was so often the case in a big drugs trial, the witnesses were addicts, homeless, vulnerable and very

likely to disappear. The police had just arrested the fifth defendant and joined him to the case. Now it was time, the judge had
said. The trial must finally begin.

'So, what's it actually about?' she asked.

'Oh . . .' We shuffled forwards to the front of the queue.
'Well, they are all charged with conspiracy to supply heroin,
kidnapping and false imprisonment, and then my guy and
another are charged with three counts of rape.'

'Shhhhhhh!' She held up her hand, whipping back her
head to shoot a look at the line of people waiting behind us.
'You can't say *rape* in the post office!'

Daniel was a big man, comfortably over six feet tall, slightly
overweight, and with cropped brown hair. He wore a sweatshirt embossed with his employer's logo, which also appeared
on the outside of the van he drove. Now Dan climbed into this
van to begin his drive home through the streets of outer
London. He arched his back, easing out stiffness from the day's
labours. It was Friday and his week had been a long one. He
turned on the rap CD in the van's player and edged the volume
up. As he drove back to the block of flats where he and his girlfriend lived, Dan's mobile phone rang. It was Kit, his girlfriend's
brother. Dan liked Kit. He was several years younger, but with
his shaved head and tattoos he somehow seemed more adult,
more assured of his place in the world. They arranged to meet
near Kit's flat to smoke some weed. Dan's girlfriend was working a long shift that evening, and it was Friday after all.

Kit had a group of friends who lived on the edge of trouble
and when Dan hung out with them he felt as though he was
near something dangerous and thrilling. Some of these friends,
Kit told him, needed Dan's help. Or, more specifically, they

needed his wheels. They had to get to Southampton that evening *to do some business*. Dan weighed up the prospect of a night at home alone against one with Kit's gang, and agreed. That decision, made in a moment, would change his life.

They drove around to pick up two of Kit's friends. One of them, whom Dan had met before, was called Drax. He was small and wiry, also with a shaved head, and he introduced Dan to the other man, whose name was Scat. It was only when Dan turned to nod a greeting as Scat climbed his bulk into the back of the van that Dan noticed he had a tear drop tatted on his cheek – the mark, Dan knew, of a death. The four men smoked weed and chatted together over the music as Dan drove them down to Southampton. It was midsummer and the evening was still light as the van reached the city. Dan was directed to a few addresses, sometimes stopping and parking up, sometimes driving slowly around. If they stopped, the others would get out and Dan would wait for them in the van until they came back. Once he saw them running, jumping over a gate yelling at him, 'Drive! Drive! Drive!', and then he heard the wail of a police car in the distance. The others scrambled into the van. Dan turned it around, adrenaline surging, and kept driving until the sound of the siren had faded away.

They stopped twice more after that. When the others returned the first time, they had a girl with them. She had thin brown hair and a face blotched with fear. The van door slid open on its runner and she climbed into the back, followed by Drax and Scat. Kit climbed into the passenger seat and gave Dan directions to the place he was to go to next. The music was still playing, but now and again Dan heard snatches of what was being said. The girl called Drax by a different name – Cash – and Dan heard others too. Bruiser. Enemy. Devil. Blade. Ghost. Mr Murder. Street names for drug dealers. Names that spoke of violence and power. They had smoked all the way from London and Dan started to realize he was high, but the others didn't seem to be and so he tried to focus on Kit's directions and ignore what was going on in the van behind him.

Eventually they reached a large council estate with several tower blocks of flats, surrounded by painted green railings and scrubby patches of grass. Kit asked Dan to drive slowly around the block. On their third circuit someone in the van shouted, 'There she is!' Kit motioned at Dan to pull up beside a girl walking quickly along the pavement, wearing jeans and a sweatshirt with the hood pulled up. Kit opened his door and jumped out, followed by the others, leaving the brown-haired girl trapped inside, alone. Dan got out of the van as the three men caught up with the girl on the pavement, encircling her. As she turned round to face them, Dan saw her short dark hair, and that she was very thin, her hollow eyes and sallow skin making him sure she was a junkie. He leaned against the van and looked up at the summer sky, glad of the fresh air. He could hear the girl saying something about stealing, about going to her house, and then, as he looked back towards the group, he saw Kit and the others begin to hustle her towards the van. As Drax passed him he gestured to the driver's side. 'Get in, then,' he ordered. Dan looked at him, hesitated, then opened the door and climbed back behind the wheel.

The following morning Dan woke as an indigo dawn began to break through the bare windows. Outside, the grey London streets were empty. He felt a rough dryness in his mouth, blood rushing to his head as it began to pound. He was, he realized, still drunk. It took a few seconds for him to remember where he was. In a flat – someone else's flat – on the bare mattress of a bed. Kit was asleep on a chair by the window, half dressed. The second girl they had picked up in the van lay on the bed with Dan, asleep. They had, Dan remembered, dropped the first girl off after picking this one up. He looked at her back as it curled away from him, her legs drawn up to her chest. What was her name? He noticed that she had, at some point, put her clothes back on again. Maria; her name was Maria. Dan thought suddenly of his girlfriend and, as a series of images spooled through his mind like a film reel, he felt panic start to swell. He remembered the van parked outside and that he was supposed to deliver it back to his boss that Saturday morning. He rolled away, off the bed, steadying himself before he picked up his clothes. He noticed that there was a condom lying wilted on the bedroom floor. Leaving it, he walked into the living room. Drax and Scat lay asleep on two sofas. There was another man, also asleep, whom Dan had been asked to pick up when they had decided to drive the girl from Southampton back to London and to this flat. He walked past the three of them and let himself quietly out, unnoticed.

Later that afternoon Maria stood in Waterloo station by a phone booth and clicked in some coins. She had found them at the bottom of her handbag; they had fallen through a hole in its lining and she had crouched on the floor of the station, using her fingers as pincers to draw them out. She tried to steady herself as she waited for her girlfriend, Lola, to pick up the phone. She wondered if she should have found a place to smoke a hit first. The heroin that one of the men had given her that morning was starting to wear off, and she could feel the fringes of pain begin to creep along her skin. She knew that Lola would be worried about her; that she would have called their friends, telling them that Maria had been taken by the dealers, that she was terrified they were going to do what they had done to that other girl when they drove her to a junkyard, stripped her, and beat her black and blue. Please, thought Maria, please, just don't let Lola have called the police.

Lola picked up the phone and, when she heard her voice, Maria started to cry. For the past two years Lola had given Maria safety and shelter and food and money and love – above all, love – the like of which Maria had never known. Now she had messed it all up. Lola knew that Cash and the others in the gang were dealers. Lola had bought drugs from them herself once – a few tabs of ecstasy. What Lola didn't know was that Maria was selling heroin for them. The first two drops had gone okay. Maria had sold the drugs and met up with Cash in a fast-food place. She had given him the money and he had loaded her up with another £1,000-worth of gear to sell. Cash knew Maria would smoke some of her stash – that was their deal – but as long as the money kept coming, he didn't care. But then Maria had a hard week. Her benefits were £150 per week, but her habit was now at £60 a day. Her addiction had consumed her body and mind for the last ten years. One leg had swollen to twice its size with cellulitis and her veins had collapsed. Sometimes she felt as though she might die without the drug. And there, in front of her, was the money from the first few deals and the magic powder that could make her feel human again. So Maria spent Cash's money and smoked his drugs, and tried to hide from him until he and his gang finally found her, as she always knew they would.

'Where are you?' said Lola. 'Are you all right? What's happened?'

Maria drew a breath, told herself to focus.

'It was Cash. I'm okay. I'm getting on a train home now

from London. Please – just don't tell anyone or do anything, all right?'

She hung up and walked through the station to her platform. When she saw the guard turn and walk towards the train, she took her chance and jumped the gate. No one stopped her. She rounded her shoulders and got on the train, looking for the nearest toilet. When she found it she sat on the seat and reached for the lighter and foil in her bag. A minute later she was leaning back, letting her head rest against the wall, feeling the warmth start to spread into her limbs as the drug flooded through her.

I sat next to my leader, Joe, in Winchester Crown Court. We were crammed into three rows of benches – barristers in the first two rows, solicitors in the third – with a fortress of files separating one legal team from the other. The trial was about to start.

Dan – our client – had put forward the same defence as Kit. Maria had got in the van. She may have been frightened – she had smoked the drugs she was supposed to sell after all – but there was no violence. Kit had directed Dan back to a flat on the outskirts of London, then he and Dan had left and gone out drinking. They had come back to find everyone asleep except Maria, who was withdrawing and wanted heroin. Kit had said no: she couldn't pay for it, that's how she'd got into this mess. Both men said it had been Maria's idea to trade sex for drugs. She had suggested it; she had supplied the condoms. Dan had gone along with it. The next morning Dan had left before anyone else had woken. He did not deal drugs. He was not part of any gang. He was innocent.

The fifth man, who had recently joined the trial, was, the

prosecution said, the most dangerous of them all. He was the man the others had picked up on the way back to London; the one who had led the torture to which Maria said she had been subjected. The ringleader, the mastermind. Mr Murder. The police had been looking for him for months and now they had him. But Mr Murder had an audacious defence. He had chosen to plead guilty to the charge of conspiracy to supply heroin, but deny kidnapping and false imprisonment. He was, he admitted, a drug dealer, but he had not been in the van that evening. No, no, he said. That must have been another man. Because he was no ordinary drug dealer – he was the biggest one the south coast had ever seen, and he would not waste his time on a petty little drug run like this one.

The jury filed into court as our high court judge peered down at the courtroom. Of the ten barristers before him, four of us were circuiteers who had joined the Western Circuit – one of six legal geographical areas distinct from London. With the exception of my leader, Joe, I knew the others well. One was Kit's barrister, Mark. Popular among his contemporaries, he was slightly but authentically eccentric. I sometimes caught him sketching portraits of a witness or the judge in his notebook, closing it gently if he thought anyone was watching him. Another was his junior, Lucy, who was as elated as I was to have the chance of a junior brief. The other barristers were all from the capital and were affectionately known as 'The PLCs' – The Proper London Counsel – by all the circuiteers.

At the back of the large, wood-panelled courtroom, the five defendants sat in the dock, Dan among them. I had smiled at him when he came up from the cells and into court, and he had nodded in return, jostling and laughing with the other defendants as they took their seats. I wondered if he was faking it, this ease with the justice system. The closest he had come to a courtroom before now was a minor theft offence many years ago. I watched him alongside those whose criminal experience was so much greater than his own and wondered if time in prison was all he had needed to become indistinguishable from them.

The members of the jury were taking their oath, one by one, in front of the men whose fate lay in their hands. Some flicked glances towards the dock; others openly stared. I knew why. When lined up next to each other, the five defendants were an impressive sight. With little to do in the eighteen months spent waiting for their trial, they had passed long hours working out in their cells. Now their torsos strained against the fabric of their sweatshirts and, as they sat back on their chairs, legs spread, their power radiated across the courtroom.

Once the jury were sworn in and introductions completed by the judge, the prosecutor, Philip, leaned across the defence advocates and began to give his opening speech. Three of the defendants, he explained, had already pleaded guilty to dealing drugs but denied the other charges. Dan and Kit – he gestured towards the dock with a wave of his arm – denied them all. Tomorrow the jury would hear from the complainant, Maria, and she would make them sure, Philip said gravely, that all five men were – beyond any reasonable doubt – guilty.

Maria stood in the witness box the following morning looking frail and thin, shielded from the dock by a screen. She was wearing a grey jumper and black polyester trousers which were an unnatural fit as though, in a panic that she had nothing to wear, she had borrowed them from someone much larger. Maria was no stranger to a courtroom, but it was the dock that she was familiar with, not the witness box. She looked out at us with an expression that was hard to read. Guarded, tough, suspicious of us all.

Philip began slowly to draw out her evidence. She had not wanted to go with the defendants that day, she said. She had been afraid they would hurt her because she owed them money. She had protested. They had dragged her inside the van and hit her. The threats, the violence, the negotiations over where she was going to get the money to repay them had continued all the way to London. They had taken her to a flat almost bare of furniture and with no electricity. That's when two of the men had left to go out drinking, and the other three had tortured and beaten her. When these men had eventually fallen asleep, the two other men had come back. She said she had been withdrawing from heroin by then, but denied that she had agreed to have sex with the men in return for drugs. She was not a prostitute, she said – or at least, not then she wasn't. She had struggled and resisted and told them no, but they had taken her into the bedroom and both had raped her. Afterwards one had given her some heroin to smoke. When she woke up, one of the two men had gone. She had been beaten again and told she must sell more drugs to pay back the debt she owed. She could not see that she had any choice. She was loaded up with a new stash of drugs to sell then dropped at the railway station to find her own way home. She knew who the defendants were – she recognized most of them from previous drug drops. She had picked them all out at an identification procedure. All except one. Mr Murder.

After the court had finished for the day and we were packing up papers, Lucy turned to me. 'Jesus,' she said. 'I mean, if that's true – what she just described – it's pretty bloody bad, isn't it?'

It was pretty bloody bad. It was also, I was as sure as I could be, true. The sadistic beatings Maria had described held a level of detail that could only have come from experience. What I did not know was whether Maria's beating had happened that night, in that flat, or whether she had transposed it from another time in a life full of chaos and crime, homelessness and prostitution. Or maybe it had happened to someone else, someone who had told her in the way she had just told us. For the other barristers and I, unlike the jury, knew what evidence was coming. We knew which witnesses from Maria's world were going to come to court – some freely, some against their will – to tell their own stories. We knew that once these stories had been told, the jigsaw pieces of Maria's case just might not fit together quite so well.

It was Lola – not Maria – who had called the police the night Maria arrived home. Maria refused to make a statement and said she did not want to talk to them. The officers who went to her house said Maria had a bruise to her right eye, but no other marks on her face. It was not until the following evening that Maria told Lola what had happened and that she had been raped. Lola immediately called the police again and arranged for Maria to come in for a vulnerable witness interview and a medical examination. Maria then described to the police and doctor a prolonged and vicious beating and gave details of a rape in which she had continuously struggled. Yet when she was examined the only injuries the doctor could find were the bruise under her right eye and a wide patch of reddening to her left cheek. She had no bruises, marks or abrasions to her legs, head, chest, back, arms or anywhere else, externally or internally. Nothing was there, except the sad and fading scars she had previously inflicted upon herself.

Maria, it transpired, had tried to destroy the evidence that could – and did – identify her alleged rapists. Lola had discovered Maria's clothes in the washing machine after Maria failed to start the cycle correctly. She had taken them out, found semen stains on both her jacket and her jeans, bagged them, and handed them to the police.

Maria had denied again and again that she was a prostitute. She was in a lesbian relationship, she said, with someone she loved and who loved her back. She had only started walking half-lit streets at night in search of payment after – indeed because of – the rape. But that was not what the other witnesses said. Oh yes, agreed one, Maria was a prostitute all right – same as she was. She had been for years. Everybody knew it.

There was one final piece that did not fit. The police had offered Maria and Lola witness protection for as long as it took for the trial to be over – longer if necessary. They would get food vouchers and subsistence payments as well as the guarantee of safety. It was many days before they took up this offer of protection. In evidence, Maria admitted that during the whole of this time – in between her interviews and examinations – she was still dealing the drugs that Cash had given her when he had dropped her at the railway station in London. She met buyers, took their money, then handed it over to Cash in return for a second batch of drugs. It was only after she had got this second stash that she went with Lola into witness protection. She took the money she had made from selling half of the batch and the rest of the drugs with her, despite the rules that said she could not.

The evening after Maria's evidence I read my notes over and over again. I could not work out why she would lie. She had so much to lose. These men were not the only ones in their gang: there was always someone higher up the chain, running the show, ready to punish those who turned. I was used to unanswered questions in almost every case, but there was usually a reason why someone would come to court and make something up. A reason that explained why they would take this risk. And, as I read through Maria's evidence again, I found it.

Towards the end of her evidence Maria had used a phrase which struck me. Lola had given her an ultimatum, she said, the night before she decided to accept the police's offer of witness protection. She'd had enough, Lola said. It was Cash or her. If Maria didn't stop dealing, then it was over. Lola would kick her out and she'd be on her own, again. I drew a circle around the words in my notebook. That was it – that was the thread to pull on. If Maria lost Lola she lost everything. Lola was more important to Maria than being arrested for perjury or wasting police time. She did not care about prison or being in trouble with the police – her world had been shaped around these things. Lola was even more important than a lifetime of watching over her shoulder for Cash's gang if she gave evidence against them. I realized that this was not just a tale of deprivation and exploitation. It was, at its heart, a story about love. Maria knew that if she confessed to getting into the van or to exchanging sex for drugs – to doing what she had, in effect, already been doing behind Lola's back – then that would be the end of two years of safe reprieve. Maria had not been trying to wash out the semen stains to hide them from the police; she had tried to wash them away to hide them from Lola. The redness that marked her face two days after her return but had been absent the night the police came was a new injury. It had come from the argument with Lola when she had glimpsed Maria's double life. What could Maria possibly say to explain the semen and her absence – except: I was taken, I was beaten, I was raped. And once she had said it she had to stick to it, not for fear that she might get in trouble with the police, but in the certain knowledge that, otherwise, she would lose Lola.

At 9 a.m. the following day, I trailed through the late-January wind to court. The brutalist façade of the courthouse was speckled with flint and in the morning gloom of winter it had a menacing feel to it. I was aware of a quiet thrill of excitement as I walked into court with my new theory. Joe was not yet there, but I found Mark in the robing room, flicking through his notes. He looked up and greeted me. I sat down opposite him and told him what I thought.

'I mean, I don't know – it's not like that is what our client has said, that Maria is lying to Lola, not us. It's not our instructions. It just seems to – I don't know – fit. Do you think?'

'Yes,' replied Mark, deliberately. 'I do think.'

Mark's cross-examination of Maria came before ours. As he stood to begin, Maria's face was set, her jaw squared in defiance. His style was respectful, firm, stealthy and very effective. Maria scoffed in denial every time he challenged her, but the explanations she gave just opened up new ways to expose her. The jury learned of other allegations of rape Maria had made which were almost identical in detail, and which she later retracted once they got her what she needed. To her claims of weakness and fragility they were shown evidence of the violence she had meted out on others. And they were told of the many and varied reasons why Maria might have decided to take up the offer of witness protection long after she was offered it: reasons which had little to do with any desire for reformation. Her evidence fell apart, piece by piece. I found myself looking away, avoiding her humiliation. I realized I felt none of the satisfaction I often did when watching effective cross-examination, for Maria was so obviously a victim that no matter what the truth was, there could be little pleasure in witnessing her exposure. She denied everything Mark said, but I could see there was little fight left in her. She was worn out.

Mark paused. Lola was the only reason, he suggested, wrapping up, that Maria had made this allegation. Lola, whom she said she still loved even though they had now broken up – something Maria blamed on the stress of the case – was the answer to it all.

Maria's denial was exhausted, her tone flat. She looked beyond Mark and said, almost to herself, 'I thought if I didn't go through with it I'd lose everything. But I've gone and lost it anyway.'

After the other defence barristers had finished their questioning, Philip re-examined her. Maria resumed her denials, her assertions, and maintained to him that although she had not wanted to come to court, although she still did not want to be there, she was telling the truth. What else, I thought, looking at her words in my notebook, could she possibly say?

Joe and I sat in a small conference room in the cells on a pair of nailed-down chairs, looking at Dan. The prosecution's case was over. The jury had heard it all. Over weeks and weeks, they had sat and listened to the evidence. Reams of text messages of drug deals in street slang read out by Philip in stilted tones, much to the mirth of the jury; cell-map sites and CCTV plotting the calls to estates in London and along the south coast, and the journeys between the two. Then came the prosecution witnesses. Street-level drug dealers, there to confirm it was the defendants who had given them heroin and crack cocaine to sell in return for drugs. They were an army of the people that life had forgotten, who climbed up the steps to the witness box with crutches and eye patches and lost limbs, and told the tale of what it is to be beholden to these drugs. Some were forced to come to court and, once in the witness box, were too terrified of the defendants to give their evidence. Two came from their own prison cells, one refusing a screen to shield him from the defendants because he was, as he put it, *banged up with them anyway.*

And now, it was the defendants' turn.

Joe leaned across the metal table and said the words I had said to clients many times before. Dan did not have to give evidence. No one could force him, not even the judge. He had answered 'No comment' in his interview, but he had written a prepared statement which outlined his defence and which had been read out to the jury. The jury had heard the questions put to witnesses by Joe, and therefore knew what Dan was denying and what he said had happened. But nothing was better than a defendant telling his story in his own voice, standing in the witness box to be weighed and tested. This would be his only chance. If Dan did not give evidence, Joe warned, then the judge would tell the jury – as the law says he must – that they could draw an inference from his silence. An inference, if they wished, of guilt. But when he learned that his co-defendants may not give evidence, Dan leaned back, his decision made. He was not going to either. He looked relieved and I wondered, not for the first time, how so big a man could be so weak. It was fear, of course, but of what? Fear of speaking of things of which he was ashamed? Fear of getting it wrong – of not having the right words at the right time? Fear of clever people's tricks? Fear of lies unravelling? Or was it fear that if he told the truth worse things than a prison sentence lay in wait? I wanted to say to him *You are different from them. They have nothing to lose by going inside. You have everything. You do not look like, sound like, act like them. You do not have a criminal record many pages long. You wore your work uniform, drove your work van. You do not have a street name. You did not try to hide yourself.*

It is not your fist that is accused of punching, nor your palm of slapping, nor your foot of kicking. You have a girlfriend, you have a job, you have a life. Fight for it. But he knew all this from Joe and so I wrote a note of Dan's decision in my book, asked him to sign it as a record that he was going against our advice, and followed Joe out of the cell.

Back in the courtroom we all stood when the judge walked in. As the other advocates sat down, I noticed one stayed on his feet. Mr Murder's barrister. He had said very little in the trial so far, asked few questions, challenged only what he had to. Now he turned to the judge and, as his client left the dock and walked up to the witness box, confirmed that Mr Murder was going to give evidence. It was to be the performance of a lifetime.

He was the youngest of the five defendants, but he stood in the witness box and commanded the room. It was not just the other defendants who were under his spell as they sat in the dock, watching him with faces of studied blankness. The rest of us – barristers, judge and jury – were gripped by him too. His power was magnetic, fascinating and terrifying. He was also one of a small selection of defendants I have met who are, I suspect, truly dangerous. The prosecution said he was Cash, and Ghost, and Mr Murder, and Bruiser, and all the other names that were exchanged between the dealers. As he explained to us during his evidence, a name never belonged to one person. Cash was the guy you called for drugs, the guy you met on the street corner, the guy who came to your door when your debt grew large enough. It was, he said, more than anonymity. It was a *franchise* – one based on ensuring confidence in his customers. They knew Cash's gear was the best, no matter whether Cash was one man or ten. Although he didn't call them customers. He called them cats. Cats who needed feeding. The takeover of a new drugs patch would happen slowly, methodically. London was too full now – there were too many gangs already fighting over turf; but the towns outside it were ripe for the taking, full of junkies who craved good-quality gear. There were fewer guns and less competition. His strategy for taking over was well practised. He would pretend to be a junkie for a while, live rough, come to know the places where the dealers went, and then, when the time was right, he would start to introduce his own supply.

'Did you ever take the drugs yourself?' his barrister asked him.

Mr Murder looked as though he had bitten into fruit and found it rotten. 'No way. I would never touch that stuff. It's filthy.' Not for the likes of you, I thought, watching him. He had a beautiful face. Olive skin, high cheekbones, mesmeric feline eyes. He had changed into a suit and open-necked white shirt, and I thought of Maria in her borrowed clothes and wondered if she had ever really grasped the contempt that people like him had for people like her. When they asked her to try a new batch of heroin had she ever thought, '*You* try it. *You* take the gamble', or had her mind been filled only with desire for the drug, with no room left for doubt. The risk of addiction or overdose or death was not one this man would ever be prepared to take. But the risk of getting caught? Yes, he was prepared for that. It was an inevitability, eventually, he said. But it was also a price worth paying. He could make more money in a month dealing drugs than in a whole year doing a normal job. He could buy cars, clothes, watches – whatever he wanted. At the age of twenty-one he had – he imagined – earned more money than his father had over a lifetime. He could do prison – he had done it before. In fact, that was how he had met the man who got him into the game. He might lose control of his patch, but his reputation would be bolstered, his contacts fostered by those other dealers he met in prison. When he was released he could try to take it back or move on somewhere else. He simply did not care about being caught. Which is why he was telling the court now, today, that he had not been there in that van. He was the only one Maria had not identified, and that was because he had never met her. He was Mr Murder, the Devil, Ghost, Bruiser – he was at the top of the tree. He would not bother taking some junkie prostitute off the street for the sake of a mere £1,000. His arrogance and contempt were as breathtaking as they were chilling.

When this man of a dozen different names had retaken his seat in the dock, Kit stood up. Only then did I realize that, in the lunchtime adjournment, Mark must have persuaded him to give evidence. As Kit left the dock, walking stiffly, his eyes fixed straight ahead, I looked at the other defendants and for the first time I saw how high the stakes were for giving evidence. Dan's face was grim, his jaw clenched. In his face I saw his fear: fear of what Kit would say, but also fear for Kit – and I finally understood that to turn against a dealer was worse than going to prison. It could be a death sentence.

Kit fidgeted in the witness box, his eyes flicking between Mark and the jury. He did not look at the dock. His evidence was no surprise. He, unlike Dan, had given answers in his numerous police interviews and he stuck more or less to these. He was just a drugs runner, he said, acting under orders, not part of any conspiracy or plan. The sex had been Maria's idea. She wanted drugs, he had them, and this was her way to pay. She had provided condoms and then, the following day when Dan had gone, she had given him a blow job in return for more drugs. That's why his semen was on her jacket and on the backs of the legs of her jeans. She had been naked the night before – there was no way it could have got on to her clothes then. Yes, he said, the four of them had been in the van that day. And the man they collected on the way to London? Kit shifted, cleared his throat. When he spoke his voice sounded weak. It was the fifth defendant. Mr Murder, Bruiser, the Devil. It was him. He, you see, was the one in charge of it all.

And then it was all over. Now it was the lawyers' turn – their chance to sift through the evidence, offering up those nuggets they wanted the jury to see in their closing speeches. *Look here!* one would cry. *No! Over here!* said another. I watched the jurors' faces as they were pulled this way and that by elegant words of persuasion until, at last, after nearly two months, it was all over.

After a jury have been sent out in a long trial, we fall into a sort of suspended space. Nothing more can be said or done and fate must play her hand. A term-end feeling of lightness takes hold and, in a case full of the kind of camaraderie that builds among those marooned in a place for weeks on end, it becomes easy to forget why we are there. Easy, amid the long lunches and chatting and waiting, to stop thinking about what might happen when the jury file back into the courtroom and give their verdicts.

Late in the afternoon on the fourth day of their deliberations, we were finally summoned back to court. It was not a verdict. The jury had a question. They were confused. They wanted the judge to repeat the legal direction on the definition of consent.

A few years before this trial the law had changed. It altered the burden of proof in law for specific circumstances of rape and the definition was now hugely complicated. If the prosecution could prove that a complainant was being held against her will when she had sex with the defendant – and that the defendant knew she was being held against her will – then the burden of proof switched. He was guilty of rape until proven innocent.

However, if the defence had raised sufficient evidence about the issue of whether or not she had consented to sex, then the burden switched back to the prosecution. They then had to prove that she had not. In one sense the law was logical. The same statute defined 'consent' as an agreement by choice from someone with the freedom and capacity to make that choice. Someone held against their will could not have had a genuinely free choice over whether or not they had sex. But the way the law expressed itself and the technical detail of the evidential burden switching back and forth was dense and convoluted. But this is the law and the judge was obliged to read it out.

The judge repeated the direction, slowly. I watched the frowns deepen upon the jury's faces. They looked tired. I wondered what factions had developed among them, who had argued, who had aligned themselves with whom. With breaks for illness and bad weather, they had been locked in the same room for nearly a week. They filed out again and an hour later another note came through. *We still have not reached a verdict upon which we are all agreed. Can we go home now, please?*

At midday the next day the judge called us all into court. The jury had been out for nearly thirteen hours in total. Unless counsel objected, he intended to give a majority direction and tell them that if ten of their twelve could agree on verdicts then he would accept that instead of unanimity. As we debated, the usher hurried into court and up to the judge's bench. He leaned forward as she reached up to whisper something. Then he sat back. 'No need,' he said. 'We have a verdict.'

The jury filed in. They looked exhausted and tense. The foreman stood and was asked by the court clerk if the jury had a verdict on which they were all agreed. Yes, he nodded, for all but one defendant.

My heart pulsed. It was Dan; it must be Dan. The court clerk read out the charges, one by one, for each defendant. The foreman gave the jury's answer in reply. Drax. Guilty of kidnapping, guilty of false imprisonment. Scat. Guilty of kidnapping, guilty of false imprisonment. Kit. Guilty of drug dealing, guilty of kidnapping, guilty of false imprisonment. Guilty of three counts of rape. He got to Dan. My head felt light. Guilty of drug dealing, guilty of kidnapping, guilty of false imprisonment. Guilty of three counts of rape. It was Mr Murder. They could not decide on Mr Murder.

The judge gave the jury a majority direction and sent them out again. An hour later they came back with a new lightness to them. The foreman stood again as the clerk put the questions to him. On the charge of kidnapping, how did they find the defendant? *Not guilty.* On the charge of false imprisonment, how did they find the defendant? *Not guilty.*

From behind me, a lone shout shattered the silence. *Thank you, thank you, thank you!* I turned to look. Mr Murder was on his feet, grinning, punching the air. Dan was sitting on the end of the row, his face blank. Next to him Kit had his face in his hands. As I listened to the sounds of victory coming from his co-defendant, I wondered whether Kit understood that this jury, unwittingly or not, had just saved his life. For had it been Kit who was leaving the dock and not Mr Murder, that would surely have been the end of it.

A month later Kit's junior barrister, Lucy, and I stood in a lace-curtained hotel in Winchester, colleagues in black tie and long frocks gathered around us. There was a circuit dinner that evening and the smells of scent and hairspray and anticipation were thick in the overheated room. On top of a ring-marked chest of drawers was a small television.

'Here it is – turn it up!' Lucy cried. On the screen a local newsreader, lipstick bright, introduced our case by name. The screen went dark as grainy footage of a van driving along an empty road began to play.

'Oh my God! They've done a reconstruction!' someone yelped. At that moment the word 'reconstruction' appeared in white text at the bottom of the screen and the room erupted into laughter and applause. The shot moved from van to street and a stock film began to play. The footage, shot at hip height, followed a gang of shaven-headed men, their hoods pulled up, their strides loping. They walked in slow motion along a street in an anonymous town. One turned to look at the camera. The face under his hoodie had been fuzzed out with a round, black spot. In slow motion he pointed his first two fingers at the camera and made a shooting gesture. A voiceover began – the cadence and bass similar to those in blockbuster trailers in cinemas. *They came: from London. Their purpose: drugs. Their intention: crime.* Across the screen flashed five mugshots of the defendants in black and white. 'I mean, they do look pretty terrifying,' someone muttered. Dan's picture was second from the left. I could not take my eyes from his face. *After a trial lasting nearly three months, a jury had little trouble in finding the defendants guilty of the kidnap, false imprisonment and rape of a local girl. They were sentenced today at Winchester Crown Court. Now this London gang will terrorize our streets with violence, drugs and guns no longer.*

'Wait – guns? What?' scoffed Lucy. 'And they haven't exactly got it right about who was found guilty of what . . .' But she was hushed by the others in the room as the screen cut to a reporter wearing a suit and a jazzy tie, standing outside the courthouse. He leaned in towards the camera as he spoke, a large fuzzy microphone in his hand.

'Yes, Suzie, thank you. Today, at Winchester Crown Court, a judge imposed three life sentences on each of the two men convicted of multiple rapes.' As he spoke the screen cut back to the mugshots of the defendants, one by one, as the reporter confirmed their names and the sentence each had been given by the judge that day. Scat – fourteen years in total. Drax – thirteen years in total. Mr Murder – seven years for the supply of drugs. And then Dan's and Kit's faces flashed up in turn. A total of three life sentences each.

I could not get the mugshot of Dan out of my mind. Not when we left the hotel, or throughout dinner that night and drinks afterwards, or for weeks and weeks. I had never seen that photograph before. The police must have released it to the press. When, some months later, I walked up the steps under the large porch of the Royal Courts of Justice for the hearing to appeal Dan's sentence, it was this mugshot I held in my mind.

Two hours later the high court judges in their oak-panelled court granted my appeal against Dan's sentence. He – like Kit – would no longer serve three life sentences, but sixteen years instead. The appeal judges said they did not consider either defendant sufficiently dangerous to warrant the other kind of sentence they could have imposed: an indeterminate sentence for public protection. This was the sentence that would, even after it had been abolished, cram prisons with inmates locked up for years beyond their release date because of their inability to prove their rehabilitation. As I listened to the appeal judges discuss and discount it, I did not appreciate at the time that Dan had in fact avoided a fate worse than life imprisonment. A sentence that was not what it seemed. A sentence that had no end.

After the appeal hearing was over I went down to the cells

below court to see Dan and to explain what had happened. I went to say goodbye. I was alone – Joe was involved in another trial. Dan was, as he always had been, affable and polite.

'I really appreciate it, Sarah. Thank you, for everything you've done.' I found it hard to look at him and concentrated instead on calculating his new release date in my notebook. The time he had already served would be taken off, I explained, and he would spend the rest of one half of the sixteen years inside. Then he would be released on licence for the rest. He would be given a list of licence conditions: reporting, signing in and so on. If he committed another crime, he would go back to prison to serve out the rest of the sentence. He was thirty-one when he was first remanded. His sentence would finish when he was forty-seven. Most of his middle life.

I walked over the crossing outside the Royal Courts of Justice and went, on impulse, to a nearby newsagent on the Strand. I bought a lighter and a packet of cigarettes, turned back on myself and, one after the other, smoked several of them standing underneath the awning of a café, cradling the coffee I had bought as cover. I rarely smoked and almost never during the day. The act of doing so in the morning, somewhere that I was likely to be seen by someone I knew, felt both rebellious and childish. I stared at the Gothic Victorian beauty of the building opposite. I could not make out the detail of it from where I stood, but I knew that, on top of the central arch at its highest point, was a statue of Jesus. I thought of Dan, the television mugshot now replaced by the face I had seen a few minutes earlier. I thought of Maria, and of the sorry procession of witnesses who had followed her. I thought of Mr Murder. And I thought of our imperfect justice; of a system striving for righteousness even though our humanity ensured it was, so often, beyond its reach.

I rolled over the case in my mind. The evidence seemed so

familiar that its gravity had lost its sting. Did I believe every-thing had happened as Maria said? No, I didn't, because the other evidence didn't support it. But did I believe that a vulner-able addict driven by a gang of violent drug dealers to a flat in a city she did not know and could not reasonably have left may have offered them sex while she was withdrawing from drugs in an effort to pay for more? Yes, I did. Did I think it was rape? Yes, I did. I thought of the words from Mark's closing speech, which had haunted me since I heard them. *These were raw, commercial, sordid acts of relief for the two defendants who bought them from her. That was the reality, otherwise every sin-gle punter Maria went with would risk being called up in court on a rape charge.* Did I believe that every time a man picked up a prostitute whom he knew was selling herself to feed an addic-tion that controlled her, or to pay a pimp, or both, he was committing rape? Yes, I thought, stubbing out my cigarette on the paving slab, grinding the butt with my shoe. Yes, I did. It was these women who risked having to sign cautions for solic-iting until the police grew tired of warning them off and added another offence to their list of convictions. But it was the men to whom they sold themselves – who must know the circum-stances they were exploiting – who were really guilty of a crime. I did not, nor would I ever, know the truth of Dan's involve-ment: how often he had met the gang before, what he knew, what he really believed. But I did think that he was guilty.

My mouth was dry and I drained my takeaway cup, the taste of scorched coffee mixing with old smoke. I turned left, down an alleyway towards Temple, and headed towards cham-bers, ready to pick up the next day's case.

9

Helena

Brighton County Court

Children Act 1989
Section 1 – Welfare of the child

(1) When a court determines any question with respect to—
  (a) the upbringing of a child; or,
  (b) the administration of a child's property or the application of any income arising from it, the child's welfare shall be the court's paramount consideration.

CONDENSATION MISTED my view out of the train window. It was early and the world outside was still in darkness. Two A4 files with tabbed pages sat, unopened, on the train table in front of me. They were the result of twelve months of bitter arguments between my client, Helena, and her husband, Ed, over their three-year-old twins. I was on my way to Brighton County Court, where a judge would decide their children's future for them because they could not. Tucked into the top of one of the files were the documents I was obliged to prepare for this final hearing. While typing them, I had realized that over the last year not a month had passed without husband and wife swinging verbal punches at one another in a courtroom. Their divorce had, by law, encouraged them to turn to blame. They were required to list examples of why the other's behaviour was unreasonable whether they wished to or not, and so the tone was set. Six applications, fifteen court appearances, two appeals – an exhausting and costly fight, even if the arguments themselves were all too familiar to those who heard them. And all for something which, experience had taught me, was likely to elude both parties long after today was over. Because what they really wanted – above resolution, even above achieving their demands – was their *day in court*. They believed that the only way bitterness could release its grip was to have this person – whom once they had loved more intimately than anyone, but who now appeared a stranger to them – answer to their crimes. They wanted to expose this person before someone with official independence, who would, they hoped, turn and say '*You* are the good one, the

better person, the better parent.' My job has taught me to understand the power of a judgment; how a compromise will not grant
the vindication that drives some people to court. They need to be
able to say *The judge made me*, because that means that they
have not, as they see it, agreed to lose. It is not until it is over that
they realize that no one – not me, nor the judge, nor the law – is
able to give them the release they so long for.

I stared out of the window in the suspended quietness of
the nearly empty carriage as the train pulled away from Victoria Station and the city began to bleed into suburbia, dreading
what lay ahead. I realized I could make out Christmas lights,
tiny orbs of red and green glowing in the windows of the houses
visible from the railway line. At my feet, tucked under the table,
was a weekend bag of clothes. Tonight, when the case was over,
I would catch another train home, back to my parents. For
today was not only the climax of twelve months of work; it was
also Christmas Eve.

Helena and Ed had met eight years earlier in the sticky city heat
of midsummer. They married six months afterwards and, for
the first time that winter, snow fell in their seaside city, as
though the world had saved its chilled confetti as a gift. The
ceremony took place in a small room furnished with a large
wooden table and four metal-legged chairs, their seats covered
in worn pink plush. Helena wore a yellow dress and said she did
not care about the civic melancholy of the place. Afterwards
they went with their quartet of witnesses to a restaurant, where
their booking had been overlooked and Ed rowed with the staff.
Eventually a table was found and Helena became effusive with
gratitude, whispering an apology on behalf of her new husband,
taking care that he overheard her.

Their twins were born after the desperate agony of miscarriage and rounds of IVF. Afterwards these longed-for babies seemed to sit within the cracks that had opened in their parents' marriage. Throughout their young lives the children never truly knew familial peace, but it was not until they turned three and Christmas wreaths and trees and lights filled the family's terraced street that the war began in earnest. On Christmas Eve, after threatening for months that he would do so, Ed left. As other parents conspiratorially took bites from fireside carrots and half-drank glasses of milk, he thundered down his front path, a shopping bag of clothes banging about his leg. The twins slept through the row despite its intensity and volume, and Helena was left alone to lay their stockings by their beds, holding her breath so she did not wake them with her sobs.

The next day Ed came back to the house, demanding to see the children. *It was Christmas Day!* he cried. Helena's attempt to slam the front door was blocked by his foot and there was a tussle. Ed, without warning, let go and the door sprang back, striking Helena in the face and causing hot tears of pain and shock.

As I scanned through the papers in the train's bright artificial light, I wondered again where the twins had been when the police arrived that Christmas morning, responding to Helena's call. There was little mention of them in the officer's short report, which reduced the altercation to a single paragraph. Were they watching from the stairs, or in their room among the debris of unwrapped stockings, listening to this adult world of shouting and strangers' voices? They were absent from everyone's account of the incident and I was reminded of something a judge once said to me, in answer to my submission that my client was only thinking of her children. 'Miss Langford,' he sighed, 'if the people who appeared before me actually put their children's interests before their own, my court would be an empty one.'

After the police had calmed him in their car, Ed, horrified by the blue lights reflected in his neighbours' windows, accepted the caution they offered. It was not a criminal conviction, the officers explained. If he admitted it, then that would be it – the matter would be over. They warned him to leave Helena and the children alone, and to seek his remedy through the courts.

Ed retreated to his mother's house on the other side of town to wallow in his fury and prepare his fight. In his absence, Helena began to plan a new life without him, back among the fields of her childhood. As she researched schools and looked for somewhere to rent near the house where her parents still lived, she prepared herself for the solicitor's letter that Ed had threatened would come. She knew he would demand to see the children and she knew that she was going to refuse, for reasons she had magnified in her mind. She told herself he was volatile, unreliable – that she had a duty to protect her children. But her refusal was, in truth, founded on another reason she could not admit: that this brave new world frightened her and this was one way she could regain some control.

When Ed's letter arrived she read it with shaking hands. Among the accusations of poor parenting and allegations that she was teaching the children to hate him, Helena realized that she was wrong. Ed did not just want to see the children. He was going to do everything in his power to take them from her.

Three months after Ed walked out, my instructing solicitor, Emily, showed me into the strip-lit conference room in Brighton County Court where Helena was waiting to meet me for the first time. She half-stood as I entered the room, the wooden bracelets on her arm clacking together as she held out her hand. She retook her seat and crossed her legs, the tip of her ankle boot clicking a nervous rhythm against the metal table leg. One of her hands moved unconsciously to the beads on her necklace, which she began to finger as though it were a rosary. I sat down opposite her, pushed my file out of the way across the table and wondered, as I always do when I meet clients for the first time, what judgements she was forming of me as simultaneously I formed my own of her. Did she take in the black suit, low heels and pulled-back hair? The files, the notepad, the pen? Was she relieved that I looked like a lawyer? Did she think I would be older? Did she hope I was a bitch?

I watched her as she hesitated, unsure how to say all the things she so wanted me to understand, desperate to explain the cavernous gap between the person she had read about in the papers before us and the person she believed herself to be. Lawyers, like politicians and journalists, were not the kind of people Helena had much contact with. They, she believed, hovered over the carrion of other people's lives, making money from their misery. She, in her middle-class bohemia, had no need of them. She was intelligent and reasonable; she read biographies and broadsheets, visited galleries and independent cinemas, ran local book groups, shopped at farmers' markets. She took good, mid-price wine to supper parties and thumped the table about perceived political injustice with friends just like her as she drank it. Yet, somehow, Helena found herself in a courthouse sitting opposite a lawyer – *her* lawyer! – unable to explain exactly how she had reached this point. The only possible answer was clear to her. It was all Ed's fault.

At Helena's feet was a large cloth bag filled with paperwork containing her record of grievances, carefully highlighted and underlined to help recall all the slights and wrongs meted out by her husband. Her notebook lay open on the table in front of us, filled with pages of her writing. Into the spiral binding she had clipped a pen: a thick multi-biro with a circle of different coloured nibs. Later, as she sat beside me in court, I would watch her click through the colours as she made notes, trying to work out how she divided the choices. Green for lies? Red for injustice? Yellow for truth? Looking at her notebook, I wondered which of Ed's secrets, confided in intimacy, she had betrayed. Confession changed to accusation: the meaning twisted, the context missing. Had he – now sitting in his own conference room with his barrister just across the hall from us – done the same? I have seen it often. Those threads of confidence which once had bound the two together now used to strangle one another instead. Sometimes I picture my clients and their ex-partners going through their statement – a final check, requested by their solicitor before signing to the truth of it – and imagine how those paragraphs of revelation must cause their heart to race with treachery. But then they remember: *To hell with it, he asked for it. If he's going to stoop that low, then so can I; two can play at that game. He deserves everything he gets.*

I opened my notebook. I had drawn, as I always do when preparing these cases, a family tree: inked lines mapping out the myriad complicated familial connections, which the court can choose to keep or to cut. Underneath this I had listed the key dates from the case. One I had underlined: 24/12. A quartet of numbers so loaded with nostalgia and magic, now to be remembered by Helena as the day her family finally broke.

I smiled at her, willing her to listen rather than talk, and began the speech I always give. This first hearing today was *just a directions hearing* – a short appearance, probably no longer than half an hour. There was no bewigged judge elevated above the court, nor rows of benches – it was just a room, the judge behind her desk, some tables in front of her, pushed together to form a large rectangle. We would sit on one side, Ed and his lawyers on the other. The judge would have seen a letter from the Children and Family Court Advisory and Support Service (CAFCASS), which we would be shown in court. Helena nodded in confirmation: yes, she had spoken to a man on the telephone, but he had seemed in a hurry, it had all been too rushed, she hadn't got to tell him everything she wanted. It was just an initial risk assessment letter, I said, to flag up anything the court needed to know about. CAFCASS were independent social workers who were there only for the children – to give them a voice and the court an independent view. Their role was not to decide which parent to believe; that was the judge's job alone. I waited for the words to sink in, knowing that when we were given a copy of the CAFCASS letter in court I would have to deflect Helena's rage at the *pack of lies* that Ed had told.

I also knew that, after reading the letter, our judge would turn to each of the parents and try to persuade them to put their arguments aside and reach an agreement for the sake of their children. Anticipating this, I would have to try to persuade Helena to settle something – to offer Ed some contact with the children – but her anger seemed too great. Ed had stopped paying the rent when he left, she said. She had been warned that her landlord might evict her. She spoke of her desire to move away. She had found a nursery – a village Montessori with a forest school. I shot Emily a look and she quietly shook her head, as though she did not believe Helena would go against the advice I knew she must have given her and unilaterally move her children, without telling Ed. Her parents,

Helena said, were willing to help her rent a small cottage, but she didn't want *him* to know that. Ed would come after her parents' money, she knew he would. Not that they were rich, but he had been chippy with them throughout their marriage and if he knew they were helping her he would just use it as an excuse not to pay her anything. And he should pay: he was working full time and she could not bear the cost of both children alone. She looked at me. If she did want to move, did she even need to tell him? He was the one who had stopped paying the rent – he was forcing her out! Couldn't she just go: restart her life? What business was it of his where she lived? She was worried he would turn up at the house at any moment, as he had on Christmas morning. She thought he might be spying on her, trying to collect evidence against her. It was just the sort of thing he would do, hide in his car, watching them, making notes in a stupid little book.

Helena leaned across the table. Ed, I must understand, had only brought this application to spite her. I didn't know what he was like but she did. How could he possibly think he could be the primary carer, look after the twins by himself and hold down a full-time job as well? He loved his work too much: he had always put it first; there was no way he would give it up. She couldn't remember a time when he had taken the twins by himself. He had no idea how to parent. Helena's mother had said she could help with childcare if Helena were to find some part-time work. Ed's mother couldn't do the same: she worked herself; she wouldn't be able to spare the time. She might be prepared to let the children see Ed if his mother was there, but that was it. He could not see them alone because for him it was all about control – it always was with him. Of *course* she didn't want to stop him seeing the children – he was their father after all, even if he didn't act like it. He was obsessed by the idea that she had only wanted children and not him – he would say he was nothing more than a sperm donor. Sometimes she wished he had been, then it could just be the twins and her. Their little team of three. Ed was so strict with them, always telling them off, correcting them. Blowing up everything into a drama. He wanted to quash their spirits, whereas she wanted them to grow up free, confident in themselves. They were, she concluded, quite frankly much better off without him. I wondered if she saw me flinch.

I watched Helena wrap herself in self-righteous loathing as she justified the decisions she wanted to make. I found myself in familiar territory – at a loss to know how to convince her that her children were half of their father, just as they were half of their mother. The law did not recognize his right to know them, nor hers, but rather the children's right to know each parent. Their right to know their provenance. To know whether the way their hair curled or their tongue rolled, or their inability to sing in tune or their skill with a tennis ball, or their broad shoulders and long middle toe came from the delicate strands of DNA that each had passed on to them. They needed to be given the chance to see, when they placed their hand next to his or hers, that it was identical in shape and form. To wonder how far back they could trace the ancestry of that hand: had it held a gun, tilled a field, gripped the handle of a brush to scrub a family's clothes? When they were old enough they would be free to reject a parent for their own reasons and cut them from their lives, but no one had a right to make that decision on their behalf. Unless the judge decided that a parent would harm them – emotionally or physically – then the law would try to protect the children's ability to have a relationship with both of them. But I could tell from the indignation and fury that simmered off Helena as I spoke that she did not want to hear, or accept, this truth.

I also suspected that, although Ed's barrister and I would try that morning to negotiate with one another for as long as the judge let us, neither parent was going to be prepared to agree to anything at all. Too often I had read the papers in a new case and thought, *This one must surely settle!* Many people get divorced and cry and grieve and curse. They pluck out books from bookcases, divide wedding gifts, work out who will take the car and who the cat. They create a shield of cooperation around their children through tight jaws, all without crossing the threshold of the courtroom. Surely these two could do it too? Later, at court, our pantomime efforts to reach an agreement would begin. My opponent and I would dart back and forth between our clients' conference rooms and our own, passing on demands, conditions, bottom lines and ultimatums. If, unusually, the court list was light and the judge amenable, they might be persuaded to hear a short argument on a minor urgent conflict. But when their decision was made, it would be final. The matter was then decided with no chance for me or my opponent to ask for further evidence on the point or to request a different compromise. But, mostly, I had to rely on each lawyer's ability to turn an antagonistic request into something that sounded like an opportunity. I knew that once one party conceded the other would often soften and they would pull one another towards hesitant agreement. Too many times, however, I would scuttle back and forth for nothing. Client, opponent, client, opponent, into court, more time granted, back to my client, opponent, client, opponent. The clauses and exemptions and preambles of our draft order would grow increasingly elaborate. Then, as the ushers began to lock up the courtrooms and the waiting room in court grew quiet at last, the pressure would seem to suffocate us all. One party would refuse to agree a vital concession, or change their mind about a paragraph already agreed. *No way!* they would cry. *This is too much. I'm not doing it. Let's just let the judge decide.* But by then it would be too late. The court day was over. The judge had no time left to hear evidence and arguments in order to make a decision. He had allowed us to negotiate outside court on the condition that, when we next were before him, it would be with a Consent Order that resolved the case. Now we would have to go away and come back another day to go before a judge who would make a decision in lieu of our agreement. In the interim, the parties would be stuck with whatever unsatisfactory arrangement had brought them to court in the first place. And so both parties and lawyers would leave court frustrated and exhausted – the last seven hours of explaining and cajoling and arguing, the lack of lunch, the dehydration and pounding head, all for nothing. I looked again at Helena, feeling the anger pulsing from her, and knew to keep my expectations low.

'Mr Forrest,' the judge turned to Ed's barrister, cutting him off, 'we are only here for the first directions hearing in this matter. No speeches, please. Just tell me exactly what it is that you want me to *do.*'

I looked at Simon Forrest and was grateful he was there. Most parties in these kinds of private family disputes are no longer eligible for legal aid and so either have to fund their lawyers from their own pocket, or – as is increasingly the case – represent themselves as litigants in person. It is difficult to justify why other people should be taxed to pay for a barrister to put forward, on behalf of grown men and women they have never met, some of the arguments I have made. Whether a child should be picked up at 1 p.m. or 3 p.m.; whether a particular birthday present or the contents of a card are inappropriate; or whether half-term holidays should be alternated or split in half. But any money saved by parties representing themselves is off-set by the cost of hearings that take far longer than they should or – had they been given the early advice to which they are no longer entitled – which should never have made it in to a court-room at all. I have sympathy for those who choose to represent themselves against a barrister. They are outgunned and they soon know it. Fear or suspicion ensures they often refuse to talk to me before we go into court, whether or not I explain that the judge will want us at least to try to agree the issues that divide us. In court, the judge will attempt to convince them that, no, I have not passed anything to him without giving them a copy; yes, they do have to show me any new evidence they want the judge to see. I have waded through applications and statements with annexes and appendices of lengthy inter-net printouts, covered with highlighted and bolded text. It is exhausting. I can only imagine how much worse it is for the judges now that over a third of cases going into the family court have no lawyer there at all.

I was just as grateful that Simon was not a 'McKenzie Friend' – someone brought by a litigant in person into the court-room to offer them moral and practical support. I can understand why a party would ask the judge for permission to have a McKenzie Friend present. But as the number of people represent-ing themselves has soared, so has the ability of pressure groups – with tales of courtroom conspiracies and secrecy – to exploit the situation to advance their own agenda, and to charge the party they are helping for their time and expenses, despite no legal qualifications or regulations that might hold them to account. I have spoken to litigants in person who have realized too late that the principal interest of their professional McKenzie Friend was to put his own literature and arguments before the judge, rather than providing support or assistance to the individual. In one case, both the judge and I were caught out when a McKenzie Friend presented himself as the party. I had already spoken briefly with him outside court – believing him, based on what he said, to be my opponent. Once in the courtroom, he rose to speak. It was my client, tugging at me from behind, who confirmed that my real opponent, her ex-husband, was the man sitting down – not the one with the beard addressing the judge. Justice had been hijacked, but maybe, in the eyes of this McKenzie Friend, that was exactly the point.

Helena had been able to rely on one of the caveats to the legal aid restriction, which grants funding to those who could show that they, or their children, have been victims of domestic abuse. Ed's police caution on Christmas Day had been enough for that. Ed, however, had to pay for his own barrister. He had instructed Simon through a direct access scheme, which enables clients to escape the ticking clock of a solicitor and agree an overall fee directly with a barrister. I could see by the number of files that Simon had brought to court – in comparison to the slim bundle Emily had sent me – that Ed was determined to get his money's worth.

Simon spoke at length of Ed's despair that he had not yet been able to see the children and his fear that Helena intended to flee with them. Her clear intention, he said, was to frustrate contact between the twins and their father, no matter what order the court imposed upon her. The current situation was untenable and needed the most urgent resolution. I felt Helena bristle next to me. She longed for me to interject, to defend her, outraged, and spray my own accusations around in return. There was little merit in doing so. The judge, as Simon knew well, was not going to make a decision about the case today. Simon was posturing – transferring, no doubt at his client's

request – a little of the rage and vitriol to which Ed had subjected him while we waited for our hearing.

'I have read your client's application,' the judge continued,
'and the Schedule Two letter from CAFCASS. I know what the
issues between these two parents are. I assume, from what you
have said, that you have not managed to resolve any of them in the
time available this morning – which is, I might add, a great shame.
So how, Mr Forrest, do you suggest that we move forward?'

'An interim contested hearing please, Madam.' Simon
glanced briefly towards me. 'The mother has refused the father
all contact with the children . . .' I opened my mouth to object
and Simon, seeing me, corrected himself. 'The mother, only this
morning I should add, has offered some contact on the basis that
the paternal grandmother is present when it takes place. But we
say supervised contact is completely unnecessary and the father
does not see why he should agree to it on these terms. Therefore
this matter must, I'm afraid, go to a contested hearing sooner
rather than later so that the father has at least some contact with
the children in the interim while we await a final hearing.'

I looked at the judge. 'I do not intend to be drawn today,'
she said, 'into the merits of the mother's contact offer, save to
say I am surprised your client would choose not to see his children at all over seeing them on his terms.' Simon drew breath
to interrupt her, but the judge held up her hand to silence him
once more. She carried on. 'As for the allegation that the mother
intends to move, I trust, Mr Forrest, that you have advised your
client that the mother is free by law to move wherever she
wishes. Only an order from the court can prevent her from
doing so, and I cannot see that your client has applied for such
an order, nor that his current application raises the issue in
any way.'

Without waiting for a reply, the judge turned to me. 'And,

Miss Langford, although I do not intend to go into the validity of the father's suspicion that your client intends to upend the children at this turbulent time, I will say that, were she to do so, this court would take a very dim view of it indeed. She has a responsibility to ensure that the children maintain a relationship with their father and their extended family. Any move by her which threatens this is unlikely to be seen, by any future court, to be in the children's best interests. I hope you have explained this to her?'

I could have told the judge of Ed's refusal to pay the rent, of the eviction letters, but there was little point. I had raised it all with Simon already and the judge had made it clear she would not be drawn into arguments today. I nodded.

'Well then, it is with great regret that I shall list this for a half-day contested interim hearing. The court lists are, as ever, over full. Having just listed a final hearing in another case, the earliest slot to allow for evidence and judgment that I would be able to offer you is in twelve weeks' time. It is, I'm afraid, unlikely to be back before me again. I can give you no more than three hours, so please bear this in mind when drafting statements, which must be filed by both parties in four weeks.'

She didn't add, *Now get out of my court*, but she may as well have.

So, as I feared, Helena left her first hearing frustrated and dissatisfied. Now she had a new date to circle in the diary – a contested hearing, where both she and Ed would give evidence and a judge she had never met would decide whether she got to tell the children that they were allowed to live with her, or whether she must go home and begin to pack their bags.

Less than a week after the first hearing, Helena received an eviction notice from her landlord. Ed still had not paid the rent. Maintaining to herself that she had little choice, she moved immediately with the children to the cottage near her parents and used the money they had offered her to pay the rent on that rather than pay off the arrears on her house. She enrolled the twins in a new nursery, only telling Ed afterwards. When Emily sent an email updating me, I read it with my head in my hands, knowing it only compounded Ed's argument that she was trying to exclude him from the children's lives. I thought of Ed – furious that his children were now living in a place of which he knew nothing – and waited for him to make his move.

Ed's application came only days afterwards. He demanded that the children be immediately returned to their old home and nursery. He paid off the rent arrears and moved back into their house. Then he changed the locks and refused to let Helena in to collect the rest of her and the children's belongings. The children could return to live there, he declared, but she couldn't. Now it was Helena's turn to be outraged. She made her own application to occupy their former home and remove Ed from it, as far as I could tell for no other reason than because she could.

Each party's emergency injunction had been made without the other knowing and was granted in the other's absence. An urgent hearing was listed in court a week after the orders were made, so that the other party could put forward their objections and the court could see whether the orders should continue or be dismissed. The two matters were joined together and so we all, once more, made our way to court. To our joint surprise, Simon and I teased out some progress. Ed agreed that he would allow Helena unfettered access to the house to collect her and the children's things, if she, in turn, withdrew her application and agreed to sign over the lease to him. She willingly agreed. She had no interest in it, she declared. Her focus now was on creating a new home for herself and the children. As we were inching our way towards an agreement about the twins' nursery, the usher appeared in our conference room, black gown flapping about him as he pressed us into court and before the waiting judge.

The circuit judge, senior and experienced, was unimpressed to find this new hearing in his overburdened court list and could not be placated by the agreements we had reached that morning. I bore the brunt of his wrath. Given that proceedings had begun and a contested interim hearing was listed, Helena's actions were divisive and underhand, he raged, and she should not be allowed to get away with such behaviour. He made an order compelling her to return the children to their old nursery, many miles away from her new home. With a flourish of rage, he attached a penal notice to it and an order that she must pay Ed's costs. After the hearing had finished and the judge had thundered off, we retreated from court. Helena, astonished, nodded mutely as I explained what, and how serious, a penal notice was. If she failed to comply with the order, I warned, she could be arrested, held in the police station overnight and produced in court the next morning to be punished. Although my appeal against the penal notice was successful, Helena, admonished, began to make the long drive every day from her new home to the children's old nursery.

Eventually, in spite of themselves, a routine of sorts established itself as both parents eased themselves into their new lives. The credit for this lay almost entirely with the two grandmothers. Ed's mother – terrified at the prospect of no longer being able to see her only grandchildren – managed to do what I, Emily, Simon and even the judge had all failed to do. She persuaded Helena – through her own mother – to agree that the children could stay with her and Ed at her house for one, then two, of the days that they were at nursery. Ed was irritated that Helena would still not allow the children to be alone with him, and cynically credited the extended nights to Helena's new long journey, but his agreement to this new arrangement broke the deadlock.

As the cogs of the court machine slowly began to push their case towards the next hearing, Helena and Ed's tentative agreement was marred by new arguments. An allegation that he had knocked her phone from her hand and smashed it as she tried to record him shouting at her; an assertion she had been rough with the children, dragging them by their hands to her car without allowing them to say a proper goodbye to their father. Abuse here, threats there, in texts, in emails; all recorded, all reported. Over the next two months, Emily and I would meet in the advocates' room on the top floor of the courthouse and try to keep up. Once again, resolution appeared in the form of the two grandmothers. They decided that they, rather than the parents, would stand on the doorstep and hand over the children with smiles and bags and instructions. I once thought I saw them sitting together in the window of the café opposite court. Two women, once connected only by their children's vows, now united by their failure to keep them.

The contested interim hearing was listed on a Friday in June. Faced with the prospect of many more months leading up to a further contested hearing to decide the truth of their new allegations, Helena and Ed finally agreed, moments before we went into court, to deal with the allegations by giving undertakings – solemn promises that they would not harm the other, in word or deed, or otherwise be held in contempt of court. The wording was so familiar to both barristers that we did not even need to discuss it before we each wrote it down on the undertaking forms: 'neither party shall denigrate the other in front of the children, nor allow anyone else to do so'. So normal; so terrible.

Shortly after 11 a.m., the hearing began. Our judge was experienced and patient, and dealt with those who appeared before him with dignity and care, but even he appeared worn down by both parties' inability to give evidence without taking every opportunity to cast a slur at the other. Faced with their intransigence, he took the least contentious route. With a little over a month left before the children began their summer holidays, he simply split their time in two. This, he concluded, was equality, which should not give either parent cause to gripe while they waited for the final hearing and a more permanent solution. The twins, now used to regular sleepovers away from their mother, would spend Sunday to Wednesday with Ed and Wednesday to Sunday with Helena. There were no grounds, now undertakings had been given, for the children to have to see their father with their grandmother present, although she would still have to collect and care for them when he was at work. Until the issue could be decided at a final hearing, they would stay at their current nursery and Helena would collect them from there on a Wednesday. The summer holidays were to be split in half: one week with her, one with him, and so on. The order was meant as a clear message that neither parent was less or more important. They were equally responsible and equally powerful. I explained to Helena afterwards, as she stood before me, unsteady with anxiety, that I suspected it was also a test. If Ed truly expected to care for the children by himself at the same time as holding down a full-time job, then this was a taste of how hard it would be. In the same way, Helena had unilaterally decided to move miles away and this was the court's way of reasserting the cost of that decision. As the parties would not compromise, everything, the judge had said, was to be split – time, cost, journeys to and from both homes. Was it just, this Solomonic ruling? I did not know, but it was at least a resolution, something these two parents – and their children – needed even more. And it was up to them to make it work.

They didn't, of course. Helena feared Ed's ability to prove himself as the primary parent and went out of her way to claw back time whenever she could. Ed, furious that the judge had granted Helena every weekend when he was the one who worked, spat out tired arguments about judicial bias towards mothers. No grievance was left unaired. One or the other was always late; the twins were sent back in dirty clothes, or without their bags for nursery or the soft toy rabbits that soothed them to sleep. Money to refund travel costs was not paid; telephone calls from the children were made on loudspeaker and monitored by the other parent. On it went, in letters, back and forth, listing the slights in solicitors' prose.

When faced with the catalogue of new grievances at the next directions hearing, the judge, exasperated, said he considered the issues significant enough for a full CAFCASS report in time for the final hearing. I can only imagine how the social worker assigned to the case, paid for by the public purse, must have frowned as she read through both parents' evidence.

It wasn't snowing, but it smelled like it. I had watched the day grow dark out of the window of the courtroom and, as I walked back to the station, the sudden drop from the artificial heat in the building to the chill outside made the cold seem to penetrate even more deeply. It was the last Friday before Christmas. All those in court, from security guard to usher to judge, had been full of seasonal farewells. But rather than join the throngs packing up and heading home, I spent the weekend weeding all Helena's grievances from her statements, in preparation for the final hearing which would start on Monday. On Christmas Eve.

The CAFCASS report had arrived that morning, a week late. I noticed the author's name with relief. Samantha Jones was a social worker I had come across before and would, I knew, have written a fair and reasonable report: sensible and balanced and firm. Both parents' views had been carefully recorded, but the truth of their allegations left to the court to decide.

The twins had turned four that September and, although they were considered too young for their views to be given great weight, the judge had still asked Samantha Jones to speak to them. I ran a pen under the words. Felix and Laura, she said, were – all things considered – happy and balanced children, in spite of their parents' conflict. Credit should go to both grandmothers for doing their best to protect the children from it. However, the children had been emotionally harmed by their parents' acrimony. They remembered when Mummy and Daddy shouted at each other – when Daddy got angry, they said, his face was scary, and Mummy cried, which frightened them. The summer had been fun. They liked going on holiday with Mummy and then with Daddy. They liked their nursery, but they wished they could go to one in the village where their new neighbours went. The cottage with Mummy was much smaller than their old house, but they liked sharing a room. They really liked seeing Granny and Grandpa all the time. They also liked seeing Grandma and staying with Daddy, although their old house looked different now because Daddy had thrown lots of things away. They were very excited about Christmas. Mummy had let them decorate their tree themselves and their friends in the village were having a party. They wanted to see both Mummy and Daddy at Christmas. They wanted to stay in their new cottage, because they wanted to go to the party. They wanted Daddy to go to the party too, but they were a bit worried if he did in case he and Mummy shouted at each other, which scared them.

I stopped reading the report and let the words sink in. I was reminded how easy it was to represent a client and unintentionally push their faceless children to the back of my mind. By the end of a case I knew the minutiae of these little people's lives – who had to sleep with a nightlight on, who wanted to wear a princess outfit every day, who was getting into trouble at school, who got car sick, who loved trains, who had started to wet the bed – but throughout they remained in abstract. I would read a CAFCASS report with a critical eye for how it could help or hinder my client's case, but then I would come to the part where the child's voice rang out, and I would feel a shock of guilty sadness as I realized that it was the first time I had heard them.

I turned back to the report and read the final pages. As was so often the case, Samantha Jones had referred to Helena and Ed as 'the mother' and 'the father' throughout, as though this depersonalization helped her write in the unemotional language of the professional. The twins needed security and stability, said her report. The constant weekly journeys to and from both parents' homes were taking their toll. Geographical distance meant that shared care was not a realistic option. They were of an age when preparations had to be made for school, and the court had to come to a decision about which parent the children would be with during the week. The father had worked full time since the children were born and continued to do so. His mother had made herself available for some of the week, but the court could not – and should not – ask her to give up her job to look after the children full time. They were now four, very active, and although the parents and court should be exceptionally grateful for her help, full-time care of them was not in the paternal grandmother's best interests, nor, more importantly, the children's. The mother intended to get some part-time work to fit around the children's education, but was available to care for the twins with the support of both her parents. She was in stable accommodation with no rent arrears and, although small, the cottage was more than adequate for the children's needs. She had researched local schools and had established a supportive network of friends for the children who attended the nursery to which she wished to send the twins.

An inaudible inhalation lay in the space before Samantha Jones's final conclusion. She recommended that the court make an order that the children live with their mother during the week and go to stay with their father from Friday to Sunday every other weekend, every half-term and half of all holidays. The twins were now at nursery every day – it was not fair that they should spend none of their weekends with their mother, nor was it fair that she should bear the brunt of the daily grind but fail to enjoy any leisure time with them. In due course, the parents must work together to agree which school the twins would attend, local to the mother.

I closed the report, placed my hand on top, and imagined both Helena's elated relief and Ed's fury when they read it. I thought of the conference Simon Forrest would have to have. I knew what it took to field a client's anger – rage confused with fear and loss. I also knew that, although Simon was likely to advise Ed that the judge would probably follow the report's recommendation, Ed would undoubtedly refuse to accept this.

If the judge was going to make that order, then so be it, but Ed was never going to agree to let the children go.

The final hearing was supposed to have been listed before the same judge who had made the order for shared care. But when I got to court after the cold walk down from the station, I found that – for reasons no one could explain – we were before the circuit judge who had imposed the penal notice on Helena in fury at her unilateral move. When we went into court, Simon – as I would have done, had I been in his position – reminded the judge of the last time he had dealt with the case. I watched him as he looked at Helena, sitting beside me, and my confidence in our case began to leak away. *Shit*, I silently cursed, as Ed walked up to the witness box and took the oath. *Shit, shit, shit.*

When we broke for lunch, Samantha Jones had yet to speak. This was unusual. Often a judge would be at pains to ensure a CAFCASS officer was never at court longer than they needed to be, and would take their evidence first so that they could be released. This time, the judge asked her to sit in court and listen to both parties give evidence. I watched him for some clue, but he remained expressionless. What was he doing, I wondered? It was rare that a judge disagreed with the recommendation in a report, but I had seen it happen. Did he hope that the CAFCASS officer would hear something she could use to justify a change of heart? All the judge needed was an admission from her that she had not considered a particular scenario, or had heard some new evidence which now altered her view. With some gentle leaning by him, she might buckle and change her mind.

We shortened our lunch break to thirty minutes. Helena

wanted to sit and pick apart the morning's evidence, but I rebuffed her and sat alone in the advocates' room, scanning my notes. I started to think more carefully about what Ed offered – about the benefits of the children staying in their old home and nursery, with a father who could financially provide for them and a grandmother who had more than demonstrated her support. The judge had already decided that Helena had little respect for Ed or for the court – that much was clear from the last time he had dealt with the case. Simon might be able to convince him that Helena was determined to erase Ed from the children's lives; that she would never comply with any orders that the court made. I winced as I scanned through my notes of the evidence she had given that morning, reading again her long list of complaints against Ed. I closed my book. I should go and find her, remind her that the CAFCASS report was a recommendation, not an order. Warn her that the judge did not have to follow it if he could justify a decision not to do so. Urge her not to be complacent; that this judge could, and would, take the children from her and give them to Ed if that's what he felt was in their best interests. But, as I stood to go and find her, Simon appeared. There was no time; the judge wanted us all back in court.

In evidence, Samantha Jones maintained her recommendation, but was balanced when she did so. She conceded that Helena did not support the children's relationship with Ed; admitted she had concerns that Helena might refuse to obey court orders compelling contact with the children's father. But, she said, she hoped that if the court gave Helena the reassurance of an order in her favour, this might provide her with the confidence to support their relationship with him once things had settled down. I looked at the judge, watching him as he wrote a note and slowly underlined it.

After Simon and I had given our closing speeches, the judge said he would like a break to consider, before he gave his judgment. Outside court, Helena called her mother, who was looking after the twins, to tell her that she was going to be late; that they still did not have a decision. She finished the call and turned to me. I feared she had been able to tell by my tone during my closing speech that the hearing had not gone well. Was the fact that the judge needed more time to decide a good sign, she asked, or a bad one? I drew a breath. 'Either,' I said. 'The judge might want to ensure he gives a judgment so detailed that there can be no criticism by either party that he has failed to consider anything.' I paused. 'Or he is preparing his explanation as to why he is not following the CAFCASS recommendation.' Helena stared at me, blankly. Softly, I said she had to ready herself in case the judgment went against her. Expect the worst, hope for the best. If the ruling went against her we could try to appeal, but this experienced judge would make sure his judgment was watertight. I could not guarantee that we would be successful.

I watched Helena as panic swallowed her, and thought of all the times I had seen a parent realize that he or she had lost. If the result was not expected, then their animal howls would echo in my head long after we had all left court. I excused myself, unable to look at her any longer, and went to wash my hands. I looked at myself in the mirror as I did so and ran through the day. Had I missed something out, thinking it unimportant? Had I been too soft on Ed when cross-examining him? How would the judge do it? Surely he would not order her to pack a bag and hand the twins straight over to Ed tonight, on Christmas Eve? Unless, of course, he was worried that she might, once again, take them away, but this time somewhere they could not be found? There was a knock on the bathroom door. It was the usher. We were to go back into court. The judge was ready.

The courtroom seemed cold, as though someone had turned on the air conditioning to rid the room of the stifling smell of hours of evidence. We all stood as the judge came back in. He did so, as always, in a distinctive style. Slowly, deliberately, his hunched walk making him look older than I expect he was. He would nod at those standing before him without looking up, then sit, open his notebook, take out his pen, remove the lid and, glancing at the clock on the courtroom wall, write down the time. Only then, when he looked up and towards us, would we know that the hearing had begun and we could speak.

This time the judge did not look up, but instead began reading his judgment from his notes, setting out the facts of the case, the history of the hearings. I scribbled a note of his words to distract myself from the clenching tension I felt. When, at last, he reached his conclusion and said that the twins should live with Helena, I felt her start to shake next to me with the effort of controlling silent tears.

I arrived at my parents' house later that same evening, long after the hearing had finished. I sat at the kitchen table, forking through warmed-up shepherd's pie, and forced myself to type the attendance note before Christmas took hold. I emailed it to Emily, then closed my laptop. Involuntarily, I thought of the twins. I wondered whether they were in their night clothes, pink-cheeked from a bath. Or maybe, by now, they would be asleep, their mouths softly open in the way sleeping children have, as though they had tumbled from a painting. I wondered if Helena had hidden her tears of relief from them or whether she had allowed herself to use them for her comfort and held them, their small hands inching around the back of her neck.

Then, for a moment, I thought of Ed, alone in the house where his home had once been. I got up, zipped the papers and my laptop back into my bag, and went into the sitting room where my family was waiting for me.

The final hearing was not the end, but it was the beginning of the end. In the months afterwards, I found myself back at court arguing about schools, holiday destinations, vaccinations and even, one depressing afternoon, circumcision. But, eventually, the gaps between hearings became longer. About a year after the final hearing I heard from Emily that Helena had begun a new relationship. Expecting this to be the start of more applications from Ed, I braced myself. I waited for demands of a criminal records check, a ban on staying over when the children were there, an agreement that they must never be alone in this new partner's care. I waited for Emily's email, but none came.

Over a year passed before I saw Emily in the waiting room of Brighton County Court. She was talking to another barrister and I wondered if I had been replaced. No, she said: there were no more applications. Ed was engaged. His girlfriend was pregnant and the baby was due in the new year. The twins were ecstatic, according to Helena. It was over, finally.

Six months or so after that, I got married. In the month beforehand, a new protocol was introduced into the family courts which changed the name of the orders handed down by judges. Custody Orders had already been replaced with Residence Orders and Contact Orders and these were now to be called something new: Child Arrangements Orders. They would spell out how the children's time was to be divided between each party, and remove the ability of a parent to wave an order and say *They belong to me!* I wondered whether it would really make a difference? We could pretend – the lawyers, the judges – that we had neutralized the battle, but I doubted that the parties would be fooled. They would still interpret an order in terms of time divided and importance accordingly bestowed. It would not matter if the order said the children were to 'live with' their father every other weekend – he would still feel robbed of them. Someone felt they'd won, and someone felt they'd lost, and I was unsure whether justice had anything to do with it.

I thought about all those times I had told someone I practised family law and watched them draw a breath before describing their own battle with the person they once loved. I knew the account I was being told was selective, designed to win me over so I had to agree how disgracefully the other party had behaved. Eventually I would find a way to extricate myself and wonder at how quickly this stranger had transformed before me and how repelled I was by it. I used to wonder how it was that I had ended up here, an agent and instrument not of the law but of revenge and spite. I had begun to fear that I did not believe in this system. Not, at least, in the way I believed it when I defended someone I suspected was guilty, or excluded evidence that would secure a conviction because it was illegally obtained, or watched the prison van with my client in it pull away knowing that his incarceration would be longer than his life. I accepted this because these moments were part of something bigger: a system of justice that I respected. I had often been asked, 'Does it put you off getting married, dealing with cases like that?' I knew I was supposed to brush it away and announce my objectivity. Except the truth was – yes, it had. Representing parents at war had fundamentally affected my life choices. I had imagined boyfriends' faces on the other side of a courtroom. I had wondered whether I would fight in the breathless wounded way my clients did. I had seen how easy it was for love to slip into hate, and feared that – despite my judgement of the parents I represented – in reality maybe they and I were not as unalike as I might hope. Luck threw me someone I loved, who trusted in the power and strength of marriage in a way that overcame my insecurity. I began to understand how a preoccupation with how my marriage might end had almost prevented it from ever beginning, and that this, in truth, made my clients' choices no less tragic than mine had been.

Shortly after I got married, I found myself in court representing a waif with cropped red hair and tattooed tendrils crawling up the back of her neck. She was mother to a two-year-old son and a six-month-old daughter. Their father, who lived hundreds of miles away, had refused to bring them back after his contact weekend. My client had been considered ineligible for legal aid and so, with no one to advise her, did not know that she could file an expedited application. It was therefore many weeks before her case got to court, during which time she had not seen or spoken to her young children. She had begged and scraped pounds and pence together until at last she had enough to find a solicitor, who in turn found me. This was her only shot – she could get no more money for any further hearings. Her terror fuelled my outrage, which, in turn, I laid before the judge. The judge immediately ordered that these two infant children be returned to their mother's care, instantly, that very afternoon.

The thought of this mother's tearful relief stayed with me for a long time afterwards. I began to understand better the purpose of these cases and the system of justice within them.

Parents need the law. They need the court to make decisions for them when jealousy, rage and bitterness disable their own ability to do so. But, more than this, their children need the law too. At the back of every courtroom sit small ghosts – unseen, unheard – whose future will for ever be marked by the decision of the court. These children lie at the heart of every case and this system of justice tries to protect them. It lifts the weight of their parents' battle from their small shoulders and places it upon the court's. It is a profound, humbling and troubled burden for the law to bear, but bear it it does, whenever a parent refuses, or is unable, to bear it for themselves. This is a system whose purpose is founded on making children's lives better than they would be otherwise. And that is a system in which I can absolutely believe.

10

Chris

Portsmouth Crown Court

Archbold Criminal Pleading Evidence and Practice
Chapter 4 – Trial. Part II. Arraignment and Plea, 4-253
Ordinarily, a plea of guilty may be changed right up to the moment that sentence is passed.
Only rarely, however, would it be appropriate for a judge to exercise this discretion, particularly where the accused has been represented by experienced counsel and, after full consultation with counsel, had already changed his plea from not guilty to guilty at an earlier stage in the proceedings.

I LOOKED AT my client, his eyes unblinking, staring at me across the bolted-down table of our conference room in the cells of Portsmouth Crown Court. A thought struck me with the clarity of a bell. *This man might kill me.* In eight years, this one might be the one. The one who suddenly leans across, puts both of his large, strong hands around my throat and squeezes the life from me.

His eyes were small and dark against the paleness of his thick-set face. They stayed fixed on me as I waited for him to answer my question. It was the second time I had asked it but he still did not respond. His hands rested on the table, palms down, and his body was completely still. There was nothing I could point to that made me certain he was mad, apart from the energy that fizzed off him and told of a hundred different voices and images battling inside his head. Was it these he was watching instead of me? He reminded me of a series of photographs I had seen: portraits of children playing violent video games – close-ups of their faces as they were shooting and killing in their alternative reality. I felt the flip of my baby inside me, as though he had been alerted in some unconscious way to danger. My pregnancy was too early yet to have formed a curve, but something made me want to put my hand over him, to reassure him, invisible beneath the cover of my suit and gown. But I kept my hands where they were; I did not want this man to know about my baby. I wished I had taken off the ring from my left hand, as though even that gave away too much. I wanted him to see me not as an individual, with vulnerabilities and precious things that could be taken away, but as a vehicle, an operative, a component of the court machine. I wanted him to see me not as a person, but as his lawyer.

I am tall, but this man, honed by service in the navy, could, I assessed, easily overpower me. As is usual, we were locked into our room, with two guards at the end of the corridor behind another door, laughing, joking, looking elsewhere. On the wall to my left was a dated-looking panic button. I knew of other barristers who had pressed their buzzer only to find it had not worked, forcing them to rely instead on their skills of persuasion and fists banging on the door. I wondered, even if I did reach it, even if it worked, would the cell guards get to us in time: hear the alarm, find the right key, open the door, pull him off? When I arrived the guards had scowled and fussed about my laptop, insisting that I sign it in, locking it into a cubby-hole, insensible to the time ticking ever nearer to our 10 a.m. sentence hearing. As far as they were concerned, this man, who had been brought by a van that morning from his prison cell, was nothing to worry about. He had pleaded guilty to raping his wife, sure. But two psychiatrists had decided that he was mentally sound, that he knew his own mind and actions.

Over the years I have met people who have scarred their limbs with self-loathing, tried to take their life with rope or pills, or been sucked into the blackness of depression. I have met people who shook with the ache of withdrawal, or who spoke to me through a fog of intoxication from the drugs or alcohol inside them. I have represented those whose low IQ or mental disorders have fogged their ability to understand me. But I had not before met someone in a psychotic state who had been judged sane. Sitting opposite this man, my hands resting on the top of two reports that declared him sound, all I had was my instinct – born from years of being locked in rooms with people who had done bad things – that the doctors who had assessed him were wrong. I sat still, trying to keep my face relaxed, open, and picked up my pen ready to write down his answer to my question.

I was not supposed to be there, that day, in that cell. Chris was somebody else's client. A senior barrister from chambers, Kate, had represented him at all the other hearings up until trial. Kate had also feared that her client was mentally unwell. She had discovered that Chris had been admitted to hospital before. There he had been treated by a consultant psychiatrist, who had said he was indeed suffering from an underlying psychosis, but that the symptoms were only apparent when he smoked marijuana. When no longer under the influence, he was of full capacity, able to know and understand his actions. Able, in theory, to know he had raped his wife and to take responsibility for it. Able, in theory, to understand me. After all, there were no drugs in prison. Right?

Chris had maintained his plea of not guilty up until the morning of his trial. That day, his wife had come to court as the only witness, and had pleaded in tears not to have to give evidence against her husband. He was, she was sure, unwell. It had happened before. He had joined the navy and had served all over the world. He was a good man, she said, and a good father to their two sons, but once he left the navy he had started smoking marijuana. The drug seemed to eradicate the man she knew. He would fight invisible enemies, bang her against the wall with his hands around her throat, cause her nose to bleed with a swipe of his elbow. Afterwards, when he saw the blood and tears and bruises, he could not remember any of it. She was at court only because she wanted to help him. The prosecutor must have frowned and looked at the psychiatrist's notes declaring Chris mentally fit to plead and to stand trial. He had approached Kate, and the two had edged around the difficulty until Kate wrote out a basis of plea – a piece of paper on which was written Chris's new admission that he was guilty of rape, but not in the way the prosecution alleged. Chris accepted that he had raped his wife, but not with the violent brutality she described in her statement. His basis of plea said it was rape because he knew she did not want to make love with him that night and he forced himself on her anyway. Chris signed the words Kate had written for him, and then so did the prosecutor. Chris's wife was spared the ordeal of evidence; he would spend fewer years in prison. Then Chris stood in the dock before the trial judge and the court clerk put the offence to him again. Chris was silent. Kate went to stand by him in the dock, prompting his response. *Guilty.*

Kate, in spite of the report by the treating psychiatrist, was so sure of her client's ill-health that, after the guilty plea, she asked the court to order a second opinion. She wanted a further psychiatric assessment which could say whether Chris should serve his sentence in a prison, or in a hospital. But when everyone came back to court for the sentence hearing six weeks later, neither this report nor probation's pre-sentence report was ready. And so the case was adjourned, Kate went on holiday and I found myself in her place, sitting opposite Chris in a prison cell, wondering if I was right to feel so afraid.

I had been told by my clerks the day before that the case was a simple one. The psychiatric and probation reports would be at court, and Chris's basis of plea would be attached. All I really needed to know was in the basis of plea and the reports. The wife's statement, as well as her victim impact statement, would be emailed to me. It was a straightforward sentence: the judge knew the case and would just follow the guidelines. The client knew to expect prison, although there had been a hint that the judge might make an exception, given that the wife's statement had begged for leniency.

Unable to hold Chris's gaze, I flicked open the pre-sentence report and pointed to a paragraph on the first page. 'See, it says it here,' I said, hoping that proof might enable him finally to answer my questions: *Why did you tell the probation officer and the psychiatrist that you were innocent, that the sex was consensual? Why are you now alleging that you were forced to plead guilty by your other barrister, and that this was all a trick by your wife?* I tapped the page with my finger, trying to divert his attention away from me, to get him to focus. His eyes continued to bore into me, his stare so penetrating that I felt as though he was challenging me to name his madness. After a long pause, when he eventually spoke he did so in short staccato sentences that sprayed from his mouth like bullets from a machine gun. Individually his words made sense; what he said was not jabberwocky. But his phrases bore no relation to one another. He would fixate on an insignificant topic, skitting between subjects, apparently unable to give detail or concrete facts. He would ask questions which had no bearing on the topic. And whenever I asked him of the detail of the offence he simply maintained that, as far as he was concerned, the evidence spoke for itself. He need not explain further; anyone who read the statements could see the truth.

I wondered whether he was practised at this – whether he knew the right words to say to keep the doctors from his door. Whether he realized that by maintaining that his wife was lying when she said he had smoked cannabis before the rape – by asserting that he had not – he knew the absence of drugs must make him sane at the time of the offence. Was it better, to him, to be a criminal than to be mad? Reading the reports, I thought how strange it was that so much reliance was placed on a patient's own analysis of his mental health, but this was the psychiatrists' realm and not mine, and, faced with the firm opinion of two doctors, I – and the court – had little choice but to accept what they said.

The sentencing hearing was, of course, a disaster. Chris maintained his innocence and his allegation that pressure had been put upon him by his previous barrister. The judge, on hearing this, huffed in irritation, although his own reading of the reports had warned him of the defendant's change of heart, so he did not seem wholly surprised. The judge then adjourned the case for a month so that I could prepare an application to withdraw my client's guilty plea – a request which must now be made in writing, supported by evidence, responded to by the prosecution and ruled upon by a judge. This I did. Chris confirmed that he was prepared to waive legal professional privilege and allow me access to the record of his confidential conference with Kate. Kate emailed me her attendance note from the aborted trial, which described what had happened, and I rifled through law books and skimmed through case law, trying to find something that might support my application. Part of me dreaded its success, for if my application were granted and Chris was allowed to switch his plea back to one of not guilty, I must then represent him at his rape trial. I filed my application and the case law that went with it, and waited. No reply came from the prosecution and so, at the next hearing, I went in search of the prosecuting barrister. The Crown Prosecution Service, it turned out, had failed to instruct anyone to cover the case. There was no one available to stand in, so the judge roared to a half-empty court and sent me away again, demanding that the matter be listed for a contested hearing and that Kate be there to give evidence and explain herself.

By the time a date was found that all could do, three months had passed. The curve of my baby was bigger and, even though I had learned to hide it, when I went to the cells on the morning of our hearing I looked at Chris, sitting opposite me in prison clothes, and felt again the same familiar fear. I showed him Kate's attendance note, although he refused to look at it. After a long pause, he said he had pleaded guilty only because he was told by Kate that, if he did so, he could go home, that very day, as this was what his wife had asked for. Chris suddenly bent low on the table, causing me to start, and snatched up his basis of plea, which had been sitting on my notebook. He turned it slowly over, then put it solemnly down. He looked at me, triumphantly, and slapped both his hands down on the table with a bang that made me flinch. That was not, he declared, his document. There was another page, one that his previous barrister had hidden. He prodded the page with his finger, slowly and deliberately, as though he were pressing a button. The missing page was the one he had signed, and it said he was *not* guilty. Carefully, I drew the basis of plea towards me and spun it around so it faced him. I pointed to the flourish above his printed name at the bottom of the page. Wasn't this his writing?

'No.'

I paused. 'Are you saying that this is *not* your signature?'

The intensity of his stare felt like a test. I felt my senses heighten. After what seemed an age, he looked down at the piece of paper where my hand rested.

'No, that *is* my signature.' He said it as if I had asked him something very stupid; as if our previous conversation had simply not happened.

Right. Okay. Don't let him get diverted, I thought: just stick to the points you need instructions on and get out of there and on with the hearing.

I asked him to tell me about Kate's advice, but Chris told me he did not want to talk about Kate – that I should put her to one side. The real issue, he maintained, was that his wife had invented these accusations to steal his inheritance. And there was something else he needed me to do, something more important. She had sent his navy docket to the prison. It had been lost; he could not find it, and he needed it with him. I must help him find it, he said. It was my turn to look at him in silence. I told him I would tell the solicitors about the docket and that I needed to go to find the prosecution before I ran out of time. I stood to leave the cell, rapping on the small window in the door to attract the guards' attention, willing them to come quickly and allow me to move away from the man whose eyes were boring into my back.

'Are you doing this: the case of, um . . .' the prosecution barrister peered down at the file in his hand, squinting, in need of glasses not to hand '. . . Mira?' I confirmed I was. He did not return my smile as he ran his fingers through grey hair, shifting his weight. 'Bloody CPS forgot to instruct anyone, didn't they? I've just been handed it. It's something completely daft like trying to vacate a plea, right? Your application, is it?'

'Yes. Do you have a copy? I brought spares.'

He did not, nor a copy of the prosecution's reply, and took the ones I offered him. As he flicked through the documents, reading but not seeing, he gave a low rumble. 'I mean, this says all I intend to say, really. Can't see I need to add anything further.'

It was unhelpful: his bluster, his hauteur. I wanted to be able to confide in him, to say *Look, you'll see in evidence, but my client is as mad as a box of frogs, and somehow he's slipped it past both doctors.* I wanted to urge him to tread gently, to go easy. But as he strutted and blustered I knew I could not. It occurred to me that he might not have been told that Kate was coming to give evidence; that I was in the bizarre position of calling a colleague and cross-examining her under oath in an effort to prove she had pressured my client to plead guilty. I said all this to him and agreed with his protests that he could not, surely, have anything to ask this barrister. That this was, after all, my show.

'Hello, Sarah.' I turned to see Kate approaching us. My opponent brightened.

'Hello there,' he said. 'I'm sorry that you've been dragged along to this. What a farce. Hope you didn't have to lose anything from your diary. I've just said to your colleague,' he gestured towards me with his thumb, as though hitching a lift, 'I'm not intending to say much today. It's the defence's application, so it's all down to them. Right then.' He turned abruptly, and left us.

Kate and I sat alongside one another on the low chairs outside the courtroom and waited to be called in. It was, of course, awkward, for we both knew I was about to accuse her of forcing her client to plead guilty. As we rattled through those subjects beloved of barristers trying to find a bond – legal aid cuts, those we knew leaving the profession for more secure employment, those swapping crime for better-paid work – I found myself trying to make her like me, trying to convince her that I knew the application was hopeless, that I was not being naïve in making it. At last, the usher came out of court. 'Judge is ready to call it on. They're bringing your client up from the cells now.'

It was a new judge, and although I did not know him I could see his manner was well suited to the case. He was calm,

CHRIS

pragmatic and, in the face of flapping hands and rolling eyes from my opponent, made little fuss.

'An unusual application, I concede, Mr Franklin,' he said, to the prosecutor, 'but perfectly proper. And in any event, as we know, it is not for justice simply to be done. It must be seen to be done. Miss Langford,' he turned to me, 'I have read your application – no need to elaborate. Would you call the witness, please?'

And so off we went. Kate was unruffled in evidence, but, unsurprisingly perhaps, at pains to emphasize her profession-alism. She described the process of the abandoned trial. The defendant had, she said, a tendency to become fixated on a grievance. When she first met him, Chris had instructed two solicitors and two barristers, and chose Kate because of a con-spiracy he thought the others were plotting. There had been a failed prison visit, when Chris had refused to come out of his cell to give Kate instructions. Kate said she feared Chris was mentally unfit to plead and was surprised when an existing medical report was found saying that he was. She agreed that Chris had not, in fact, ever admitted his guilt, but had told her that he did not want a trial. Kate had then told the prosecutor that her client would plead guilty before she had written down a basis and checked it with Chris. But, she said swiftly, she denied any accusation that she had hastened this decision – she had made it clear to her client that, by pleading, Chris would almost certainly go to prison. She could not explain why Chris thought that a guilty plea would mean he could leave the court-house immediately and go home. She remembered that Chris had paused when the charge was put to him in court. Kate had gone and stood by the dock, and had checked one last time that he wished to plead guilty. Chris did. And that was that.

When Chris gave evidence after Kate, he was all that he had

been in conference. I tried to coax from him the details of how the trial had collapsed, what he had understood and believed, and what Kate had told him. Although Chris repeated everything he had told me, each part of his evidence was preceded by a long silence and his cold, hard stare, and my fear that he would become distracted and fixated by something else. He repeated his assertion that a page was missing from the basis of plea, and then swung back again when the judge challenged him on it. He had expected, he said, to be able to sign the piece of paper and then go home that day, for that is what his barrister had told him would happen. But, later, in answer to another question, he confirmed that, after pleading guilty, he had expected to get a prison sentence – maybe two years or so.

When my opponent cross-examined him, he was wound around in knots as Chris made new assertions and contradictions to answers he had already given. Eventually, with visible relief, the prosecutor sat down, stating to the judge that this was my application and he had very little to add to it. Chris's answers throughout were couched by the 'Ma'am' and 'Sir' of military parlance; his back straight, chin up, jaw squared, arms clamped to his sides, as though he were undergoing inspection on parade.

Usually, when I wait for a ruling or judgment or verdict I go to see my client. I sit with them, chew over what has been said in court, prepare them for what might or might not happen next. But after Kate left, I sat outside the court door alone, typing my attendance note. I did not want to sit in a room with Chris, nor forget anything that had just been said in court, just in case afterwards Chris decided to deny the lot.

Within the hour, the judge summoned us back. I saw that he was reading from a note he had made and I wondered whether he too was worried enough about the case to want to keep a detailed record. He went on, methodically and carefully, to list the reasons why he was not going to allow Chris to change his plea.

Chris's claim that he had thought a guilty plea would mean he could go home that day, the judge said, stood in stark contrast to his evidence that he had expected a two-year prison sentence. This had exposed him; he was refusing to face up to what he had done: The long pauses in his evidence were down to a difficulty in finding answers to challenging questions. The defendant had known, for his barrister said she had told him, that he should not plead guilty if he had not committed the crime, but he did so anyway, without any pressure, and now regretted it. If a defendant was of sound mind, ably represented by senior counsel and the guilty plea was not equivocal, then the law was clear. Regret was not enough to allow him to change it. So, the judge said, firmly, he would move straight on to sentence. In a case with no aggravating circumstances or previous convictions, the sentence would be five years' custody. Given the basis of plea, he felt able to go below this. He would also reduce the defendant's sentence by one tenth, that being the amount allowed by law for a change of plea on the day of trial. The judge shut his notebook and pulled it towards him, signalling his intent to finish the hearing. Christopher Mira, he said, was sentenced to three years' imprisonment. The prosecution had not applied for a Sexual Offences Prevention Order, nor a Restraining Order, and he would not have been minded to make one even if they had, given what the defendant's wife had written. Because of the type of offence, the defendant would be subject to notification requirements for the rest of his life, but his barrister – he waved a hand at me, pushing his chair back – would explain all this. Any questions? No. Good. He nodded, turned, and left through the door behind him.

*

After a sentence hearing, I sometimes, for efficiency, take off my wig and gown and pack them into my wheelie bag before going down to the cells to see my client. When my conference is finished I can then leave and go straight home, rather than trudging back up to the robing room. I am surprised how often people say I look different without the outfit. Once or twice cell guards I have got to know have failed to recognize me, and have laughed in embarrassment after I have signed in. The costume works. Of course it does all the other things it is supposed to do as well. It lends an air of associated solemnity and gravity. It identifies who you are in court, while simultaneously making you look the same as all the others, as all uniforms are supposed to do. But more than that, it disguises me. It gives me cover. When I fasten my starched white bib, shrug on my gown and jam my wig on to my head I become someone else; someone both familiar and unrecognizable.

This time, when I went to see Chris in the cells, I did not take off my wig and gown.

In our conference I tried to explain to him that, with the length of time he had already been in prison waiting for his sentence, he would have only six months left to serve before he was released on licence. Implied within my words was a plea for him to realize that the judge had been lenient. And, to my surprise, he made no fuss. I could not, however, shake the feeling that the military man in him thought he was being given an order, and that his compliance was expected rather than his views and instructions solicited.

I ran through what it meant to have to report his address and his whereabouts to the police for the rest of his life, and that his probation officer, who would be assigned when he was released from prison, would help him. There was a long pause while he stared at me. So, when should he next report to me? he asked. No, no, it was not me, I said, placing both hands on the table, leaning forward, frowning. I was not his probation officer. I was his lawyer. His face remained impassive. But what would happen when we next went to court? he asked. I looked at him, then slowly explained that we were not going to court again – this was the end of his case. A jangle of keys in metal broke into the silence and turned his attention to the cell door, which opened in a telepathic miracle. An overweight prison guard stood in the doorframe, beckoning at us – *time to go, time to go* – they were loading the van back to prison and Mr Mira must get in it. I stood quickly, said goodbye to Chris and hastened to the main cell door as a guard walked over to unlock it, and set me free.

11

Jude

Bristol Family Court

Family Procedure Rules 2010
16.6 Circumstances in which a child does not need
a children's guardian or litigation friend

(1) . . . a child may conduct proceedings without a
children's guardian or litigation friend where the
proceedings are—
    (a) under the 1989 Act . . . and one of the
    conditions set out in paragraph (3) is satisfied.
(3) The conditions referred to in paragraph (1) are
that—
    (a) the child has obtained the court's permission; . . .
(6) The court will grant an application under
paragraph (3) (a) . . . if it considers that the child
has sufficient understanding to conduct the
proceedings concerned or proposed without a
litigation friend or children's guardian.

I stood in the entrance hall, next to a large pinboard covered in laminated notices, and wondered at the kind of smell that so often seems to belong to a school. There were the easy scents of nostalgia: new books, floor polish, gym kits, packed lunches. Underneath these was the base note of what it is to be a child, as though some fantastical perfumer had infused the pheromone scents of youth into the fabric of the building. I stood there, conspicuous in my black suit, and thought how for some children the smell might hold the prospect of misery. For others it could mean a crossing into safety away from the war raging at home. I wondered which of the two this school offered Jude – the boy I was waiting to meet.

Behind me, the main school door opened and my solicitor hurried in, smiling, full of apologies. I rebuffed them, telling him the teacher had only just left to fetch Jude from his classroom. We stood chatting until the sound of heels on wood silenced us. The double doors from the hallway opened. Behind the teacher walked a twelve-year-old boy. His hair was light brown, thick, cut neatly short. He looked directly at us with a confidence I had not expected. The grey school cardigan he wore, a crest of red and gold on its breast pocket, was over-long. It had been bought by someone, I thought, who intended him to stay at this school until it fitted him. I thanked the teacher, who was encouraging the boy to greet me. He took my outstretched hand and I was surprised at the firmness of his grip.

'Hello, Jude, my name is Sarah,' I said. 'I am your barrister.'

*

Jude could not really remember a time that his mother and father had not been in court. He was four when his mother, Monica, left him, his older sister, Martha, and his father, Nigel, in the home where they had grown up. In the face of Nigel's refusals to allow her to see her children, Monica applied to the court within the month. And so it began.

Over the following years Jude's and Martha's lives were marked by court dates and meetings with officers from the Children and Family Court Advisory and Support Service (CAFCASS), and with almost every kind of order that a court could make. At first a judge tried to divide the children's time equally between both parents, but less than a year went by before this course failed. A second long contested final hearing then took place. This judge, frustrated by Nigel's permanent hostility towards his ex-wife, ordered that the two children should move to live with Monica in her newly rented cottage near the winding River Severn in south Wales, an hour's drive from her old home in the suburbs of Bristol where Nigel still lived.

Four years then passed, all full of litigation. At a third final hearing, a different judge – faced with the opposition of both children to their mother and her new relationship and baby – hesitantly returned them to Nigel's care. He did so with a warning: were Nigel to frustrate the children's relationship with their mother again, then this order would be immediately reversed. Nigel, for reasons he felt were justified, did not do as the judge had asked and began again to edge Monica out. It started with excuses over why they could not see her, with claims of inconvenience, and soon turned to slights, allegations, accusations. The weeks when Monica would not see or hear from the children began to turn to months. When she once again brought the matter back to court in an effort to see them, both children told anyone who would listen that they hated her. Jude, then eight years old, when asked by a social worker how he felt about his mum, said he wished she were dead.

Some three years later, Martha turned fifteen. Nigel had been home educating the children but had finally bowed to fears that he was trying to isolate them and placed them back in mainstream school. This, along with Martha's age, brought with it a sense of autonomy and she started to question the established order. Slowly, she began to make contact with Monica, began to argue with Nigel. Then Martha packed her bags, left the terraced house that was her home, and moved to live with her mother and her two half-brothers. Jude, now eleven, swore that Martha now meant nothing to him. She had betrayed them both, and he never wanted to see her again. Monica, unable to get Nigel to consent to Martha moving to a school nearer her new home, was forced to drive her daughter the long daily journey. Jude had just moved up to join the same school, and so it was that Nigel and Monica now both went to the gates, waiting for one child each. Jude's home was so close to the school that he had, in the past, walked home from his primary school right next door, sometimes chaperoned by his sister, sometimes not. But Nigel could not stand to miss the opportunity of facing his adversary and insisted on picking Jude up. He would wait in the car park, leaning on his car, scanning the tarmac until he saw where Monica had parked. Sometimes he just stared at her. Other times he would seem to walk towards the school's entrance but then stop, draw out his phone and take a photograph of her. If Monica waited inside the school building, she would come out to find notes on her car – requests to tell Martha she could come home whenever she wanted. It was both nothing and everything, which was Nigel's skill. Individually innocuous; collectively menacing.

Slowly, in her mother's care, Martha began to tell stories of life under Nigel's rule. How the children had been told to say they hated Monica; how they had been instructed to misbehave when they were with her; how they feared his mood after they returned home from seeing her and all the questions he would ask them. Nigel had used Monica's new life and new children as certain proof that she did not love them any more. All this Monica had already suspected, but bolstered by Martha's pleas she now made a further application to the court, this time for Jude to come to live with her. So the two children found themselves once again at the mercy of a judge and the ever-changing pack of social workers and experts called upon to decide their future. Their case made its way into the list of Judge Francis. It would be the first time they had ever come before her, and it would also be one of her last cases, for she was soon due to retire.

A lawsuit brought by one parent against another is a private rather than a public one and would normally not involve the state. But once Judge Francis heard of the children's courtroom legacy, she appointed a guardian as a third party to represent them. Gabriella, the guardian assigned to the case, was an experienced social worker. With this experience came a belief that her voice was the most important and so, faced with Nigel who thought the same, the two clashed in a power struggle that threatened to take centre stage. But, in truth, Gaby was right. The law saw her both as the children's messenger and as their protector, and so her words came to the court with greater weight than those of a parent who came to the courtroom with their own agenda. In her report, Gaby described parental alienation, implacable hostility, poison dripped into small ears until the parent the children should love had grown rotten in their minds. Her view was clear. The judge needed to act urgently and with great care to ensure that any damage Nigel had wreaked on the children's relationship with Monica was not permanent. Martha was safe, and the shredded bonds with her mother had started to mend. But Jude must be removed from Nigel's care before his relationship with Monica was broken beyond repair.

But Jude said no. No, he would not go; no, he did not agree. Gaby, he said, was wrong. His mother had left them, deserted them, made a new family for herself, and now Martha had too. He hated them both. He wanted to stay with his dad. If they made him go then he would just keep running away until they left him alone.

I will never know what was in Judge Francis's mind when she read the report of Gaby's conversation with Jude, but her ruling went to the heart of the law. It was not enough to make the right decision. The only way those within this flawed system can feel they have been given justice is if they feel heard. And so Judge Francis decided that if Jude objected to what Gaby said on his behalf, then he should be entitled to say what he wanted for himself. While Gaby must continue to give a voice to Martha, this young boy, just turned twelve and sufficiently competent to understand what was going on must have his own solicitor and barrister to make representations in court on his behalf. Yes, she said, she was aware that the final hearing was only nine days away, but a solicitor willing to take on the case could be found then and there at court, and they in turn could instruct a barrister to represent Jude in the final hearing. She was sure someone could be found who could manage to get themselves up to speed. That was how I came to be standing in a school shaking the hand of a boy who, for the next year, would be my client.

There were times during the following months when I questioned the judge's decision. I was wrong to do so. She knew exactly what she was doing. She gave Jude a voice and, in doing so, gave him power – even if, in court, we doubted whether the words he spoke were actually his own.

It was my solicitor, Ben, who suggested we meet Jude at school. He had already been to see the boy once at his house and said to me afterwards that Nigel had lingered in the background, listening. He had been polite, of course, but Ben believed Jude could not speak freely with the spectre of his father in the room next door. School offered a neutral space, free from eavesdropping ears. And yet, when I left the small room into which we had been shown by the teacher for our conference and went in search of a loo, I saw a man waiting in the entrance hall. He was short and thin, and was pacing back and forth across the lobby. I said hello, and he nodded at me and sat down on a seat. I knew it must be Jude's father, come early to collect him. Once Nigel knew where we were, he moved to walk up and down the hallway outside our room. His form flashed past the glass aperture in the door and I felt a shift in the atmosphere, like a change in the sea's current. Afterwards Nigel said he had not known when we would be finished – he needed to come early to make sure Jude was not left alone; and he could not hear anything, nor had he wanted to. As in the dozens of excuses that flowed from him in court, each statement was individually believable, but, when put together, a different picture formed.

Jude sat next to me in our conference room, with Ben on my right quietly taking notes. As I explained my role, the process of evidence, the final hearing coming up the following week, Jude watched me carefully. I told him I was separate from Gaby; I was not a guardian. Her role was to listen to children and explain the court process, but then to give the judge a professional view on what should happen next, even if this were at odds with what the child was telling her. But I was his barrister and I would put forward the case he wanted. I did not say that it was my duty to do this even if I did not believe him, or whether or not I suspected the words he spoke were not his own. I must fight his corner, even if I feared he had been pinned into it.

In front of me lay a file, unopened, and within it a deluge of criticism levelled against the father he said he loved more than anyone else in the world, with descriptions of Nigel as a strange and frightening man. Then there were the statements – dozens upon dozens of them – and reports from the school and guardians and social workers involved in the previous applications. A recent social services investigation had concluded that their threshold had not been crossed for state intervention, but still listed the ways in which they thought Nigel had caused his children harm. The file was united in its censorship of this man with whom Jude shared his DNA, his building blocks, his blood. How could I be responsible for introducing this grave young boy to the complex world of which he had felt only the edges?

And so I didn't. I told him what the others wanted, what they said Jude had said, and a summary of their worries. Then I let him talk. It seemed he had been waiting for this chance for many years. He had written it all down, he explained, to help him. Some of the words were underlined, some in bold where he had scored over the letters with his pen. Within the note were references to things I had not told him. Details of reports I did not know he had seen. Explanations of incidents he had not witnessed. Afterwards, as I climbed into Ben's car for a lift back to the station, I asked him whether he had shown Jude those parts of the bundle. *Of course not*, Ben said, and we both looked back at the road as the rain bashed down on the windscreen.

Bristol Temple Meads railway station rises from its cobbled hill like a temple of locomotive worship. Its clock is set within a Gothic watchtower high above the warm, carved limestone, surrounded by pinnacles. The building looms over the fore-court, while inside a vast glass and cast-iron roof dreams of long-gone steam and protracted farewells. Platforms and tunnels are clad in the livery colours of the Great Western Railway; cream and brown tiles echoing with the steps of war-weary families taking longed-for holidays to the coast. Its romance holds you, as though by stepping on to its platforms you might find yourself wearing a stole and hat, carrying a small leather suitcase, raising a gloved hand to your mouth to protect your lungs from the smog.

The Family Courts, built only a few years ago, are modern. They lie away from the grandeur of Bristol Crown Court and the winding cobbled back roads, just off the business district of Victoria Road. The entrance is within a large atrium, at the end of which a bank of lifts transport you in stainless steel through the layers of justice that rise above them.

Some weeks before, I had stood in the courtroom before Judge Francis as she tried to decide whether or not Jude should come to court to give evidence at the final hearing. We had all agreed, at least, that Jude should not sit through all five days. I should attend, and telephone him after school to go through the relevant parts of the evidence. When I had told him of this decision afterwards he had accepted it in the way a child does, although I suspected that, had I given him the choice, he would willingly have come to court and watched it all. But what is heard cannot be unheard and I was glad he would not be there to hear a procession of witnesses pull his father apart. But the giving of evidence is different. It is true that there are judicial guidelines that encourage judges to meet the children about whom they are making decisions in their chambers. They are told to explain their job, what their powers are and, if they feel they can, why they have come to their decision. I have been in cases where a judge has seized this chance, so the child or children go through a secret door behind the judge's chair and return bolstered, not quite believing it. The judge usually follows them looking relieved, glad perhaps that it is over and no one has cried or hated them. They have, they hope, proved themselves as human beings as well as makers and enforcers of the law.

But Jude was a party to the case. He had every right to give evidence if he wished. When I had explained the possibility of it he had looked up at me with shining eyes – *I would love that* – and my heart had dropped. Judge Francis had listened carefully as I explained this to her, then nodded. In that case, he must. He could do so by video link, then afterwards come into court, should he so wish, to hear what his future might be.

The evidence began with Monica. I realized, as she climbed into the witness box and took the oath, that it was the first time I had really heard her speak. Her hair was tawny red and piled on top of her head, frizzy wisps of it escaping in a crown around her hairline. She wore a long green skirt and a Chinese-collared jacket, black and woven with coloured birds. Her voice was high and soft. As Nigel took violent notes throughout her evidence, I could not help but wonder how the two had ever been matched.

While Nigel was giving his evidence, I found it difficult to look at him. He was not like witnesses I had seen before, who stumbled on the details of their explanation or said they could not remember, or who slithered and slipped away from questions. He was precise, detailed, confident and, most of all, angry. He spoke frequently of his right – his legal entitlements – to make the choices he had made. They were, he said, after all *his* children. He scowled and shook his head in rage when Monica's barrister asked him questions, and his eyes flicked, time and time again, to his ex-wife, sitting quietly on her bench, as if he were filled with disbelief that anyone could think her a better parent than him.

He had been meticulous in his preparation: brought with him folders of his own, charts, records, print-outs highlighted with Post-it notes. I glanced across at his barrister, sympathizing with him, as he flicked through the lists of questions Nigel had printed out for him to ask. Nigel believed he had done everything he thought would help him win. He had kept a record as the websites advised; meticulously collected evidence to support what he suspected; written it down, carefully timed and dated, all ready for his *big day in court*. Another big day in court.

Maybe his previous experiences in court had taught him to behave like this? I was experienced enough to know that there were professionals who glossed over their mistakes. That they could maintain they had called when they hadn't, could interpret distress as aggression, could fail to send a necessary letter or complete a vital task, safe in the knowledge that their version was more likely to be believed than that of an irate parent. I understood his desire, in the face of this system, to record everything. To trust no one. I could also see why Nigel would feel confused that, instead of being rewarded for such precision, he was now accused of psychopathy, of bullying, of controlling behaviour. He believed that the professionals, whom he thought should support him, had instead spent their time and energy trying to discredit him and none at all investigating the chaotic flimsiness of his ex-partner. As I watched him grip the edge of the witness box, I wondered how I might feel, standing there, my children in the balance, thinking that these people could never take it seriously enough. But through his fixation on being proved right, Nigel had lost any ability to ask what it was all for; to stand back and see the damage that his battles had caused the two people he claimed to love the most.

When he stepped down from the witness box after nearly two days of evidence, the very fabric of the courtroom felt worn out. Gaby gave her evidence next, and Nigel made no effort to subdue his reaction to it. The psychologist who came after her caused him so much consternation that the judge had to warn him to be quiet or leave the courtroom.

And now, at last, it was Jude's turn. He and I sat opposite one another in a conference room, away from our court. He was due to give evidence after lunch. He was wearing his school uniform, for that was where he had been all morning. In the context of the court environment it looked entirely out of place, almost shocking, but Jude remained completely composed. I watched him, trying to decide if I had a sense of whether this statue-like calmness was his natural state, or whether, as others had concluded, it was a practised stillness, a watchfulness grown out of years of learning that he must be careful of everything he said. I knew a lot about him, but unlike other children I had spoken to in court proceedings, I knew none of the colour. I did not know what his favourite subject was at school, what book he was reading, the kind of music he liked, what he would spend his pocket money on. I wished I had had the time, when meeting him, to talk about subjects unrelated to his case. Maybe then I could have persuaded him that he need not be so careful – that he must not feel he had to write down every question I asked so that he *had a record*.

After we had gone through his statement again, I walked with Jude to the small room where the video link would take place. He would be beamed into court, protected from looking at the expressions of anyone other than the person asking him questions. As I made sure his face was in the right place for the camera, that we could hear the court clerk and that she could hear us, I realized he was not nervous but excited. It occurred to me suddenly that, maybe, this was because he was going to get to prove his love to his father. He was going to be able to show him how good a son he could be. Never, I reminded myself as I walked back to court, composing myself, underestimate the desire of a child to please a parent.

Judge Francis strode into court and everyone rose in greeting. Although we had been before her all week, her presence still struck me. Her short, swept-up hair was thick with silver streaks and she wore earrings made from two discs of battered gold. She had, I noticed, put on lipstick after lunch. It was carmine red, and a phrase came into my mind. *War paint*. She knew that, this afternoon, a child was about to look her in the face and ask her to do something that almost everyone in the courtroom said would hurt him beyond repair. She also knew that this child would later sit before her, alongside both his parents, and listen to her decision on which one could take him home.

Jude's face shone out from a screen, wheeled into court for the purpose. The camera swivelled from the court clerk to the judge and then to me. Jude was leaning forward slightly, his eyes staring fiercely down the lens at us. He looked so young. I felt my throat tighten and glanced quickly down at my notes, pushing the emotion away. The next ten minutes were both terrible and wonderful. In one sense, what Jude said was unremarkable – he had already filed a witness statement and the specifics of his evidence were all in there. No one really wanted to cross-examine or challenge him on it, save to question whether what he said he wanted was for him or to please his father. The floor, therefore, was his. He spoke of his loyalty to his father, how everyone had got it wrong, how his dad was a good dad and he loved him. When he had finished, I was just getting to my feet when I heard a noise to my left and, instinctively, looked over. Monica was sitting completely still, staring at the screen. Her hands were resting on the desk before her. They were, I noticed, shaking.

'Does Your Honour have any questions for Jude?' I asked, quickly turning back.

Judge Francis leaned forward and the camera switched to frame her face. Her voice was calming. 'No, I don't, Jude. But I just wanted to know if there was *anything* else you wanted to tell me before I make my decision?'

Jude looked to one side, thinking, and then looked back. 'I think, just to say thank you for letting me speak. I have wanted to speak for a very long time. I am really glad I did.'

Dusk was falling outside the courthouse. The security guards who hovered at the desk behind the entrance had locked the doors. Usually, if there was any sign that anyone might delay the shutting of the court they would swagger over – *Court's closing now, Miss* – and linger nearby, jangling keys, hurrying us along. They wanted to be away, out of here, back to their lives. Tonight was different. They stood in a huddle by the security arch, keeping their distance. Although I had not told them, someone may have whispered that, upstairs, there was a twelve-year-old boy in a room who might refuse to leave. That elsewhere there was a father who had left court in fury as soon as the judge had begun her judgment, but that he might come back and, if he did, no one knew what he would do.

I was not with Jude but in a room nearby, surrounded by the other barristers in the case, my mobile phone in the middle of a table. We were all talking into it. On the other end, on loudspeaker, his deep voice bouncing off the breeze-block ceiling, was Lord Justice Kolbe. He was a judge of the Court of Appeal and the only possible person who could grant a suspension of the order that Judge Francis had just made returning Jude to his mother's care that evening.

Lord Justice Kolbe was, apparently, the duty judge. It had fallen to him tonight to hear emergency applications for an order to be stayed after the court had closed. As we went around the table in turn, trying not to interrupt one another, I could not help but wonder where he was when we had burst into his Friday night. Had he been in the bath, or eating supper, or fallen into a doze in front of the TV? The thought seemed both undignified and entertaining. I forced it away as I set out a summary of the case as concisely and quickly as I could. Judge Francis had granted a Residence Order to the applicant mother, I said, to take effect immediately. The child was to be returned to her care today against his will. I therefore asked him to suspend the order by granting a stay, so that we might make a swift application to the Court of Appeal to overturn the ruling.

Oh, what a position to be in. In the silence down the phone the judge balanced what he knew. There was a competent child who had just been told to leave court with a parent whom he declared he hated. But if the experts were right, to grant a stay and send him home with his father now could be worse than

263

dangerous. But the judge did not need to make a fresh decision – he just needed to apply the law. The bar for a stay was high and we had not crossed it. He would not suspend the order. We could file a paper application to appeal instead. After his ruling was over he said goodbye and I did too, which felt odd, the informality of it grating against our subject.

Jude remained expressionless as I told him the result of the telephone call. He did not cry or protest or refuse to go. Instead, when Monica came down the steps to meet us by the front door of the courthouse, he looked straight down at the floor, blocking her out. She said his name softly, but he did not look up. Maybe it was best if she went ahead, we said, and Jude could follow in the social worker's car.

We waited outside as, behind us, the security guards gratefully locked the courthouse doors. Ben and I watched the second car pull away and I looked at the figure of Jude in the passenger seat. He seemed suddenly tiny, and I willed him not to look at us, for I was not sure I could bear it if he did. But he did not. As the car pulled away his eyes stayed fixed ahead.

Jude was transformed. I could not place it in specifics – his hair was the same chestnut brown but longer, messier; his eyes still a ferocious blue. I noticed for the first time, now he was standing next to her, that they were exactly the same colour as Monica's. It was more complex than his looking relaxed, subtler than the fact that he kept smiling. It was as if he had been plugged in.

I stood there, looking at him, in the corridor of the Royal Courts of Justice. Behind us was a door, and behind that sat three lord justices waiting to hear my application to appeal Judge Francis's decision. In my hand I held my application, my carefully drafted skeleton argument and the case law that I claimed supported my position. My stomach felt tight with nerves. Nigel's solicitor had arrived alone and had already told me that she did not think Nigel would come today. He had been very upset at the end of the final hearing, she said, and had hinted at doing something. Something which I knew neither of us would articulate out loud. He had not turned up for their appointment to discuss the possibility of an appeal. His telephone was off; she could not reach him. She was going to have to come off record after today and he would then be on his own.

Monica said she would leave us to talk, and went to stand around the corner with her solicitor, chatting. Then, Jude looked straight at me and said he had changed his mind. He wanted to stay where he was. He wanted to stay with his mum. We spoke about Martha and his two half-brothers and Monica's partner. We spoke about his new home, the school to which both he and Martha had moved. We spoke, briefly, about Nigel, but it was hard for him and I could tell he did not want to talk about it. It was enough for me to hear him, to see him, to know that he was sure. And so we went into court and I withdrew my appeal and the lord justices, relieved to be unburdened from the decision, beamed at Jude and sent us away.

A year after the final hearing, I stood in the taxi queue outside Bristol station waiting for my turn, using my late pregnancy to justify a ride to court. Today was the final direction hearing in Jude's case. The judge had come out of retirement to hear it and, I was told, had done so gladly. Jude would not be at court, but in my bag was the position statement I had drafted setting out what he had told me he wanted the court to know. That he was sad his father had not come to the contact sessions the guardian had arranged or tried to get in touch and that he missed him. But that he was happy. He was happy at his new school, he was happy he had lots of friends, he was happy living with his two half-brothers and with Martha again. At the end of the document was a sentence which may have been the most significant I have ever written: *Jude wants the judge to know that he thinks she made the right decision.*

After the hearing I found myself walking in the opposite direction to the station. Ahead of me church spires and cobbled streets led to the old part of the city. To my right Bristol Castle loomed out of green trees in its park. The view was filled with memories and associations, not just of university and old cases but of the other cities and buildings to which my job had taken me. I looked down at the mesmeric reflections on the surface of the river. This was one of the last cases I would do before I left to have my baby and I wanted to savour it. It was rare, this chance to find out what happens afterwards. After I tie the pink ribbon round my files and sign the brief and send off the attendance note and put the bundle in the wire tray in the clerk's room to be billed, my part in the play is usually over. I was glad to have had the chance to see and speak to Jude since the decision that changed his life; glad I had spoken to him for today's hearing and heard the lightness in his voice. It was not until now that I had also been able to concede how relieved I was. I had not allowed myself to imagine all the other possible outcomes of the risk Judge Francis had taken. How wrong it could have gone.

I thought of the baby inside me, weeks away from his arrival. I had expected the physical vulnerability of pregnancy but not the emotional one. It was as though the armour I had grown to do my job was loosening. It troubled me. I had begun to suffer a fear of crying in court, of being too moved and, through this, revealing weakness. I had also not yet grasped the politics of pregnancy. I knew to disguise it, lest the work stopped coming – clerks and solicitors assuming there was little point handing over a case I would not be around to see through. I had felt the ever-present speculation about when I would come back to work; how I would balance the heart-tugging demands of a child with never really knowing when I would be home, or how early I would have to leave the follow-ing day, or how late I had to work to prepare tomorrow's case. I had heard that time taken off for holidays and school plays and unwell children may be punished. How, in some chambers, the clerks would acknowledge it out loud – the boys will go any-where we send them so they deserve the good briefs, irrespective of talent and ability. But I did not know back then that out of sight really was out of mind. Or that, at one point, it would be suggested to me by a man I had never met that my best course might be to 'step back' from the law.

I also had not realized that I would need to separate myself from my job to mother a baby. Nor, conversely, did I know how I would miss the courtroom with an ache and that I would long to return. I would miss the ability to lose myself entirely in the dissection of a case. I would miss the swoop of relief or shock at a jury verdict or judgment. I would miss the ever-present camaraderie, the feeling of togetherness against the odds, an unspoken acknowledgment of our allegiance to a job where there are many reasons to admit defeat. I would miss my cli-ents. Not all of them, but enough.

I turned and walked across the bridge, over the road and up through the narrow market street lined with stalls and cafés until I came to the road where the crown court stands. Part of me wanted to slip in and watch a trial, but I felt foolish doing so in front of those who might wonder why I had turned up as a tourist. Instead, I thought of those cases and clients that had changed me. I became aware of a familiar sensation. It was the same feeling I have whenever I tug my black gown over my shoulders and settle my wig into place on my head. It is a quiet but solid respect for the law – its history, its purpose, its ambition, its place.

We pride ourselves on our legal system. We know we should be proud because foreigners choose to come here to use it. They do so knowing that the judge before whom they appear cannot be bribed or threatened or bullied into doing anything other than applying the law. That sense of integrity extends throughout the system, not just for those who use it but among those who work within it and try to preserve its dignity and efficacy. As a result, our courts dispense justice with a degree of equity that means they are still considered among the fairest in the world.

We are in danger of taking this inheritance for granted. Great damage has already been done. Our legal system is regularly threatened and often wholly unsupported by those whose duty it is to protect it. Changes in its function and its funding have gouged chunks out of the high legal principles that we presumed were inviolable. Access to justice for all, no matter what your background or your bank balance. A high-quality judiciary, both to enforce the law and to make it. A fair, swift and equal hearing. We may believe that we are a long way from the corrupted legal systems that encourage foreigners to litigate in our courts rather than their own, where only money or political favour can ensure your freedom or a favourable judgment. We would be mistaken. While the legal system is in need of reform, the cumulative effect of poorly targeted funding cuts over several decades has seriously compromised the criminal law and threatened the principle of good and fair justice both for victims and defendants. Access to the family and civil courts for those without means is now skeletal. Falling pay and overwhelming workloads have meant that finding new judges is as difficult as keeping the ones we already have – something made no easier by public attacks from those who should know better. The law, and by extension the country, is threatened by an insidious form of corruption that is just as damaging as the more obvious kind. The gradual but irreparable erosion in trust in our legal system and its ability to dispense justice is a situation against which we must all protect ourselves, for, should we slip further into it, all of us will pay the cost.

Lawyers often say the law is important even to those who are unlikely to set foot in a courtroom because, as the truism goes, none of us knows what life might throw at us; any of us may become the unexpected victim of a terrible crime or a false accusation. But the law's reach is far wider than this. The decisions made in courts across our country touch our daily lives somehow, no matter how far removed we think we might be or whether we notice. Our ability to buy and sell and to invest are made possible by a legal system that is trusted to enforce a contract fairly. From the cost of our insurance to our ability to hold our government and its institutions to account, good and bad decisions by the law reach us all in the end. The law seems removed because the archaic rituals and language of the courtroom belie the fact that our legal system is a living thing. It deals with the most contemporary of problems, reflecting society back at itself. This is why everyone should have an interest in protecting what we know our justice system can do at its best.

The law is human justice, designed and enforced. It will therefore always be imperfect. It makes mistakes, it is slow, sometimes chaotic, sometimes illogical. It cracks and – at times – crumbles. But it remains a pillar upon which our country is founded. Were it to break, the stability of our nation would break too, and we would all be the poorer for it.

I turned away from the courthouse and walked slowly along the street. I realized that, without explicitly comprehending it, this feeling I had just recognized had been with me since I first walked into a courtroom. Pride. I am proud to be part of something I think is important. I am proud of something that, at its most elemental, underpins our law-making institutions and, therefore, our democracy, our lives and our liberties. I am proud, in short, to call myself a barrister.

Notes on the Law

1 Dominic

3 '. . . how to represent a child': Mandatory training for all advocates who practise in proceedings involving children has been recommended and the regulatory body for barristers, the Bar Standards Board, is currently considering this requirement.

4 '. . . old enough to be a criminal': In England and Wales, the age of criminal responsibility is 10 years old. This is lower than in any other country in Europe, including other parts of the UK. For example, in France it is 13, in Germany and Italy 14, in Denmark and Norway 15, in Spain 16 and in Belgium 18. In Northern Ireland it is 12 (with exceptions for very serious crimes) and in Scotland children are not prosecuted below the age of 12. A number of neurodevelopmental studies have said that children below adolescence (13–14 years) cannot be compared to adults in terms of their brain's ability to control their emotional responses and actions (*Rules of Engagement: Changing the Heart of Youth Justice*, Centre for Social Justice, 2012). There have been numerous calls from a wide number of organizations, governmental and otherwise, to raise the age to 12 in England and Wales as well. The United Nations Committee on the Rights of the Child has repeatedly said that the minimum age of 10 years is not compatible with our obligations under international standards of juvenile justice and the UN Convention on the Rights of the Child.

4 '. . . leading in only one direction': Although the number of juveniles going into custody has dramatically reduced over the last decade, the number of those who do who then go on to reoffend within a year of their release has increased to just below 70% (*Proven Reoffending Statistics*, updated 27 July 2017). See also note for page 20 below ('. . . not to send them to prison').

5 '. . . would pay me £125': Criminal barristers are predominantly paid from the public purse through legal aid. In the crown court, the advocate's fee is fixed. In the magistrates' court, the defendant's solicitor will pay a sum to any barrister they instruct out of their case fee. There is no set rate for this, although in 2008 the General Council of the Bar recommended a minimum gross rate for magistrates' court appearances of £50 for hearings, £75 for a half-day trial and £150 for a full-day trial. In a survey carried out by the Young Barristers' Committee in 2016 amongst those practising for seven years or under, many received less than this.

8 '. . . stopped and searched, again': Section 1 of the Police and Criminal Evidence Act 1984 grants police a power to stop a person (or vehicle), ask them questions and search them. The police are entitled to do so only if they have reasonable grounds to suspect that the person is carrying illegal drugs, a weapon, stolen property or something that could be used to commit a crime. The police are obliged to confirm their name and police station, what they expect to find, the reason they want to search you, why they are allowed to, and that you may have a copy of the record of the search. There is no obligation on the person either to stop or to answer the police's questions. Only 17% of all section 1 'stop and searches' lead to an arrest (*Police Powers and Procedures 31 March 2017*).

16 '. . . admissible by law into the trial': Every defendant walks into the courtroom an innocent person. Those determining their guilt – magistrates, judge or jury – cannot know anything of their previous convictions, for fear that this may impact on the way they deal with the evidence. However, a judge may allow evidence of a defendant (or witnesses') previous convictions, or other reprehensible behaviour, to be put before the jury if a 'bad character' application is granted. The evidence has to pass a number of statutory tests, but the most common one is when the evidence shows that the defendant has a propensity to commit the kind of offence for which he is currently on trial (i.e. he has previous convictions for similar offences), or that the evidence shows he has a propensity to be untruthful. The law prevents a judge from allowing bad character evidence in, even if it passes the tests, if he thinks it would make the hearing adversely unfair.

16 '. . . working knowledge of the sentencing guidelines': The Sentencing Council for England and Wales was established to draw up guidelines for every offence, designed to ensure national consistency between judges and courts. They are said to be 'guidelines not tramlines', although the effect is to reduce significantly the autonomy of the judge, who would have to have a good reason for departing from the guidelines without fearing a referral to the Attorney General's Unduly Lenient Sentence Scheme, or a defendant's appeal. The guidelines often break specific offences into different levels of seriousness, depending on the facts of the case. Within each of these levels, the guideline sets a sentence starting point, and a bracket indicating a minimum and maximum sentence. It then lists common aggravating and mitigating factors which tip the needle up or down from the starting point. It is fair to say that, although they have been successful in largely ensuring national consistency where before there was little, they have also been blamed for significantly increasing the length of sentences and, in turn, the ever-swelling prison population (85,409 in October 2017). The overall maximum sentence for an offence (and sometimes the minimum), however, is set by parliament. When parliament increases the sentence for one offence, the Sentencing Council must readjust the starting point in all other corresponding offences to ensure there is not a wide discrepancy which can mean heavier sentences for other crimes, not just the one whose maximum was increased by parliament.

18 '. . . one third off his sentence': The law states that every defendant is entitled to a discount off their sentence if they plead guilty before their trial. This discount reduces as the case gets nearer to trial. Since Dominic's case, the only way for a defendant to guarantee a full third off their sentence is to indicate a guilty plea in the magistrates' court at first instance before their case is sent up to the crown court (or, if it's a magistrates' court trial, to plead guilty at the first hearing). Thereafter, the discount reduces incrementally the closer they get to trial. There is a one fifth discount for someone who pleads guilty before the first day of trial, one tenth discount for anyone who pleads guilty on the first day of trial, and no discount for someone who pleads guilty once the trial has begun. Critics of the new scheme say that, far too

NOTES TO PAGES 20–25

often, the defence will not have sufficient disclosure from the prosecution at this early hearing fully to understand – and advise on – the evidence and the defendant's prospects of success at trial. Until this disclosure is produced, they are unlikely to recommend a guilty plea, even though this might cost the defendant a reduced discount if, having seen all the evidence, he then does plead guilty.

20 '... pre-sentence report': A pre-sentence report (PSR) is a document prepared by probation to assist the court after a defendant has pleaded guilty. One is prepared in most cases, unless a long period of custody is inevitable. The probation officer will interview the defendant and then write the PSR setting out the offender's history, remorse, vulnerabilities and commitment to change, as well as making recommendations for any kind of community sentences that might be available or suitable. The PSR is a recommendation to the court, and the judge need not follow it.

20 '... not to send them to prison': Britain has the highest prison population in western Europe at 85,409 (*UK Prison Population Statistics* briefing paper, April 2017). Although the reoffending rate in adult offenders is the lowest since 2004, generally offenders with a large number of previous offences have a higher rate of proven reoffending than those with fewer previous offences. The reoffending rate for those released from short sentences has been consistently higher than that of people released from longer sentences. Adults who served sentences of less than twelve months reoffended at the very high rate of 65.5%, compared to 29.9% for those who served determinate sentences of 12 months or more. For adult offenders starting a court order (community sentence or Suspended Sentence Order), the proven reoffending rate was 33.9%. This would suggest that Community Orders are more effective than prison at reducing offending, and short prison sentences are ineffective at creating any kind of rehabilitation, although there is no way of knowing differences in offender characteristics and the type of sentence given (*Proven Reoffending Statistics*, October 2017). See also note for page 4 above ('... leading in only one direction').

25 '... technically, I have to do it': Barristers operate under a system known as the 'cab rank rule'. They are obliged to take the next case that comes their way if they are qualified and experienced enough to do it and their diary is free. This system prevents barristers picking and choosing cases based on their merits or value. If you are next, then you are up. Where there is a clash of cases, a barrister and their clerk will weigh up the competing duties to each client to see which case should take precedent.

25 '. . . barely cover my train fare': If a defendant is alleged to have breached his community sentence (i.e. by failing to attend an appointment) he will be summoned back to court for a breach hearing. The advocacy fee fixed by statute for a breach hearing was, and remains, £85.11. My fee for Dominic's hearing – less chambers' fee of £17.44 and train fare of £57.10 – would therefore be £10.57 before tax.

2 Derek

30 '. . . let them go with a caution': Rather than prosecuting minor offences, a caution allows an offender to be dealt with without prosecution. It is available only for minor offences, and the offender must admit his guilt. A caution is a legal warning, not a conviction. A conditional caution has, as the name suggests, conditions attached to it. If the offender breaks these, he can be prosecuted for the original offence. Cautions may have to be disclosed to employers in particular kinds of jobs, and are also made available to the Disclosure and Barring Service (which replaced the Criminal Records Bureau).

30 '. . . public interest to charge them': Every prosecution case must pass a two-part test. Firstly, there must be sufficient evidence to provide a realistic prospect of securing a conviction against each suspect, on each charge. If there is not enough evidence, the case stops at this point. The second test asks whether prosecuting the case is in the public interest. Even if a conviction might be likely, if prosecution is not in the interests of justice, then the offence must not be charged. Police are able to make this decision to charge in respect of some minor offences. In all other offences, the papers have to be reviewed by a Crown Prosecution Service lawyer, who applies the two-stage test and decides whether or not the police should charge. See also note for page 30 above.

30 '. . . before a judge and jury': A 'summary offence' can be heard only in the magistrates' court. An 'either-way offence' can be heard in either the magistrates' court (before three lay magistrates or a district judge) or the crown court (before a judge and a jury). An 'indictable-only' offence can be heard only in the crown court. All cases start in the magistrates' court. The magistrates' sentencing powers are limited up to six months' custody for one offence, and up to twelve months' custody if there are two separate offences which are dealt with by consecutive sentences. If a likely sentence will exceed the magistrates' powers, it will be sent up to the crown court. A defendant charged with an either-way offence also has the right to choose trial by jury over trial in the magistrates' court.

32 '. . . the offence of "gross indecency" ': The Criminal Law Amendment Act 1885 first prohibited gross indecency – defined as any sexual contact between men, either in public or private. The offence was eventually repealed by the Sexual Offences Act 2003, which also created Section 71 – Sexual Activity in a Public Lavatory (see note for page 32 below). In 2017, under the Alan Turing law, all men who had been convicted in the past of gross indecency due to consensual, private sexual acts were pardoned.

32 '. . . meeting in public lavatories for sex': Section 71 of the Sexual Offences Act (SOA) 2003, Sexual Activity in a Public Lavatory, is summary only, punishable by up to six months' imprisonment, and not an offence that requires the offender to register his details with the police. It is committed if a person is in a lavatory to which the public (or a section of the public) has access and intentionally engages in sexual activity. The person can be alone, their motive and intent are irrelevant, no one needs to have been caused alarm and distress as a result of the sexual activity. The offence comes from the 1967 SOA Act, which decriminalized private homosexual acts but prohibited homosexual activity in a public lavatory. The 2003 Act made the offence gender-neutral. However, between 2012 and 2017, 92% of people apprehended by the British Transport Police for the offence were male, at a rate of more than one a month.

34 '. . . to back up his client's story': Section 34 of the Criminal Justice Act 2003, which came into force shortly after Terry's trial took place, obliges the defendant to give notice to the prosecution of any witnesses they intend to call, including their names, addresses and dates of birth.

36 '. . . law conversion course': There are two routes to becoming a lawyer. The first is to study a law degree and then to decide whether to undertake the Legal Practitioner's Course and become a solicitor, or to undertake the Bar Vocational Course and become a barrister. The second is to study a postgraduate law conversion course, which takes one year, and then go on to undertake either the LPC or the BVC. To become a solicitor, the LPC has to be followed by completing two years of a training contract within a law firm. However, anyone who has completed the BVC is able to call themselves a barrister whether or not they have then gone on to complete their year's worth of pupillage or have been accepted as a member of a chambers.

36 'Inn of Court': There are four Inns of Court: Lincoln's Inn, Inner Temple, Middle Temple and Gray's Inn. Originally constructed as places of education, where barristers would hone their skills by debating at various dinners, they still fulfil a hugely important role. Every barrister must join one of the four Inns, and it is this Inn which then 'calls' them to the 'Bar' when the barrister has finished their academic training. Barristers must still go to a minimum of twelve dinners a year at their Inn of Court, and the Inns also provide other training both during and after qualification. They are also crucial in providing scholarships to members to help with their academic fees.

38 '. . . ever-decreasing rates of publicly funded pay': The average fee income for a full-time barrister working on legal aid rates was £56,000 in 2014–15 (before tax). This had fallen annually from £69,000 in 2012–13. In 2014–15, 39% of barristers received less than £50,000 (*The Composition and remuneration of the junior barristers under the Advocates' Graduated Fee Scheme in criminal legal aid*, published by the Ministry of Justice, 17 December 2015). The figure represents claimed fees, not earnings – costs such as travel, chambers' expenses, training and insurance still need to be deducted (between 20 and 30%). Barristers are self-employed and receive no pension, holiday, sick or parental-leave pay other than that which is statutory.

38 '. . . technology made it obsolete': In 2016 the Crown Court Digital Case System was rolled out nationally. Now a barrister is emailed their brief by the CPS or solicitor and all disclosure or other material is uploaded on to the system.

41 '. . . principle of open court': The openness of judicial proceedings is a fundamental principle dating back to the Middle Ages and now enshrined in Article 6(1) of the European Convention on Human Rights – the right to a fair trial. Any citizen or reporter can go into a criminal courtroom, observe and take notes. Anything said in open court is a matter of public record.

3 Saba

45 '. . . orders with respect to children': Over the years the name of orders made by a family court under Section 8 of the Children Act 1989 has changed. What were once termed 'Custody Orders' became 'Residence' and 'Contact Orders' and then, through the Child and Families Act 2014, the law was amended to 'Child Arrangements Orders' in an attempt to prevent parents asserting that one parent had greater importance than the other in the child's life. This umbrella term is now used to cover any orders which set out the division of a child's time between each parent.

57 '. . . a variety of cases': Magistrates who have undertaken the necessary training have the power to decide upon a wide variety of family cases – both public and private – unless they involve more complex issues, in which case they will be allocated to a judge. There is now a single family court system encompassing all family cases and, in theory, cases are allocated to the appropriate level of tribunal – magistrate or judge – when they are issued.

59 'Children and Family Court Advisory and Support Service (CAF-CASS)': This is a non-departmental independent public body whose officers are social workers independent from the local authority. They are appointed by the court at the beginning of a case to speak to both

parties and see if there are any welfare or safeguarding concerns in respect of the children, in case the court wants them to be involved further. They will conduct a brief risk assessment, then write a letter to the court reporting what each parent has told them and whether they have discovered anything of concern in the social services and police records. If not, this will be the end of their involvement. If welfare concerns are raised, either at the beginning of a case or at any point before the final hearing, the court may ask CAFCASS to prepare a Section 7 report. This is a full investigation by the CAFCASS officer, who will speak to the children about what they want, if they are considered old enough. The CAFCASS officer will conclude the report by making a recommendation to the court about the kind of orders the court should make.

59 '. . . finding of fact hearing': A finding of fact hearing is a trial within the family proceedings, which is used to determine whether allegations made by one party against the other are true. Both parties make statements, give evidence and are cross-examined. Unlike a criminal trial, the court makes its decision on the balance of probabilities, in that it has to decide whether what one party alleges is more likely to have happened than not. These findings are then used to inform the court's decision on the application.

60 '. . . representing himself': There is currently no accurate record of how many defendants represent themselves in criminal proceedings, but anecdotal evidence suggests it has risen since the introduction of means testing for criminal legal aid representation, particularly in the magistrates' court. A report published by the charity Transform Justice in 2016, entitled *Justice Denied*, cited a survey by the Magistrates Association in which 25% of defendants who came before its members in 2014 were unrepresented. The report stated that 'Interviewees had witnessed unrepresented defendants not understanding what they were charged with, pleading guilty when they would have been advised not to, and vice versa, messing up the cross-examination of witnesses, and getting tougher sentences because they did not know how to mitigate.' The Ministry of Justice is currently conducting an inquiry into the situation in the crown court.

60 '. . . cross-examine on his behalf': Sections 34–40 of the Youth Justice and Criminal Evidence Act 1999 prohibit a litigant in person in a criminal trial from cross-examining a complainant in proceedings for sexual offences, or a child, but there is no such prohibition in the family court. If Saba's hearing were to take place today, Asif would not qualify for legal aid (see note for page 60 below). Although her evidence could be given behind a screen or via a video link, Asif would have to cross-examine Saba himself in court. In 2017 an updated Practice Direction (PD12J) stated that a judge should 'be prepared where necessary and appropriate to conduct the questioning of the witnesses on behalf of the parties, focusing on the key issues in the case'. This requires the judge, who must then rule on the truth of the allegations, to ask questions of one party on behalf of the other. Judges, practitioners and charities have all asked parliament to replicate the criminal law prohibition on cross-examination within the family court, and to provide funding for an advocate to cross-examine on the alleged perpetrator's behalf.

60 '. . . representing himself': The Legal Aid, Sentencing and Punishment of Offenders Act 2012 (LASPO) significantly restricted legal aid to a large number of civil cases, including most private law disputes in family cases (i.e. any case where there is not state intervention). An exemption is available for victims of domestic abuse. Those who can produce 'trigger evidence' to prove they are the victim of domestic violence are entitled to legal aid. Applications can be made for legal aid in 'exceptional circumstances'. Between April 2013 and March 2014 only 57 applications were granted. Those excluded from qualifying for legal aid include parents whose first language is not English. Were Saba's case to take place today, she would qualify for legal aid on the basis of her history of domestic violence. Asif would not qualify for advice or representation and would have had to cross-examine Saba himself (see also note for page 60 above ('. . . cross-examine on his behalf')). LASPO has resulted in a significant rise in the numbers of individuals representing themselves in hearings. Ministry of Justice figures for 2017 show that 18% of all family cases had legal representation for both parties; 36% had no lawyers involved at all.

61 '... want to come to court': The courts are growing increasingly alive to the power of unrepresented litigants in person to make repeated and baseless applications in an effort to harass their ex-partner. The court does have the power to restrict this. Section 91(14) of the Children Act 1989 empowers any court dealing with a Children Act application to prevent future applications being made without permission of the court. This is called a Barring Order. This, however, is a power which is used sparingly by the courts and only after a litigant has already made numerous and groundless applications.

4 Raymond

73 '... and his seventeen-year-old sister, Daniella': If someone under the age of 18 is charged along with an adult, their case will be heard alongside the adult's in the criminal court, not the youth court.

74 '... plea and case management hearing': This is now called the plea and trial preparation hearing. It is the first hearing in the crown court at which a defendant may enter their plea, and is used to timetable the trial and any other directions. At this hearing a defendant is required to submit a defence case statement, which sets out the specifics of their defence – i.e. which elements of the evidence are challenged. This ensures that, if evidence is not challenged, it can be agreed, and the witness then does not need to come to court. The prosecutor will simply read out the undisputed evidence.

78 'The closer to trial, the less credit you get': See note for page 18.

83 '... Daniella's guilty plea': Daniella's conviction was admissible into evidence as proof that she had committed the offence, under Section 74 of the Police and Criminal Evidence Act 1984 (PACE 1984). However, Section 78 of PACE says that if admitting the conviction would have such an adverse effect on the fairness of the proceedings that the court ought not to admit it, then the judge can refuse to allow it into evidence. It is up to the trial judge to rule whether admitting a co-defendant's guilty plea may carry such weight in the minds of the jury that it would unfairly impact on the defendant's trial.

90 '... *must throw it out!*': After the prosecution case has finished, the defence are entitled to make a 'submission of no case to answer' if they think that the prosecution's case against them has not raised any evidence that the defendant committed the crime, or is very weak. If the judge agrees that there is no evidence that the defendant has committed the crime, he must stop the case. If the judge thinks that the evidence is tenuous, weak or vague, or inconsistent with other evidence, then he may stop the case if he thinks that a properly directed jury could not safely convict on this evidence.

93 '... compensation for the DVD player': The Criminal Injuries Compensation Bureau (CICB) financially compensates blameless victims who have been victims of violent crime with money from public funds. Since its inception it has paid out more than £3 billion, making it among the largest compensation schemes in the world. The rules of the scheme and the value of the payments awarded are set by parliament and are calculated by reference to an injuries tariff. It is not necessary for the person who caused the injury to be identified or convicted in order to receive a payment, but victims must report the crime and cooperate with the police and any prosecution. The efficacy of the CICB has been called into question by cases such as the false allegations made by Jemma Beale against 15 different men, a man known as 'Nick' who made false allegations against senior army and political figures, and an unnamed man who made allegations against a fire chief – all of whom were paid large sums by the CICB despite most of the allegations not being proved in court.

5 Rita

102–3 '... to apply to their sentence': See note for page 18.

103 '... names on the indictment': The indictment is the legal charge sheet in a crown court which contains the name of the defendant(s) and the specifics of the charge of the offence.

109 '... end of the prosecution's case': See note for page 90.

117 '... directions relevant for our case': *The Crown Court Bench Book and Specimen Directions* is a court book dealing with jury and trial management and summing up and sentencing in the crown court.

118 '. . . from common law': The law of England and Wales, of Scotland and of Northern Ireland is made up both of statutes made by parliament and of common law. Common law is a history of convention and legal decisions given by judges in the appeal or supreme courts which are binding, until they are overruled by a new judgment from the same, or a higher, court.

118 '. . . of one mind, of one will': A husband and wife cannot, in law, be guilty of a conspiracy if only the two of them conspire to commit a crime. The same rule now applies to civil partners. The law says that where a husband and wife are charged with conspiring with another, the jury should be directed to acquit the husband and wife if they are not satisfied that there was another party to the conspiracy.

122 'Unless they had misunderstood it': In February 2010 the Home Office published a paper entitled 'Are juries fair?' It remains the most comprehensive study into the workings of a jury in England and Wales published to date, involving over 68,000 jury verdicts across all crown courts. Ultimately the study was positive about juries. However, it also looked at jurors' understanding of a judge's legal directions in a trial. Whilst over half the jurors in the study thought the judge's directions easy to understand, it turned out that only a minority (31%) actually understood the directions fully. A written summary of the judge's directions on the law given to jurors at the time of the judge's oral instructions improved juror comprehension: the proportion of jurors who fully understood the legal questions in the case in the terms used by the judge increased from 31% to 48% with written instructions. There is no requirement for judges to hand juries written directions.

6 Maggie

127 '. . . and the guardian's barrister': The guardian is a separately represented social worker whose role is independently to represent the interests of the child. Their duties should involve holding the local authority to account, making sure that their care plan is the best one possible and sometimes acting as an intermediary between the parent and the local authority if communications with the social worker have broken down.

128 '... your informed consent': Under Section 20 of the Children Act 1989, the parents/mother of a child can agree to the local authority *accommodating* the child for a temporary period. Accommodating means more than housing – it means providing for their care. This arrangement can mean the child staying at home with its parents and interventions from the local authority; more often it means the child moving into temporary foster care. Section 20 does not mean that the local authority has parental responsibility for the child, and the child's parents are entitled to withdraw their consent at any time. If they do, the local authority must return the child immediately to the parents' care. The local authority can ask the police to exercise their emergency powers to remove the child (up to 72 hours under Section 46 of the Children Act 1989) if the circumstances allow for this, or can make an application to the court for an Emergency Protection Order or an Interim Care Order (see note for page 129 below). The courts have been concerned about local authorities relying on Section 20 consent and allowing the temporary situation to become a permanent one without issuing proceedings or providing support. There are also concerns around whether parents properly understand what Section 20 consent means, and it is the social worker's responsibility to ensure that they do.

129 '... in the local authority's care': An Interim Care Order (ICO) places a child into the care of the local authority during care proceedings, before the final hearing takes place. The order gives the local authority parental responsibility over the child, which supersedes the parent's parental authority if there is a disagreement about the child's welfare. The order allows the local authority to decide where the child lives and who has contact with him. To make an ICO the local authority has to prove facts which establish that significant harm has already been caused to a child, or there is a serious risk that the child will suffer significant harm in the future, or which show that the child is beyond parental control. Sometimes parents admit that the threshold criteria have been crossed. If they do not, the local authority has to prove the allegations on the balance of probabilities. The court must first agree that the threshold has been crossed and, if so, whether it is in the child's best interests to make an order. This is not inevitable, although it is likely.

130 '. . . it will never go back': A paper published in 2016 by Professor Karen Broadhurst, lead researcher at Leicester University, et al., found that once newborn babies were removed in care proceedings from their mothers/parents, only 10% were returned. ('Women and infants in care proceedings in England: new insights from research on recurrent care proceedings', *Family Law*, Vol. 46, No. 2, 7 February 2016, pp. 208–11.)

130 '. . . happening to her next baby': Professor Broadhurst's 2016 paper also found that one woman in four who has her child removed by the state returns to court to have a subsequent child removed. In respect of those women who returned to court for a further set or two sets of care proceedings, 70% of the infants involved were aged less than one year, and nearly 60% were aged less than one month. The conclusion drawn was that there is a tendency on the part of local authorities to issue proceedings very early in the life of an infant where there is a history of previous proceedings.

130 '. . . attach to the order, as usual': When magistrates make an order they are obliged to attach the facts and reasons upon which they based their decision to the back of it. The appeal courts have recognized the fact that there was a widespread practice of the local authority drafting these *facts and reasons* on behalf of the magistrates. The High Court said that this practice was 'patently wrong, must stop at once and never happen again' *(Re NL (A Child) (Appeal: Interim Care Order: Facts and Reasons)* [2014] EWHC 270 (Fam)).

131 '. . . rebuild the family': The fundamental principle of adoption remains that, where there is opposition from the parents/mother, the

making of a Care Order with a plan for adoption, or of a Placement Order, is permissible only where, in the context of the child's welfare, 'nothing else will do'.

131 '... blue eyes matched his jumper': Peter Connelly (also known as 'Baby P') was a 17-month-old boy who died in London in 2007 after suffering more than 50 injuries over an eight-month period, during which he was repeatedly seen by the children's services and health professionals. Peter's mother, her boyfriend and his brother were all convicted of causing his death. The case caused shock and concern, partly because of the magnitude of Peter's injuries, and partly because Peter had lived in the London Borough of Haringey, North London, which had already been subjected to an intense review seven years earlier following the case of Victoria Climbié, an eight-year-old who was murdered by her guardians. From 2008–9 (the time of the Peter Connelly case) to 2012–13, care applications rose by 70% (*National picture of care applications in England since Baby P*, as published by CAFCASS).

131 '... supposed to care for them': According to the Office of National Statistics crime and justice figures, 24 children (under 16) were killed by a parent or stepparent in the year ending March 2016.

131 '... any other country in western Europe': Figures from Professor Karen Broadhurst in her 2016 report.

132 '... helping her learn how to do so': In 2017 the courts raised the query of whether a local authority should spend on issuing proceedings (the cost of issuing a care application is over £2,000) and on psychological evidence (on average more than £2,000) when the expenditure is incurred before attempts at therapeutic support in respect of the parents or mother have been made. (H. H. J. Wildblood QC, *A Local Authority v The Mother & Anor* [2017] EWFC B59, www.familylawweek.co.uk/site.aspx?i=ed180307.)

134 '... no parental responsibility for her': Parental responsibility means the legal rights, duties, powers and authority that a parent has in relation to his or her child. If a man and woman are married they automatically have parental responsibilities. If they are not, the father must have his parental responsibility rights granted by the court. A local authority can be awarded parental responsibilities.

135 '. . . to be Aaron's mother': Parent and baby foster-care placements are a way of keeping mothers or parents with their babies within family-based placements. The foster carers do not necessarily provide parental care (except if asked to), but teach the parent to develop their own skills. They also observe and record how the parent looks after the child and work with other professionals to identify support that might be needed in the future. The placement is an alternative to a more institutional mother-and-baby unit where there are several mothers and supervising staff. Placements generally last 12–24 weeks but may be extended if longer-term support is required.

136 '. . . her interim resolution hearing': This is the directions hearing before the final hearing in care proceedings, and a last opportunity for the parties to narrow the issues and to see if any agreement can be made, which might avoid the need for a full final hearing.

137 '. . . provided for the hearing': In any family proceedings, the applicant is obliged to provide the court with the bundle of case papers no later than two working days before any hearing. They must also provide the court and the other parties with a number of documents no later than 11 a.m. on the day before the hearing. These include a case summary, a statement of issues to be determined by the court, an up-to-date chronology and a position statement by each party, including a summary of the order or directions that they are asking the judge to make. The courts have recognized that these obligations are not always complied with and have said that this is unacceptable, that orders for costs should be made against the party or lawyers in default, and that in flagrant cases defaulters may be publicly identified in open court (*Re X and Y (Bundles)* [2008] 2 FLR 2053).

139 '. . . looking for adoptive parents': Twin-tracking is the practice of progressing adoption plans at the same time as pursuing other options for children. Although it works well for children's timescales and means that there is as little delay as possible between the order being made and the child being adopted, critics of the practice say it

exacerbates the perception – if not the practice – of the local authority having already closed its mind to any possibility of rehabilitating the child with the family.

141 '. . . where others fail': A publication by CAFCASS stated that there are considerable local variations in the number of applications per 10,000 children. Some local authorities have seen increases of up to 500% (note that this is apparent in areas where the numbers are relatively small) and decreases of up to 46% since the case of Baby P. Ofsted rated 77% of 69 local authorities inspected 'inadequate' or 'requires improvement' in November 2015. The report concluded that the statistics showed that good leadership was more a factor than size, levels of deprivation and funding in providing a high quality of children's services.

142 '. . . in recurrent care proceedings': In Professor Broadhurst's study, a review of women who had been involved in repeated care proceedings showed that in 36% of cases, proceedings involving the removal of one child overlapped with proceedings involving the removal of a new baby. The average time between pregnancies for women who were involved in two sets of care proceedings was 13 months, although for some women it was only 6 months between the birth of one child and the conception of the next.

143 '. . . twenty-six weeks imposed by the legal framework': By law, care proceedings must finish as soon as possible or take no more than 26 weeks. If the court anticipates proceedings will not finish in this timeframe, then it can extend it but has to give a judgment explaining why. Just over half of all cases are disposed of within 26 weeks. Some professionals feel that the current timetable will never be long enough for a parent to show meaningful change sufficient to ensure their child can be placed back in their care.

143 '. . . thirty-three thousand pounds each year': The National Audit Office stated a council foster-care placement in 2014 was in the range of £23,000–£27,000, compared with a range of £41,000–£42,000 for a placement with other providers.

143 '. . . what kind of placement is undertaken': The average cost of removal per mother was £200,000 (for an internal foster placement)

and £300,000 (for an external foster placement). In respect of a mother who had had eight children removed, the cost was between £500,000 and £800,000 to place her babies. The average cost of assessment of parenting capacity of a mother was £4,000. (Figures from 'The Serial Removal of Children from Young Mothers – is this right?', Maureen N. Obi-Ezekpazu, *Family Law Week*, 18 May 2014.)

145 '... *disguised compliance*': A term used within the care system to describe parents who say they are willing to change and engage, but are paying lip service to professionals and neither see the need, nor intend, to do so. Published case reviews highlight that professionals sometimes delay or avoid interventions due to parental disguised compliance. However, David Wilkins, senior research fellow at the University of Bedfordshire, argues that disguised compliance and resistance result from the situation rather than the individual, and suggests social workers should be more reflective and reflexive in their approach ('We need to rethink our approach to disguised compliance', David Wilkins, www.comunitycare. co.uk/2017/03/16/need-rethink-approach-disguised-compliance/.)

148 '... for a further year': Supervision Orders give the local authority the legal power to monitor a child's needs and progress while the child lives at home. They also place a burden on the local authority to offer a parent support. Unlike a Care Order, a Supervision Order does not give the local authority shared parental responsibility, nor allow them any special right to remove the child from their parent. The parents keep parental responsibility but mustn't act in any way against the Supervision Order.

7 Peter

155 '... a legal slap on the wrist': See note for page 30 ('... let them go with a caution').

155 '... the Crown Prosecution Service': See note for page 30 ('... public interest to charge them').

156 '... levels of perversion': The categories cited in this chapter as 'levels' were amended on 1 April 2014 to categories A, B and C. A

merges Levels 1 and 2; B is any image involving non-penetrative sexual activity; C is other indecent images not falling within A or B.

156 '. . . sentencing guidelines were clear': See note for page 16 ('. . . working knowledge of the sentencing guidelines').

156 '. . . treated in law as such': All defendants under 18 years of age are dealt with in the youth court. Had Peter been charged when he was 17, his case would have been heard in the youth court. Guidelines published in 2017 have clarified that, where a defendant turns 18 in between committing an offence and being convicted (as in Peter's case), it will rarely be appropriate that a more severe sentence than the maximum that the court could have imposed at the time the offence was committed should be imposed (in Peter's case, two years' detention). However, a sentence at or close to that maximum may be appropriate.

159 '. . . pre-sentence report': See note for page 20.

160 '. . . a Criminal Records Bureau request': In 2012 the functions of the Criminal Records Bureau (CRB) and the Independent Safeguarding Authority (ISA) were merged under the Protection of Freedoms Act to form a new body, now called the Disclosure and Barring Service. A DBS check enables employers to check the criminal records of current and potential employees in order to ascertain whether or not they are suitable to work with vulnerable adults and children. For individuals working in certain positions, a valid DBS disclosure is a legislative requirement.

162 '. . . alongside whom he would be incarcerated': To date, parliament has taken the view that sentences for indecent images must be deterrent as well as punitive. This is, in part, to try to 'starve out' the market for the buyers of indecent images so that the makers will slow their trade. This policy has been ineffective: there has been an astonishing rise not only in the number of images being downloaded, but the number of offenders imprisoned. Child sexual abuse prosecutions rose by 82% over the past decade. They made up one third of all convictions for sexual offences in England and Wales in 2016–17. Police forces nationally are operating beyond capacity due to the number of reports.

162 '. . . Sexual Offences Prevention Order': Since Peter's case, Sexual Offences Prevention Orders have been renamed Sexual Harm Prevention Orders. These prohibit a defendant from doing anything described in the order. The court may make an order if it thinks it necessary to protect the public, or any particular members of the public, from sexual harm from the defendant.

162 '. . . his details every year': Colloquially known as 'The Sex Offenders' Register', Part 2 of the Sexual Offences Act 2003 brought into law a retrospective provision that requires offenders to notify certain personal details to the police in their area. These include any address at which they might stay for more than seven days, foreign travel plans, whether a child under the age of 18 is staying in their household for at least 12 hours, bank accounts and credit-card details, and passport and any identification documents. They must do so within three days of their conviction and every year thereafter. Failure to do so is a criminal offence punishable by the court by up to five years' imprisonment.

8 Daniel

174 '. . . imposing strict time limits': Custody Time Limits (CTLs) define the time that a defendant awaiting his trial can be held in custody. Less serious offences (summary and either-way offences) have a CTL of 56 days. More serious offences heard in the crown court have a CTL of 182 days. A CTL may be extended, or further extended, for a defined number of reasons, including the court ordering two or more charges, or some other good or sufficient cause. The prosecution must have acted with all due diligence and expedition.

181 'Our high court judge': More complex and difficult cases are dealt with by high court judges. They usually sit in London, but also travel to major court centres around the country to try serious criminal cases, important civil cases and assist lord justices to hear appeals. High court judges are given the prefix 'the Honourable' and referred to as 'Mr/Mrs/Ms Justice Surname'. In criminal proceedings they are known as 'red judges' because of the colour of the robes they wear.

181 '... legal geographical areas distinct from London': Barristers who practise outside London are divided up geographically into six legal circuits. Those who practise within a circuit are able to join that circuit as a member. The circuits are: the Midland Circuit, the Northern Circuit, the North Eastern Circuit, the South Eastern Circuit, the Wales and Chester Circuit, and the Western Circuit.

182 '... shielded from the dock by a screen': Witnesses who are vulnerable, intimidated or victims of a serious criminal offence are able to give evidence in a way that is designed to relieve some of the stress associated with giving evidence. These methods are called special measures. For example, the witness can give evidence behind a screen or over a video link, or their evidence can be pre-recorded so that they do not have to then give it again in court. Special measures apply to prosecution and defence witnesses, but not to the defendant. They are granted only after an application has been granted if the judge thinks that special measures are likely to maximize the quality of the witness's evidence.

189 '... read out to the jury': In his police interview, a defendant may sign a 'prepared statement' which sets out, in brief terms, his defence or what he denies before he then goes on to answer 'No comment' to questions put to him in the interview. This prepared statement can later become evidence in the same way that the transcript of his interview would. A court can draw an adverse inference from a defendant's silence in interview.

193 '... specific circumstances of rape': The Sexual Offences Act 2003 made a number of changes to the offence of rape. If it is proved that any of a number of specific circumstances existed at the time of the rape, and that the defendant knew those circumstances existed, then the complainant is taken *not* to have consented to intercourse. One of those circumstances is when the complainant was unlawfully detained. The burden then flips to the defendant to put forward evidence, which raises the issue of whether or not the complainant did, in fact, consent to intercourse and whether he reasonably believed that she consented. If the defendant puts forward enough evidence to raise these two issues, then the burden flips back again to the prosecution to prove beyond reasonable doubt that she did not consent and that the defendant did not believe she consented.

197 '. . . convicted of multiple rapes': A life sentence sets a minimum tariff that has to be served before the defendant will be eligible to apply for parole (early release). The average minimum term is around 15 years. However, life sentences last for the rest of a defendant's life, so if they are released from prison and commit another crime they can be sent back to prison at any time. A whole-life term means there's no minimum term set by the judge and the person is never considered for release.

197 '. . . indeterminate sentence for public protection': The imprisonment for public protection (IPP) sentence was a form of indeterminate sentence introduced by the Criminal Justice Act 2003. It was abolished in 2012. It was intended to protect the public against criminals whose crimes were not serious enough to merit a life sentence, but who were regarded as too dangerous to be released when the term of their original sentence had expired. It was composed of a punitive 'tariff' intended to be proportionate to the gravity of the crime committed, and an indeterminate period which commenced after the expiration of the tariff and lasted until the Parole Board decided that the prisoner no longer posed a risk to the public and was fit to be released. There was no limit to how long prisoners could be detained under an IPP. In effect, offenders served longer in prison than had they been given a life sentence. In 2007 the high court ruled that the continued incarceration of prisoners serving IPPs after tariff expiry where the prisons lacked the facilities and courses required to assess their suitability for release was unlawful. In 2010 a joint report by the chief inspectors of prisons and probation concluded that IPP sentences were unsustainable with prison overcrowding in England and Wales. As of 2017, over 3,000 prisoners remain incarcerated under their IPP sentence. Three quarters of them had completed their minimum term and hundreds had served five times the minimum.

199 '. . . sign cautions for soliciting': In England and Wales it is an offence for a person persistently to loiter, or solicit, in a street or public place for the purpose of offering services as a prostitute. Norway, Sweden, Iceland, Northern Ireland and Canada criminalize the sex buyers. England and Wales have no consistent police approach to soliciting. In Leeds, for example, the police and council have controversially decided not to apply the law between 7 p.m. and 7 a.m. in a particular area. There has been at least one murder of a prostitute since this decision was made. In Suffolk, however, after a number of prostitutes were murdered, a zero-tolerance approach was taken to kerb-crawling and, copying the Nordic approach, multi-agency support was put in place for women, virtually eliminating street prostitution and murders. Nottingham also targets the sex buyers, decreasing the number of sex workers on the streets in 10 years from 300 to 50. An all-party parliamentary report called 'Shifting the Burden' was published in 2016, recommending the reversal of criminalization from the women who sell sex to the men who buy it, but as yet the government has not taken up the proposals.

9 Helena

202 '. . . encouraged them to turn to blame': If separating couples want to get divorced without waiting for two years (or five if the other person does not consent), one person must submit a petition detailing how the other is at 'fault'. A study published in 2017 found that 60% of English and Welsh divorces were granted on the basis of adultery or unreasonable behaviour. In Scotland – where a divorce can be obtained after one year if both parties agree – this figure was 6%. In a national opinion survey, 43% of people who had been identified as being at fault by their spouse disagreed with the reasons cited for the marriage breakdown, and 37% of respondents denied or rebutted the allegations made against them by their spouse. The study found no empirical support for the argument that fault may protect marriage. In countries that have a 'no-fault divorce', including Scotland, there has been no long-term recorded increase in the number of divorces applied for annually. We already have something tantamount to immediate unilateral divorce, but that method unnecessarily encourages acrimony

between the parties. A number of judges, charities and interested groups have called for a 'no-fault divorce' to prevent separations between couples escalating due to the requirement to blame one another.

205 '. . . accepted the caution they offered': See note for page 30 ('. . . let them go with a caution').

208 '. . . (CAFCASS)': See note for page 59 ('. . . Children and Family Court Advisory and Support Service).

208 '. . . without telling Ed': The law states that a parent is free to move anywhere within the jurisdiction without the permission of the other parent. There is no presumption of favour of the status quo – each case must be decided on its own merits. However, if both parents have parental responsibility (see note for page 134), then each parent is entitled to be consulted upon any significant changes in their child's life with a view to coming to an agreement. If a parent thinks that the other may relocate with the children, they are able to bring an application to try to prevent them from doing so.

210 '. . . right to know each parent': Section 1 of the Children Act 1989 sets out the 'welfare principles' that the court must apply in every case involving a child. These principles ask the court to presume that involvement of a parent in the life of the child will further the child's welfare if this parent can be involved in the child's life in a way that does not put the child at risk of suffering harm. The presumption does not apply if there is some evidence before the court in the proceedings to suggest that involvement would put the child at risk of suffering harm, whatever the form of the involvement.

212 '. . . are no longer eligible for legal aid': See note for page 60 ('. . . representing himself').

213 '. . . a McKenzie Friend': This (named after the case that first permitted them into court) is a person who has been granted permission by the judge to accompany a party into court. They are there to support and assist the party, but cannot speak in court unless the judge has granted them permission, which is very unusual. They are not entitled to give the party legal advice. There is no requirement for them to be legally qualified or insured and they are unregulated. The view of the Judicial Executive Board is that courts should adopt Scotland's approach and ban payments. They recommended that McKenzie Friends should be more properly named 'court supporters' the better to identify their role.

214 '... direct access scheme': Members of the public may now go directly to a barrister without using a solicitor or other intermediary. Barristers who undertake this work must be qualified to do so. The client agrees a fixed fee with the barrister for the work they will do, which typically covers drafting documents and appearing at hearings.

215 'An interim contested hearing': A contested hearing in the middle of an application to decide a point that cannot wait until the conclusion of proceedings at the final hearing. Both parties will file statements on the specific point, and then give evidence after which the judge will decide the issue. The case then proceeds to final hearing on the outstanding issues.

217 '... remove Ed from it': An Occupation Order is designed to remove someone from their home so that the person making the application can return to live in it. This person must fit into a defined number of categories that establish their right to live there. The court must then perform a balancing act, taking into account the harm caused to the parties and any children by granting, or not granting, the application, as well as the housing needs, financial resources and the parties' conduct.

217 '... without the other knowing': An application for an injunction (i.e. something that prohibits an action or event) can be made without letting the other party know, either because it is an emergency or because they fear what the other party will do if they become aware of an attempt to stop them. The application will come before a judge with only the party who is making the application present. The application is usually granted, and the judge then orders both parties to return at a later date to see if the application is opposed. If it is opposed there is

then a full contested hearing to decide whether or not the order should remain in force.

218 '. . . circuit judge, senior and experienced': A circuit judge is a senior judge of the county or crown court and is referred to as 'Your Honour' in court.

218 '. . . attached a penal notice': A penal notice is a paragraph added to an order which states that if a party disobeys all or part of the order then they can be arrested by the police. They will then be brought to court and punished for their breach, if it is proved beyond reasonable doubt. It is essentially treated as a contempt of court.

219 '. . . to deal with the allegations by giving undertakings': Undertakings are formal promises given to the court not to do something. If a party breaks their undertaking, they can be brought back to court to see if this can be proved. Again, it is essentially treated as a contempt of court. Undertakings are not an admission that a person has done any of the acts of which they are accused. They are therefore a useful way of resolving an application for a Non-molestation Order where the allegations are disputed, without going all the way to a contested hearing. The only difference between an undertaking and a Non-molestation Order is that the police cannot arrest someone for breaking an undertaking – the applicant has to bring the matter back to court.

10 Chris

236 '. . . no drugs in prison': In 2016 more than 45% of prisoners in a survey conducted by the HM Inspectorate of Prisons said it was easy to get drugs whilst incarcerated. In 2017 the Ministry of Justice reported that prison officers had confiscated 225kg (about 500lb) of drugs in one year.

237 '. . . or in a hospital': If a judge is satisfied by the written or oral evidence of two medical practitioners that a defendant is suffering from a mental disorder which makes it appropriate for him to be detained in a hospital for medical treatment, the judge can make a Hospital Order in place of sending the offender into custody. The defendant will then be sent to a secure hospital. In 2016 there were 40,161 incidents of self-harm in prisons and 120 self-inflicted deaths – almost twice the number in 2012, and the highest year on record. The Prisons and Probation Ombudsman found that 70% of prisoners who had committed suicide between 2012 and 2014 had mental health needs. In June 2017 the National Audit Office published a report which stated that the government does not know how many people in prison have a mental illness, how much it is spending on mental health in prisons or whether it is achieving its objectives.

237 '. . . pre-sentence report': See note for page 20.

237 '. . . follow the guidelines': The sentencing guidelines state that the offence range for rape is from 4 to 19 years' custody.

239 '. . . waive legal professional privilege': Legal advice privilege applies to confidential communications between lawyers and their clients made for the purpose of seeking or giving legal advice.

245 '. . . on the day of trial': See note for page 18.

245 '. . . nor a Restraining Order': For Sexual Offences Prevention Order, see note for page 162. A Restraining Order protects the person named in the order from conduct which amounts to harassment or which will cause a fear of violence. It can be made by the court both after a defendant has been convicted and when he has been acquitted if the court considers it necessary to do so.

245 '. . . subject to notifications requirements': See note for page 162 ('. . . his details every year').

11 Jude

251 '. . . (CAFCASS)': See note for page 59.

254 '. . . on his behalf': The general rule of law is that a child cannot make an application to the court, or be joined as a party to proceedings, unless he has a guardian appointed on his behalf. The guardian will then go to court on the child's behalf and represent the child's best interest. The Family Procedure Rules 2010 provide an exception to this. Rule 16 allows a child independently to instruct a solicitor, provided either that the child has obtained the court's permission to do so or that a solicitor considers the child understands sufficiently well to give instructions in relation to the proceedings. The test applied is whether the child is *Gillick competent* – whether he or she has the maturity to make their own decisions and to understand their implications. The court will make a child a party only in cases that involve an issue of significant difficulty. The courts have found a child's autonomy is of great importance and that it can be in the child's best interests to have some direct involvement in the proceedings *(Re W (a child)* [2016] EWCA Civ 1051*)*.

258 '. . . decisions in their chambers': Guidelines were published in 2010 with the purpose of encouraging judges to enable children to feel more involved and connected with proceedings in which decisions are made about their lives. In part this could mean the child meeting the judge, to give them an opportunity to satisfy themselves that the judge has understood their wishes and feelings, and to understand the nature of the judge's task. A judge will never see a child alone.

268 '. . . fairest in the world': *The World Justice Project Rule of Law Index* produces annual reports based on independent data on the global rule of law organized around 80 different factors ranging from constraints on government powers to absence of corruption and the upholding of fundamental rights. The scores and rankings are derived from more than 110,000 households and 3,000 expert surveys in 113 countries and jurisdictions. The *Index* is the world's most comprehensive data set of its kind and the only one to rely solely on primary data, measuring a nation's adherence to the rule of law from the perspective of how ordinary people experience it. The only country of a similar population size which ranks above the United Kingdom is Germany. Rankings are: 1 Denmark (population 5.7 million); 2 Norway (population 5.3 million); 3 Finland (population 5.5 million); 4 Sweden (population 5.7 million); 5 Netherlands (population 17 million); 6 Germany (population 82.67 million); 7 New Zealand (population 4.69 million); 8 Austria (population 8.74 million); 9 Canada (population 36.3 million); 10 Australia (population 24.13 million); 11 United Kingdom (population 65.64 million).

The UK fell out of the top 10 in the 2017–18 index with a score for the accessibility and affordability of civil justice much closer to the United States (ranked 19). The effectiveness of its correctional system is recorded at 0.53 – a figure lower than in the US (0.58).

Bibliography

I have highlighted a handful of reports – available free on the internet – which deal with some of the issues raised in this book. There are many more listed on www.inyourdefence.co.uk

1 Dominic

McGuinness, Terry, *The Age of Criminal Responsibility*, House of Commons Library Briefing Paper, Number 7684, 16 August 2016: http://researchbriefings.parliament.uk/ResearchBriefing/Summary/CBP-7687#fullreport

Bateman, Dr Tim, *The State of Youth Justice 2017: An overview of trends and developments*, National Association for Youth Justice, September 2017: http://thenayj.org.uk/wp-content/uploads/2017/09/State-of-Youth-Justice-report-for-web-Sep17.pdf

Prison: the facts, Bromley Briefings Summer 2017, Prison Reform Trust, Summer 2017: http://www.prisonreformtrust.org.uk/Portals/0/Documents/Bromley%20Briefings/Summer%202017%20factfile.pdf

2 Derek

Strudwick, Patrick, 'This is Why Men Meet for Sex in Public Toilets', *Buzzfeed*, 12 August 2017: https://www.buzzfeed.com/patrickstrudwick/men-are-still-meeting-for-sex-in-public-toilets-and-the?utm_term=.rmR6KGK1X8#.lcMV6P6Dxd

Business as Usual? A follow-up review of the effectiveness of the Crown Prosecution Service contribution to the Transforming Summary Justice initiative, HMCPSI Inspectorate, June 2017: https://www.justice inspectorates.gov.uk/hmcpsi/wp-content/uploads/sites/3/2017/06/ TSJ_FU_thm_June17_rpt.pdf

3 Saba

Impact of changes to civil legal aid under Part 1 of the Legal Aid, Sentencing and Punishment of Offenders Act 2012, House of Commons Justice Committee, Eighth Report of Session 2014–15, HC311, 12 March 2015: https://publications.parliament.uk/pa/cm201415/cmselect/ cmjust/311/311.pdf

5 Rita

Conspiracy and Attempts: A Consultation Paper, The Law Commission, Consultation Paper No 183, 2015: http://www.lawcom.gov.uk/app/ uploads/2015/03/cp183_Conspiracy_and_Attempts_Consultation.pdf

Thomas, Cheryl, *Are Juries Fair?* Ministry of Justice Research Series 1/10, February 2010: https://www.justice.gov.uk/downloads/publications/ research-and-analysis/moj-research/are-juries-fair-research.pdf

6 Maggie

Broadhurst, Karen, and Mason, Claire, 'Birth Parents and the Collateral Consequences of Court-ordered Child Removal: Towards a Comprehensive Framework', *International Journal of Law, Policy and the Family*, Vol. 31, No. 1, 1 April 2017, pp. 41–59: https://academic.oup. com/lawfam/article/31/1/41/3065577

Children in need of help or protection, report by the Comptroller and Auditor General, National Audit Office, HC 723, Session 2016–17, 12 October 2016: https://www.nao.org.uk/wp-content/uploads/2016/10/ Children-in-need-of-help-protection.pdf

McCracken, Katie, et al., *Evaluation of Pause*, Department for Education Research Report, Children's Social Care Innovation Programme Evaluation Report 49, July 2017: https://www.gov.uk/government/uploads/system/uploads/attachment_data/file/625374/Evaluation_of_Pause.pdf

7 Peter

Online child sexual abuse images: Doing more to tackle demand and supply, National Society for the Prevention of Cruelty to Children, November 2016: https://www.nspcc.org.uk/globalassets/documents/research-reports/online-child-sexual-abuse-images.pdf

8 Daniel

Shifting the Burden: Inquiry to assess the operation of the current legal settlement on prostitution in England and Wales, All-Party Parliamentary Group on Prostitution and the Global Sex Trade, March 2014: http://prostitutionresearch.com/wp-content/uploads/2014/04/UK-shifting-the-burden-Mar-2014.pdf

9 Helena

Trinder, Liz, et al., *Finding Fault? Divorce Law and Practice in England and Wales*, Nuffield Foundation, 2017: http://www.nuffieldfoundation.org/sites/default/files/files/Finding_Fault_full_report_v_FINAL.pdf

10 Chris

Mental health in prisons, Report by the Comptroller and Auditor General, National Audit Office, HC 42, Session 2017–2019, 29 June 2017: https://www.nao.org.uk/wp-content/uploads/2017/06/Mental-health-in-prisons.pdf

Changing patterns of substance misuse in adult prisons and service responses: A thematic review, HM Inspectorate of Prisons, December

2015: https://www.justiceinspectorates.gov.uk/hmiprisons/wp-content/uploads/sites/4/2015/12/Substance-misuse-web-2015.pdf

11 Jude

Report of the Vulnerable Witnesses & Children Working Group, Judiciary of England and Wales, February 2015: https://www.judiciary.gov.uk/wp-content/uploads/2015/03/vwcwg-report-march-2015.pdf

Rule of Law Index 2017–2018, World Justice Project, 2018: https://worldjusticeproject.org/sites/default/files/documents/WJP_ROLI_2017-18_Online-Edition.pdf

Acknowledgments

She must come first because, without her, there would not have been a book – or at least not this one. Elizabeth Day, thank you for remembering the time we walked across a Suffolk field and I told you I wanted to write. Thank you for then joining me with the firebrand force who is now our shared agent, Nelle Andrew. I am so grateful that she chose me to write this book, and I hope I make her glad to have done so.

Susanna Wadeson was prepared to hear me pitch this book despite my ten-day-old baby and half-finished proposal. She was then able to convince everyone else at Transworld of its merits. Since then she has been a constant and regular support and has delivered any suggestions or criticisms in a way which always assured me of her faith in the book and what I wanted to say.

To Dr Nick Freeman, the university teacher who noticed me, and who later gave me the reference which, I have no doubt, helped me pursue the career I told him I wanted.

To Sarah Jones, who may recognize herself in this book, but may never have known what a profound influence she had on me.

To my old clerk, Charlie Charlick, and my stalwarts in Winchester and Oxford, Stuart Pringle, Lee Giles and Russell Porter. Thanks for letting me (mostly) do the work I wanted to do, and for never making me choose between work or my children. Thanks for making me feel that I will always have a place in the chambers where I grew up. And thanks for not freaking out when I told you about this book (although wait until you hear about the telly series).

Thank you to my head of chambers, Nigel Lickley QC, and to all the other barristers in my chambers and on my circuit who have made me feel like I was part of a family rather than a profession. Thank you also to those barristers and solicitors who have set the tone for the rest of us through their dedication to their work and their clients, no matter how long the hours or poor the pay. When I was called to the Bar in 2005 many others told me that the publicly funded Bar was over and that the proposed changes to the legal system would see me out of work within a few years. I am glad I ignored the nay-sayers and listened instead to those who said that this is a wonderful profession and a position of privilege and that I could make it work. They were right.

To my parents, for the trust and freedom they gave me. Spending my carefully saved Post Office account money on travelling the globe as a wide-eyed nineteen-year-old changed me in invaluable ways and has proved a lifelong lesson. Only now do I really understand the great strength it took to let me go. It is their work ethic, and my mother's conviction of the need for financial independence, which meant I have worked since I was a teenager. Those early jobs taught me so much and I would not have chosen the path I did without them. Thank you for never pressurizing or censoring me but letting me find my own way, and for supporting my determination to become a barrister. Thank you particularly to my mother for her proof-reading abilities and her pride in this book.

Thank you to my parents-in-law for the encouragement,

praise and crucial babysitting services you have handed out in abundance.

To all my friends who have seen me through an extraordinary year, but particularly to those whose humour, love, alcohol and play-dates (sometimes at the same time) have kept me steady – in no particular order: Alexandra Gywn, Clemmie Burton-Hill and Helia Ebrahimi. Most of all, thanks to Kate Fortescue. We have navigated this weird world alongside one another through pupillage and beyond. I cannot think of a better person to remind me of the dual importance of reading all the unused material and the need to get behind the DJ booth and dance on the podium. I have learned a lot from you, and am proud to call you my friend.

Thank you to my three-year-old quicksilver son, Wilfred, whose bear-hunt expeditions to my writing hut provided light relief just when I needed it. I hope that when you one day read this you will know that looking after you has been the best job I have ever had. Thank you also to my one-year-old, Aubrey, whose short life has been overshadowed by this book. Luckily you were born with a wide smile and an open heart, and you therefore will, I hope, forgive my absences.

I have saved the most important person for last. My husband, Ben. You are one of the best people I know. Your faith in my abilities enables me to carry on when I doubt them. I trust you not only to know the answer but to have weighed it against a moral and ethical compass that few can match. During my writing of this book the outside world pitched us and our little family high and low and all over the place. The fact that there is any book at all is due, in part, to your respect for my desire to write it, and your willingness to switch from matters of state to ones of laundry and childcare. You are, as always, the star to my wandering barque. I love you (and fear you will have to learn to live with my Oxford commas).

About the Author

Sarah Langford has been a practising barrister since 2006, both in London and around the country, principally in criminal and family law. She studied English at the University of the West of England. She worked as a barmaid, legal secretary and note-taking clerk before completing a law conversion, in which she gained a distinction. She was awarded a scholarship from Gray's Inn of Court and went on to train as a barrister. She lives with her husband and two small boys in London and Suffolk.